D0206898

FEMALE IMPERSONATION

CAROLE-ANNE TYLER

ROUTLEDGE
NEW YORK   LONDON

Published in 2003 by
Routledge
29 West 35th Street
New York, NY 10001
www.routledge-ny.com

Published in Great Britain by
Routledge
11 New Fetter Lane
London EC4P 4EE
www.routledge.co.uk

Routledge is an imprint of the Taylor and Francis Group
Copyright © 2003 by Taylor and Francis Books, Inc.

Printed in the United States of America on acid free paper.

10 9 8 7 6 5 4 3 2 1

All rights reserved. No part of this book may be reprinted or reproduced or utilized in
any form or by any electronic, mechanical or other means, now known or hereafter
invented, including photocopying and recording or in any information storage or
retrieval system, without permission in writing from the publisher.

Library of Congress Cataloging-in-Publication Data
Tyler, Carole-Anne
    Female impersonation/Carole-Anne Tyler.
        p.cm
    includes bibliographical references and index.
    ISBN 0-415-91687-9 — ISBN 0-415-91688-7 (pbk.)
    1. Feminist theory. 2. Sex role. 3. Women. 4. Femininity. I. Title.
    HQ1190 .T95 2002
    305.42'01—dc21   2001019650

CONTENTS

ACKNOWLEDGMENTS

As anyone who has written a book knows, they are always collaborative endeavors, even if signed by a single author—though I am afraid I cannot blame this volume's flaws on anyone but myself. I must thank first and foremost my family, beginning with Rick Keane, who perhaps more than anyone else knows what a struggle it is to write, having been forced to live with and suffer through the drafting of this book along with me (and on bad days perhaps instead of me). I must also thank my siblings, particularly my sisters Brenda and Roey, whose questions about this and other writing projects over the years have forced me to try to clarify my thinking. To my parents I owe a great deal. Though they never had the chance to go to college they wanted their children to have an education and the chance for a better life—or at least for a better income. They encouraged me to work hard and think harder, and to continually question the inequitable distribution of opportunity in the world; I hope they see some of that reflected in this book; even if, they are still bemused by the connection that female impersonation might have to something called "English."

I have been most fortunate in my friends, colleagues, and mentors over the years and only wish I had better profited from their examples. I must thank Bob Scholes and Mary Ann Doane for shepherding me through the final stages of graduate study and commenting on early drafts of many of these chapters, as well as for introducing me to the methodologies without which this work would have been impossible. My first graduate class, with Bob—Paradigm, Schema, Episteme—introduced that discontinuity in my approach to the analysis of literature and culture, which the course treated and of which this book is the result. When I wrote up my first description of the project, Mary Ann told me I would have a hard time convincing her of any of it; I fear I have probably not succeeded in doing so, but her tough questions and scrupulous scholarship have inspired me to do the best work I could. Without the encouragement of Bob and the late Roger Henkle I might have left Brown University satisfied with my M.A. in Creative Writing; instead, they persuaded me to disregard the English program graduate advisor's warning that in the Ph.D. program one could not write a creative dissertation too many; (I hope that despite the rules some spark of creativity might have been found in that first draft and the revisions to it). I must thank many other Brown faculty for their encouragement over the years, their comments on early drafts, and the example of their own scrupulous feminist scholarship: Ellen Rooney, Elizabeth Weed, and Naomi Schor, who were kind enough to publish in *differences* what became parts of chapters and to offer extensive advice for revisions at that time; Karen Newman and Kaja Silverman, who also read drafts of some of the chapters and offered advice and support, and Keith Waldrop, who tried to instill in me some self-confidence from my earliest days in the creative writing program and shared with me some of the books that helped me arrive at this book's focus.

In addition, I am very indebted to the incredible cohort of graduate student colleagues at Brown and to the Pembroke Center Fellows, who taught me so much in small and large reading groups and informal dinners or discussions over martinis late at night: Diana Fuss, Katherine Stockton, John Murchek, Evelyn Roberts, Virginia Blum, Rey Chow, Kari Weil, Mimi White, and Lynn Joyrich. Over the years Dale Bauer has provided encouragement just when I needed it most, as well as another example of the best kind of feminist scholarship. My debt to my present and past colleagues at the University of California-Riverside is also immense. I could hardly have asked for a better circle of friends and critical interlocutors than some of the junior faculty I was hired with—Parama Roy, Katherine Kinney, and Joe Childers—or the person who hired me, Kim Devlin; I have also benefited from conversations with George Haggerty and the faculty in the gender and sexuality focused research group and in the Center for Ideas and Society seminar groups in which I have participated. Emory Elliott has been a wonderful mentor not just to me but to so many younger scholars when they were starting out. Jennifer Brody was a later but equally important UCR friend and interlocutor, as was Kathleen McHugh; they and Parama have shared my moments of misery and miraculously persevere in their friendship and support. To them in particular, and to Diana Fuss, I owe special thanks, not just for their friendship and encouragement over the years but for their willingness to read and comment on drafts and to share their own work with me; they have explored with me and in their scholarship the difficult questions about identity that have so engaged me, and this project is the better for that. I wish it were better still as recompense for their generosity and example.

Finally, I must thank the editors of and readers for *differences,* and their readers and editorial assistants; the editors of *Theory between the Disciplines,* Mark Cheetham and Martin Kreiswirth and their assistants, and Diana Fuss and her assistants for *Inside/Out*, since they helped ready for publication versions or sections of some chapters that have benefited from their editorial comments. Work on the project was in part enabled by research money or by one- or two-quarter research leaves funded by an American Council of Learned Societies Fellowship for Recent Recipients of the Ph.D., UCR's Center for Ideas and Society, and UC pretenure faculty development awards, for which support I am also grateful.

THE FEMININE LOOK

Rather than ask, "What is the attitude of a work to the relations of production of its time?" I should like to ask, "What is its position in them?"

— WALTER BENJAMIN, "THE AUTHOR AS PRODUCER"

Perhaps the most surprising idea of contemporary Western feminism is that women are female impersonators. It is already implicit in Simone de Beauvoir's famous pronouncement in *The Second Sex:* "One is not born, but rather becomes, a woman . . . this creature, intermediate between male and eunuch, which is described as feminine."[1] Still one of the best-known affirmations of gender as a social construction, Beauvoir's claim is that femininity is an act that is not the expression of a nature but a labor of production that is not without its relations of exploitation like other jobs in the modern era (*Second*, 302). As work, it binds women to the social formation and its oppressive hierarchies of sex and other differences, which together constitute a gendered identity. Yet we disavow our knowledge of this, mythologizing femininity as "natural," the outward manifestation of a biological or other inner essence that determines our desires and behavior. Walter Benjamin's efforts to theorize the relation of art, literature, and other work(s) of high and popular culture to a particular social formation alerts us to the need to similarly contextualize gender work(s). What would it mean to take seriously the notion that gender is an artifice, that the social formation mediates a subject's relation to the labor that is its very self-production in a socially mandated impersonation? How can we move beyond an analysis of the *attitude* of gender or the other identity work from which it is inextricable—of impersonation as gender with attitude—to an analysis of its *position* in a social formation, of the work it does, as well as the work it is? Will the knowledge that women are female impersonators end women's oppression? Will it end female impersonation itself? What could—or should—"this creature, intermediate between male and eunuch" become when she ceases her feminine impersonation to produce her self differently?

Beauvoir offered a salutary warning to those who would answer that question: "Let us not forget that our lack of imagination always depopulates the future; for us it is only an abstraction; each one of us secretly deplores the absence there of the one who was himself" (*Second*, 812). As she recognizes, narcissism makes for a difficulty with alterity. Although Beauvoir accepts the common wisdom that women are more inclined toward narcissism than men, it is in effect masculine narcissism as "self interest" and the desire to feel superior to others that for her explains why women are female impersonators rather than authentic human beings. Such narcissism reduces sexual difference to "opposition," the "lack" of what would make women "similar" to men. Man and eunuch, the *one* and the *other*, master and slave, transcendence and immanence—this is the sexual relation into which woman is "indoctrinated," according to Beauvoir (*Second*, 302). Woman accepts it because of her dependency on men, isolation from other women, and "temptation" to forego the "risk of a liberty in which ends and aims must be contrived without assistance" (*Second*, xxiv). Narcissism impedes the construction of a different future, with different sexual relations, whenever men or women fail to take the risk of imagining alterity and make themselves a double, whether for men, of men, or for and of "other" women, which feminism itself sometimes advocates, as I will demonstrate in this book.

What could counter a narcissism so pervasive that both victim and oppressor are said to suffer from it? Beauvoir believes the answer is what existentialism promotes as "reciprocity" or mutual recognition between "equal" subjects, who must take the "risk of liberty" and transcend themselves through "freely chosen projects" (*Second*, xxxiii). This is the same solution Frantz Fanon proposes to racism in *Black Skin, White Masks*, published just three years after *The Second Sex*. In it, he argues that the members of the "second" race respond to their treatment as inferior with an "impersonation" that only seems to confirm their differences as inferiority and suggests that equality and reciprocity would end racism.[2] However, his title conveys the limits to such a strategy, which too closely resembles the problem itself. What is "liberty" if it must be exercised in a repetition of the projects of the white self as the only, or the "natural," path to the "transcendence" of "immanence"? Immanence thereby remains the province of the black other even in his freedom, which becomes a slavish mimicry. When "equality" demands sameness, what Beauvoir terms "natural differentiation" is not possible, nor is genuine "reciprocity" (*Second*, 814). As Jacques Lacan emphasizes, narcissism cannot be undone by a philosophy that grasps the negativity of the subject "only within the limits of a self-sufficiency of consciousness . . . the illusion of autonomy" and a theory of society that "refuse[s] to recognize that it has any function other than the utilitarian one. . . ."[3] Such notions cannot explain— or help us change—the "subjective impasses" that have resulted from them, some of which Lacan details, "a freedom that is never more authentic than when it is within the walls of a prison; a demand for commitment, expressing the impotence of a pure consciousness to master any situation; a voyeuristic-sadistic idealization of the sexual relation [and, I would add, race and class relations]; a personality that realizes itself only in suicide; a consciousness of the other than [sic] can be satifisfed only by Hegelian murder" (*Ecrits*, 6).

Who really takes the existentialist "risk" in the exercise of the "liberty" of a self conceived as fully conscious, able to "freely choose" its projects? What happens to alterity when that self misrecognizes difference, both that of the Other and itself, since there is no self without the other's recognition? How is it that the impulse to murder-suicide can be overcome? Is it possible to explain and change the narcissism of oppressive gender, race, or class relations? What will succeed impersonation: the authentic being of "natural differentiation," or a different impersonation, another social construction and a new becoming (wo)man? How can feminists imagine difference differently, so as to contest the reproduction of "woman" as a support for man's narcissism or her own? It is clear that feminist theories and practices too often have failed in the imagination of the future because of a narcissism at work most forcefully in the assumption of a self that is fully conscious, autonomous, and masterful, even when feminists profess to believe otherwise. Such failures color the history of "second-wave" Western feminism beginning with that of Beauvoir herself, making it white (and middle class). Each distinctive moment in this history is a critical response to the narcissism of an earlier (or concurrent) moment, fracturing the unity and stasis of feminism, so that it is truly a "movement," "*en procès*"—in process/on trial—along with its subjects, as Julia Kristeva explains human being.[4] Through this movement of doing and undoing, assuming and critiquing all theses, including identities, women have tried to render justice to their differences not only from men but from each other.

This dialectic structures the relation between the two best-known moments of recent Western feminism, the movements centered on the demands for equal rights and difference. Impersonation is a key trope for understanding what was demanded of women by both, even as it also accounts for the narcissism of both. It is at once the problem and the solution, the countering of one narcissism with another. Such a movement suggests a negativity inhabiting narcissism itself, the "otherness" that interrupts the reproduction of the same that we might expect from self-love and self-involvement. As a difference within patriarchy, women have disrupted its self-perpetuation through the eternal return of the same patrimony in each generation, the ideas about gendered property—what is "proper" for or the property of each sex—that govern sexual difference in a social formation. But as a difference within feminism itself, women have ensured it can no more perfectly reproduce itself in each succeeding (or coeval) generation than patriarchy can. There is something beyond narcissism, which the history of feminism suggests we might call "impersonation." Yet *impersonation* becomes the very name of narcissism for what seeks to oppose it, which is another impersonation. It seems female impersonation is conformity and critique, paradoxically suggesting there is something *beyond* it that is *within* it, that puts it in process/on trial. What are women like? What would women like? These questions, which for Sigmund Freud formed the infamous "riddle of femininity," have no one answer, as the history of feminism makes clear.[5] Women always seem to be something more or other, and to want something more or other, than what is imagined even by a feminist community, which is why feminism is necessarily a *movement*, on its way to something that cannot be determined in advance.

EQUAL RIGHTS FEMINISM AND IMPERSONATION

In "Women's Time," her much-anthologized essay on Western feminism, Kristeva argues that the women's movement originated with the liberal feminist aspiration "to gain a place in linear time as the time of project and history . . . [and] the socio-political life of nations," which involved "the rejection, when necessary, of the attributes traditionally considered feminine or maternal in so far as they are deemed incompatible with insertion in that history. . . ."[6] Kristeva glosses linear or "cursive" time as masculine and obsessional, noting that liberal feminists who demanded equal rights embraced men's values as those of the nation in "a logic of identification" ("Women's," 194). She suggests that such assimilationism has come under fire from two succeeding generations of feminists. The first emphasizes women's difference from men and refuses the social contract that inaugurates and legitimizes the time of politics and history as men have conceived them. The second demands both equality and the right to difference. As Anne Phillips points out in the introduction to a volume about feminism and equality, the demand for equal rights seems to make feminism an extension of the liberal project.[7] The latter assumes a universal human nature that should be democratically available to all, a nature that theorists have increasingly argued is not natural but the social product of a First World and white capitalist patriarchy. Liberalism enfranchises the oppressed by inviting them to "recover" their natural and originary "full humanity," which realizes itself most completely in that system actually responsible for—and dependent upon—their oppression and exploitation.

The identification with the values of the oppressor as expressive of the "fully human" necessitates the belief in a state of nature whose identities, desires, and symbolic exchanges are always already modeled on those of the hegemonic culture, as several feminist philosophers and political scientists have argued.[8] By naturalizing what is a cultural production, such an "equality" negates differences and the differences they could make in the social system. As Elizabeth Grosz notes, "Equality becomes a vacuous concept, in so far as it reduces all specificities, including those that serve to distinguish the positions of the oppressed from those of the oppressor."[9] Not only is women's specific character seen as nonessential, but, as she explains, men too can claim they are oppressed by patriarchal social roles, so that the problem of sexism is subsumed under the more universal issue of "dehumanization." Furthermore, equality cannot be achieved "at the level of sexual and reproductive relations" or even at that of the social meanings attached to roles and behaviors, which differ with the perceived sex of the actors (a man's assertiveness is a woman's bitchiness, etc.) ("Conclusion," 339). It seems sexual difference just will not go away, short of transsexual surgery.

For that reason, the sex/gender distinction once so important in feminist theory has been called into question. For years, feminists asserted that sex is part of the state of nature, and has to do with the procreative body, whereas gender is a cultural production and, therefore, open to change. By repudiating gender—the feminine difference that was the product of oppression— equal rights feminists expected to recover their full humanity without having to undergo a sex change, becoming just like men without becoming men. However, something like the latter seemed to be necessary, even if impossible, as sex itself proved to be the occasion of oppression. No matter how hard women tried to impersonate men, they were perceived and treated as women. The project of eradicating oppressive gender differences would have to culminate in what Shulamith Firestone (and several feminist science fiction writers) proposed as "cybernetic communism," in which women would cease not only to raise but also to bear children.[10] Women would have to eliminate sex as well as gender.

Reacting against this, feminist "strategic essentialists" like Moira Gatens have read it as a kind of castration, a neutralization of sexual difference through the fiction of a neuter or universal body whose properties would really be those of masculinity/maleness.[11] For Tania Modleski, any refusal of feminine specificity—including that of feminist antiessentialists—is gynophobic, a disavowal of castration anxiety that may well be "gynocidal."[12] Difference feminists generally claim the signs of the procreative body as signs of a "feminine specificity" that is the ground of a difference from men and an identity with other women. But this reinscribes the state of nature they wish to critique, as bodies must submit to the inexorable procreative law of nature (and the heterosexuality from which it is difficult to extricate reproduction) in such a fashion that all the differences between women are neutralized in the fiction of a universal, "natural" woman, whose properties cannot be specified by race, ethnicity, class, or sexual orientation, since these are presumed to be epiphenomenal, like "gender" was in the sex/gender paradigm.

As compelling as Modleski is, her argument about Sojourner Truth's famous question "Ain't I a woman?" is symptomatic of just such a sexual indifference at the heart of sexual specificity. Modleski recognizes the ambiguity Truth's negative interrogative invites, but nevertheless wants to affirm a similarity between her and the white, middle-class feminists she addressed, which would be based on an identical biological "essence":

> Sojourner Truth . . . invites in fact both a yes *and* a no: "yes" in terms of her"experience," which in some major respects reduces her to her biology—to being the white man's breeder with little freedom to "fluctuate" in any (although in other respects it requires her to possess the physical strength of a man); and "no" in terms of an ideology based on a notion of frail white Southern womanhood. Given the doubleness of response required by the question . . . it seems to me politically irresponsible for (white) femininsm to refuse to grant to Sojourner Truth the status of a woman for it would then be in complicity with the racist patriarchal system that Sojourner Truth was protesting and that has denied, and in important ways continues to deny, this status to the black female . . . .
> (*Feminism*, 21)

As Hortense Spillers persuasively argues, procreation and mothering is just what black and white women have not had in common because a slave "breeder" was not a mother as the white woman was, who derived some benefits from a patriarchalized gender and kinship system in which slaves did not participate.[13] (Their children belonged to the master, who was sometimes the father too, although he did not recognize his paternity, only his legal ownership of a commodity.) While Spillers does not suggest how class might impact this racial difference, Sander Gilman demonstrates that in the nineteenth century black women and white working class women were thought to have similar genitalia very different from the genitalia of white middle-class women.[14] And the fact that women who had sex with women in pre-modern Europe were often reclassified as "hermaphrodites" and allowed to change their legal sex, as Ann Jones and Peter Stallybrass explain, suggests that there is a history, rather than female essence, of the genitalia of lesbians, which Valerie Traub notes is linked to a notion of clitoral hypertrophy.[15] Clearly, reproduction concerns more than just a natural, prediscursive sexual difference. For that reason, as Firestone knew, feminists must not stop short of critiquing procreation itself and of reinventing it along with the bodies that are its support and product. Sex and gender are discursive and cultural productions, as Michel Foucault and others have argued.[16] It is a production that quite literally incorporates race, class, sexuality, and a host of other cor-porealized differences that impact on the way the sexed body is lived or expe-rience and treated by others. Elizabeth Spelman quite rightly wonders, "Is it really possible for us to think of a woman's 'womanness' in abstraction from the fact that she is a particular woman, whether she is a middle-class black woman living in North America in the twentieth century or a poor white woman living in France in the seventeenth century?"[17] If we do not recog-nize this we will be compelled to repeat that turn away from femininity—or at least some femininities—enacted by an equal rights feminism indifferent to difference.

What is striking about the belief in a feminism that must repudiate femi-ninity is that its logic impels it toward a very specific "transsexualism," one that must alter race and class as well as sex and gender before the subject can enjoy the fruits of full humanity. At its limit is the First-World, white, middle class woman with a career, who is almost the same (but not quite) as the male counterpart with whom she identifies as "human." If she is anxious about a femininity she cannot completely eliminate, it is that of the "other" woman, which haunts her own, ensuring she will never pass for universal man. That excess of femininity she fears is the "excessive" femininity of women who are not First-World, white, and middle class, as she desires to be. In many of the discussions of the dangers of femininity that advocate "unsexing" in response to oppressive engendering, there is also an advocacy of what we might call "e-racing" and "unclassifying," although always as part of the process of becom-ing (like) universal man.

A representative critique in this mode is Susan Brownmiller's *Femininity*, a national best-seller in 1984.[18] Brownmiller's attitude to femininity is made very clear in the prologue:

> Femininity serves to reassure men that women need them and care about them enormously. By incorporating the decorative and the frivolous into its definition of style, femininity functions as an effective antidote to the unrelieved seriousness, the pressure of making one's way in a harsh, difficult world. . . .
>
> There is no reason to deny that indulgence in the art of feminine illusion can be reassuring to a woman, if she happens to be good at it. . . . Is there anything destructive in this? Time and cost factors, a deflection of energy and an absorption in fakery spring quickly to mind, and they need to be balanced, as in a ledger book, against the affirming advantage. (*Femininity*, 17)

Brownmiller relates the "fakery" of the feminine illusion to feminine competition for men, which results in what she describes as "false advertising." Such a complaint is not only masculinist but couched in the language of modern capitalism, an indication of the values informing the book's costs-benefits analysis of femininity.

Brownmiller is very critical of what she terms "the tyranny of Venus" for the damage it does to women's wallets, psyches, and bodies (*Femininity*, 24).[19] She gives a list of examples all too common for this type of analysis, which is meant to show the universality of the subjugation of women through fashion: corseting, foot binding, and the wearing of neck rings and obis, only the first of which has been a regular practice of Euro-American women (*Femininity*, 33). "The truth is," she writes, "men have barely tampered with their bodies at all, historically, to make themselves more appealing to women . . . under the masculine theory that real men do not trick themselves out to be pleasing. (They have better ways to prove their worth.) A woman, on the other hand, is expected to depend on tricks and suffering to prove her feminine nature, for beauty, as men have defined it for women, is an end in itself" (*Femininity*, 35–36). Brownmiller's anger is rooted in a belief in the natural, which for her is also the functional; both are identical with the masculine. This is evident in the repetition throughout the book of "useless," "ornamental," and "trickery" as modifiers for a femininity which she continually contrasts with the practicality and functionality of masculinity. The definition of the decorative as contingent and feminine detail is characteristic of a neoclassiscist idealist aesthetic which persisted into the twentieth century, according to Naomi Schor.[20] But in Brownmiller the decorative is equally marked with respect to class, race, nationality, and sexual orientation: the masculinity that she finds "functional" is always that of middle-class, white, heterosexual men. Hers is a modernist anti-aesthetic that, as Peter Wollen argues, orientalized and primitivized the decorative. This is particularly marked in the work of the influen-

tial Viennese cultural critic and architect Adolph Loos, who is quoted extensively by Schor as well as Wollen. He writes, "The lower the culture the more
apparent the ornament. Ornament is something that must be overcome. The
Papuan and the criminal ornament their skin. The Indian covers his paddle
and his boat with layers and layers of ornament. But the bicycle and the steam
engine are free of ornament. The march of civilization systematically liber-
ates object after object from ornamentation."[21]

Brownmiller is equally determined to liberate women through an end to
the ornamental. Her review of "progress" in male dress "reform" is like that
Loos details elsewhere, with bourgeois European masculine style as the apex
of achievement. Starting in the eighteenth century, Brownmiller writes, elegant men's wear "began its steady advance toward functional utility," which
she associates with "expert tailoring," "practical, dark colors," "good cloth
and good fit," and "the new masculine values of dynamic action combined
with serious responsibility" (*Femininity*, 86). Unfortunately, she suggests, "the
design of women's clothes did not move forward at all." In fact, she adds,
"Every wave of feminism has foundered on the question of dress reform. I
suppose it is asking too much of women to give up their chief outward expression of the feminine difference. . . . " (*Femininity*, 79). She notes that even
women in the corporate world are compelled to display their legs in skirts,
while they are forbidden to display their breasts, which must be concealed in
suit jackets; a middle class woman's exhibitionism must be both "ladylike" and
"professional" (*Femininity*, 102). Brownmiller highlights this contradiction,
but misses its class and race dynamic, which is obscured by her naturalization
of a very specific masculine style.

She has already admitted that clothing signifies class as well as gender, so
that the utility of "good cloth and good fit" cannot be considered apart from
its display of class difference, since, as Kaja Silverman has argued, exhibitionism can consolidate social hierarchies, as the fact of sumptuary laws suggests.[22]
The attention of the latter to "contingent" details undermines Brownmiller's
implicit distinction between use and exchange values, which structures her
critique of femininity as exploitation characterized by excessive consumption,
false advertising, the profits that derive from it or the waste of good capital in
bad investments that it promotes, and an unnatural competition between
women for men and between men through their ornamental women. As far as
Brownmiller is concerned, women should renounce a femininity whose
"major purpose" is "to mystify or minimize the functional aspects of a
woman's mind and body that are indistinguishable from a man's" (*Femininity*,
84). Feminists must emulate men, perhaps even become men, which is not
impossible if femininity is simply a troublesome decoration on a foundation
that is naturally masculine, as it is for Brownmiller. As far as she is concerned,

such transsexual surgery is accomplished quite simply, with a change of clothes. "No mysterious bundle of tricks is required to impersonate a man," she writes, "for masculine movement flows naturally from physiology with little modification. Female impersonation, however, relies on a suitcase full of special effects: a wig, a dress, a brassiere and a set of falsies, jewelry . . . a makeup kit . . . a girdle, nylons and a pair of high heels. . . . women are all female impersonators to some degree" (*Femininity*, 174–75). All the time and effort of excess consumption associated with femininity—its commitment to exchange value without use value and competition without responsibility—aligns it with an economic system gone awry, best figured for Brownmiller in the capitalism of Madison Avenue and the precapitalist economies of the European monarchies and the non-Western world (what Karl Marx termed "Oriental despotism," or the "fetishistic" economies of West Africa, whose valuation of material objects seemed irrational to Euorpeans, as William Pietz documents).[23] The return to nature and the utilization of use value is a return to responsible capitalism and the man in the gray flannel suit, who is not only white and middle class but straight. "Heterosexual men dress . . . to conceal their bodies, having no urgent need to attract the judgmental male eye," Brownmiller asserts when she advises heterosexual women to emulate them, as she believes lesbians have (*Femininity*, 97). Yet as she has already admitted, those same men may be dressing to be seen and adjudged as properly middle class, like the Euro-American businessman.

The suggestion that women will cease to be oppressed as women when they become (just like) heterosexual bourgeois men grows out of a logic that is both circular and startling. Brownmiller repeats the valorization of that ideal of the masculine for which feminists have criticized our society, never seriously interrogating the values associated with it. Furthermore, she does not consider the difficulty that repudiating femininity may pose; as far as she is concerned, a woman simply can *choose* to stop being feminine. But this is to forget what she has argued throughout, that femininity has been defined for women by men in their interest, so men may not wish women to change. Furthermore, women themselves may not wish to change, if ideology has structured their very desires, as contemporary ideological critiques assume. "If ideology is effective, it is because it works at the most rudimentary levels of psychic identity and the drives," Jacqueline Rose observes, an argument also made by Louis Althusser, who borrows from Lacan to develop a critique of ideology as "false consciousness," arguing that it is in fact consciousness itself.[24] Ideology is not simply lies believed by a dupe who only has to learn the truth to change; it is instead the very mechanism of subject formation, the ideas that order our being and will. Gender identities are never simply a matter of conscious choice, whether men's or women's. Women, therefore, are

not purely responsible for femininity nor purely the victims of its implemen-
tation; their construction as desiring subjects helps account for their limits as
conscious agents of change.

Brownmiller's implicit theory of ideology makes it as epiphenomenal as the
femininity that instantiates it. Beneath it is the white, middle-class, heterosexual masculinity that is the essence of human nature. What is natural or
essential cannot be transformed because it is not a product of human labor.
Brownmiller recognizes that as an impersonation femininity is at once a construction and a representation but argues that masculinity is a simple
"person-ation" or expression of humanity. Woman could be fully and responsibly (hu)man if she so desired. Yet Brownmiller also sees that "whatever a
woman puts on, it's likely to be a costume," noting the real difficulty women
have with "person-ation" (*Femininity*, 101). It would seem women are always
viewed as impersonators—but female impersonators, even when they are
miming or emulating men. Sexual difference cannot be shed as easily as
moulting feathers or old clothes. Conscious and unconscious investments in
women's remaining feminine create a real resistance to it. Nor is it clear that
women should refuse femininity if the alternative is cross-identification with
masculinity, a transvestism like that which feminist film critics Laura Mulvey
and Claire Johnston have suggested enables the female film spectator to resist
being the passive feminine object of the gaze.[25] Such a transvestism is urged
upon all claimants to a "common humanity"and the equal right to be citizens,
philosophers, and artists—subjects of politics, knowledge, and vision.
However, as Brownmiller's book reveals, that humanity is not "common" but
particular: white, bourgeois, masculine, and heterosexual. It constitutes and is
constituted by a point of view, values, and practices that masquerade as
nature, a zero degree of representation and subjectivity, unmarked by the particularity of embodiment. Masculinity cannot be the site of a purely objective
perspective on femininity, a utopic place that is literally no place. If the
demand for equal rights entails passing as a man it reinforces hegemonic values and power structures by accepting their universality; for this reason, some
critics of patriarchy have refused to be labeled feminists.[26]

Increasingly concerned with the disappearance of difference, feminists and
others have pursued what Peggy Phelan characterizes as a politics of visibility,
affirming and representing subjectivities whose specific differences from the
unmarked universal have been censored and scotomized, but also, I would
argue, by marking the unmarked as masculine, making it visible as such. As
Phelan recognizes, the project of making the invisible visible is not without
its risks. If man is too "interested" to be disinterested and see things clearly, if
"the gaze" is inextricable from the regimes of power and knowledge with
which it is allied, then difference may become visible through a voyeuristic

and fetishistic surveillance that sustains, rather than subverts, hegemonic identities and concerns.[27] Similarly, Elizabeth Grosz argues that "it is vital to ask how this difference is conceived and, perhaps more importantly, who it is that defines this difference and for whom" ("Conclusion," 339). But is it possible to achieve the "pure difference" for which Grosz calls, one that would not be modeled on metaphysical negative, binary, or oppositional structures, within which only the dominant term has any autonomy ("Conclusion," 339)? As Grosz herself says, "there can be no feminist position that is not in some way or other involved in patriarchal power relations" ("Conclusion," 342). Paradoxically, feminists must, as women, critique and redefine the feminine from within the feminine. How can femininity be reappropriated so as to signal both women's identification with it and refusal of it, given its constitution in patriarchy? What theories and practices will enable feminists to articulate different desires and interests, which are neither the same as men's or women's as they have been defined in patriarchy?

Jonathan Culler addresses these dilemmas in a discussion of reading and writing as a woman. Critically different readings depend on the possibility of a reader who is not complicitous with a patriarchal text or interpretive discourse but can resist it, a reader whose resistive difference is simply posited at the start: "To ask a woman to read as a woman is in fact a double or divided request. It appeals to the condition of being a woman as if were a given and simultaneously urges that this condition be created or achieved."[28] Culler suggests that the hypothesis of a woman reader was justified initially through the assumption of an essentially—or socially constructed—different experience for men and women that would result in different reading experiences. However, as the critique of phallocentric institutions and representations was elaborated, feminists realized that women's oppression means women do not always read their own experience differently from the way patriarchal men do. As Culler says, women "have been alienated from an experience appropriate to their condition as women," a phrase that maintains the hypothesis of a different "condition" even as it recognizes its actual absence in experience (*On Deconstruction*, 50). According to Gayatri Spivak, this is the problem of representation, a problem Marx confronted when he realized class position does not necessarily coincide with class consciousness.[29] All too often someone else has to represent or "have" class consciousness "for" the subject, just as Culler must recognize the woman's "condition" for her because at the level of her experience she is a transvestite, dominated by the apparatus (whose structure may preclude any unity of desire and interest in the subject, since interest is systemic, while desire is individual).

Spivak nevertheless insists there are no "transparent intellectuals," since their discourse mediates and indeed constitutes the other's desire for those who read their reconstruction of events and the motives of the actors involved. The transparent intellectual functions like a fetish, enabling the ideal—or transparent—speech situation, which Slavoj Žižek describes as a disavowal of the difficulty of understanding and relating to others according to the fetishistic formula, "I know very well communication is broken and perverted but still. . . ."[30] Spivak criticizes Foucault, as well as Gilles Deleuze and Félix Guattari, for just such a disavowal when they imagine the masses are not deceived about their desires but know and can speak about them through the medium of the intellectual, who would convey their wishes rather like a psychic does voices from beyond the grave: "In the name of desire, they reintroduce the undivided subject into the discourse of power," she writes ("Subaltern," 274). By assuming the masses know what they want, transparent intellectuals disavow self-difference, the "constitutive contradiction" of ideological subjectivation, whose effect is that subjects can be deceived about their own best interests because the other within, as the desire of the hegemonic apparatus, is (mis)representing them. The problems of representation—of reading and writing skills—are not necessarily resolved by representing oneself, given self-difference. Furthermore, by writing as psychic mediums, transparent intellectuals disavow the difference between self and other, which is at stake in painting portraits of the other (representation as *darstellung*, or depiction, which risks iconic misrepresentation in alienating images) and in serving as the other's political proxy (representation as *vertreten*, or delegation, which risks indexical misrepresentation in alienating, silencing, or otherwise failing to take into account some portion of a constituency). The representative necessarily identifies his desire with the desire of the other he claims to represent and interpret. The relation of knowledge makes representation perverse; it inevitably engages sadistic voyeurism and fetishism.

This is only too clear from Kristeva's description of the "moments" of feminism that are an alternative to the demand for equal rights. According to Kristeva, they express different demands, which arise from women's "time," a temporality that differs from that of production, political economies, nations, and "history" proper (linear, "masculine" time). Women's time is both "monumental" and "cyclical," the measure of female subjectivity in the structure of reproduction and its representations. These temporalities are more spatial than linear time, and conceal what it reveals as its own rupture, the obsession that drives it toward an impossible mastery: death. Kristeva argues that the second phase of feminism, attentive to "women's time," seeks "to give a language to the intrasubjective and corporeal experiences left mute by culture in the past" and demands "recognition of an irreducible identity, without equal in the opposite sex and, as such, exploded, plural, fluid, in a certain way non-identical" ("Women's," 194). It theorizes not only equality but difference —an essential difference, at once eternal and recurring. She argues that a third and more recent feminism combinines the demands of the first two moments: "*insertion* into history and the radical *refusal* of the subjective limitations imposed by this history's time on an experiment carried out in the name of the irreducible difference . . . " ("Women's," 195; emphasis in the original).

Kristeva recognizes that liberal feminism "globalizes" the problems of women and constructs a "Universal Woman" whose differences from liberal-ism's "Universal Man" tend to disappear in a logic of identification with him, as in Brownmiller's work ("Women's," 194). However, Kristeva believes that the second and third waves feminisms fracture the coherence of this construct and address "the multiplicity of female expressions and preoccupations" ("Women's," 193). Yet they do so, she says, so that "there might arise, more precisely, less commercially and more truthfully, the real *fundamental differ-ence* between the two sexes" ("Women's," 193; emphasis in the original). Can the (re)construction of the essentially feminine result in something noniden-tical? Can it avoid the "globalization" of one set of women's interests as those of all women and the construction of its own "Universal Woman"? While Kristeva states that the second- and third-wave European feminist sensibility seeks a "trans-European temporality" that seems to limit it, she has already globalized "monumental history" by suggesting that in it, European women are linked to women in places outside Europe: European women "*echo* in a most *specific* way the *universal* traits of their structural place in reproduction and its representations," which connects them to women in North America, and China, and elsewhere ("Women's," 190; emphasis added).

Kristeva's "echo" of the universal in "the specific" reverberates like—or *as*—the eternal that is cyclical, the paradox of "Women's Time" (not "Woman's Time") as she discusses differences between women, as well as between men and women. Evidently the same does not repeat without a dif-ference: the eternal is not always already, since it returns; space is split by time; an essential identity is nonidentical; Narcissus's voice is Echo's. Kristeva is suspicious of essentialism, which is not quite itself in this essay but not quite something other, for her masculinity is not the time or space (utopia) to which woman should return, as to her essence or true nature, which has been hidden beneath the veils and artifices of femininity. Yet neither is femininity that time as *one* time (the eternal feminine) or space (the globalized trans-European feminine). Any notion of a feminine essence or Universal Woman that could be (re)constructed must be suspect because, as feminist film theo-rist Mary Ann Doane reminds us, there is an "inevitable alliance between 'feminine essence' and the natural, the given, or precisely what is outside the range of political action and thus not amenable to change. This unchangeable 'order of things' in relation to sexual difference is an exact formulation of patriarchy's strongest rationalization of itself."[31] Nevetheless, the same insists in "Women's Time" so that women might be different from men, if not from each other. Kristeva knows and does not know about other differences, those between women, as she endorses and pursues an antiessentialist deconstruction, and essentialist reconstruction, of feminine identity. The multiple splittings in the essay—of space by time, of eternity by repetition, of man by "woman," and of woman by women, among others—testify to that, functioning fetishistically.

As Freud explains it, fetishism is charcterized by just such a splitting of the ego into two contradictory attitudes about an unpleasant truth, which the fetish signifes. A disavowal of that unwelcome knowledge, it signals both a recognition and refusal of it.[32] A careful reading of Brownmiller's book suggests that equal-rights feminism fetishizes differences of class and race as well as gender. However, the same may be true of second- and third-wave feminisms, which Kristeva represents as she discusses and practices them in "Women's Time" and her other work. Deconstructing and reconstucting feminine difference and sameness, feminists like Kristeva may both denaturalize and renaturalize certain identities. For them, some impersonations seem to "pass" as simple "personation," as the expression of a nature or essence of gender, class, and race through signifiers at once transparent to it (like an icon) and motivated by it (like an index). Clearly, to critique the feminine from within the feminine so as to promote difference rather than sameness is no easy task when both men and women are narcissistic. Is Echo "woman" for a masculine Narcissus—or the "other woman" for a feminine narcissist? Whose impersonations are "critical" of—or for—a narcissistic economy in second and third wave feminist reappropriations of femininity?

DIFFERENCE FEMINISM AND IMPERSONATION

Could femininity itself be the site of a real contestation of patriarchy that goes beyond the "Munchausen effect" described by Michel Pêcheux in *Language, Semantics, and Ideology*? In the latter, he recounts the story of Baron von Munchausen's miraculous rescue: after riding into a marsh, the baron managed to extricate himself and his horse from their muddy predicament by pulling with all the strength of one arm on a lock of his hair.[33] It might seem that reappropriating the feminine is another such fantastic gesture, one likely to leave women where they started, mired in patriarchy, with perhaps an illusion of having one high heel planted on secure footing. Yet the number of articles and books explicating and endorsing the deconstructive critical power of an "impersonation" of femininity continues to multiply rapidly. "Putting on" femininity is said to reveal it as a put-on or fake, a social construct, rather than a nature, subverting its ideological effect. How can women "put on" what they put on to signify their femininity, the "useless, ornamental trickery," which according to Brownmiller tricks them into, rather than out of, femininity? If femininity is already a matter of impersonation, what can make it appear as such? Does the attitude of gender work to the relations of its production change its position in them? Is gender ideology simply false consciousness, and the "mystery of the feminine" only mystification?

Perhaps the first feminist theorist to make a claim for the transgressive potential of female impersonation or "mimicry" was Luce Irigaray:

> One must assume the feminine role deliberately. Which means already to convert a form of subordination into an affirmation, and thus to begin to thwart it. Whereas a direct feminine challenge to this condition means demanding to speak as a (masculine) "subject," that is, it means to postulate a relation to the intelligible that would maintain sexual indifference.
>
> To play with mimesis is thus, for a woman, to try to recover the place of her exploitation by discourse, without allowing herself to be simply reduced to it. It means to resubmit herself . . . to "ideas," in particular to ideas about herself that are elaborated in/by a masculine logic, but so as to make "visible," by an effect of playful repetition, what was supposed to remain invisible: the cover-up of a possible operation of the feminine in language. It also means "to unveil" the fact that if women are such good mimics, it is because they are not simply resorbed in this function. *They also remain elsewhere. . . .* [34]

This passage draws attention to Irigaray's desire to be both deconstructive and reconstructive. Even as she critiques femininity as a masculine or phallocentric production she gestures toward a femininity "elsewhere" that would not be so, that would escape the reduction of sexual difference to masculine similarity or opposition and complementarity, with man the self for whom woman must be other in a nonreciprocal relation.

As Judith Butler has pointed out, unlike Beauvoir, Irigaray does not support the privileging of masculinity as the universal by urging upon women an identification with its values, whose result is male impersonation.[35] Irigaray favors instead the (re)construction of feminine difference through/as *écriture féminine* and other practices necessary for that "complex and painful process, a real conversion to the female gender."[36] It would be an ethical project like the later Foucault's "care of the self," and function in many respects like "négritude," the assertion and valorization of a distinctively black culture and identity as an alternative to the mimicry of (and assimilation to) white culture that for Fanon is the expression of a black "inferiority complex" created by colonialism. Yet Fanon was ambivalent about the value of négritude, particularly in *Black Skin, White Masks*: "However painful it may be for me to accept this conclusion, I am obliged to state it . . . [f]or the black man there is only one destiny. And it is white" (*Black Skin*, 10).[37] Because "sociogeny," the "social factor," contributes as much as "ontogeny," the "individual factor," to both black and white alienation and neurosis, Fanon argues that analysis cannot ignore the racial hierarchy, which is both socioeconomic and psychic (*Black Skin*, 11). It is therefore "the white world" that stuctures and makes meaningful even such resistive responses to it as négritude, which Fanon believes (at least at times) fixates on a mystical past at the expense of "destiny," the future (*Black Skin*, 13). Like Fanon, Irigaray recognizes and critiques the gender hierarchy that orders reality and subjectivity for women; nevertheless, she is willing to take the risk of regression by proposing an alternative feminine world and subjectivity. This realm seems to precede the masculine world both at the level of the social (as prepatriarchal, goddess-worshipping matriarchies) and the psyche (as the pre-oedipal). Mimicry is at once a sign of women's participation in this "other" femininity and a negation of their participation in patriarchy through what Lacan has termed feminine "masquerade."

Just as Fanon reappropriates psychoanalysis for his response to racism, so Irigaray reappropriates psychoanalysis for her response to sexism, at once critiquing and utilizing Freudian and Lacanian notions about subjectivity and gender. She is especially critical of the crucial role both attribute to the castration complex, whose resolution constitutes and hierarchizes sexual difference, situating women as marginal subjects in that they are less than men, which makes them less than subjects (and less than human). Not quite fully within what Lacan calls the "symbolic," the realm of true intersubjectivity instituted by an acceptance of the law (against incest), women are narcissists, like cats or criminals, according to Freud.[38] Irigaray argues, however, that men are the real narcissists and finds the theory of castration in both Freud and Lacan symptomatic of that.[39] Whereas the little boy's "imaginary" narcissism is supposed to be interrupted by "symbolic" castration, it is, instead, furthered by it at the expense of woman, who is made—quite literally—to serve his narcissistic interests in "wholeness." She "lacks" what he "has"; her penis envy reassures him of his (self-) possession. According to Irigaray and many other feminists, the image of woman as castrated and consumed by penis envy addresses masculine desires; in effect, such an image does not have a feminine enunciation, although women may identify with it, misrecognizing themselves as the origin of the fantasy it figures. As Virginia Woolf so aptly describes it in *A Room of One's Own*, woman has served as a looking glass "possessing the magic and delicious power of reflecting the figure of man at twice its natural size."[40] Woman does not see herself in that mirror at all.

The importance of the mirror image for the structure of subjectivity is highlighted by Lacan in his "return to Freud." Prompted by the work for his 1932 dissertation on paranoia, Lacan reconsidered the Freudian theory of narcissism and concluded that the ego was fundamentally narcissistic and paranoid in its structure and outlook, born from the child's (mis)recognition of the image in the mirror as its self, from which it receives the impression of having stable boundaries and mastery over its world. As Lacan says, it is "the total form of the body by which the subject anticipates in a mirage the maturation of his power . . . [and] symbolizes the mental permanence of the *I*, at the same as it prefigures its alienating destination . . . the statue in which man projects himself. . . ." (*Ecrits*, 2). This primordial subject, the ideal ego, is the foundation for the later identifications with ego-ideals which build up the ego itself. It is an uncertain foundation, however, based on a fundmental mis-recognition (*mirage*) of the self in/as the other (imago), whose fantastic qualities (unity, mastery, etc.) are appropriated to supplement the subject's own inadequacies. Because the imago, as Lacan writes, is "invested with all the original distress resulting from the child's intra-organic and relational discordance during the first six months," the imaginary is characterized by what Richard Boothby describes as "fantasies of omnipotence and utter helplessness, mastery and victimization" (*Ecrits*, 19).[41] The imaginary structures the subject's fantasy life by providing it with an image of itself to which the drives are channelled: imagos are an "organization of the passions" and as formative of subjectivity and fantasy as complexes—which in any case cannnot do without them (*Ecrits*, 19, 11). The ideal ego is, in effect, the first signifier of the drives, which remain unknowable until they are turned outward and represented by an object, aim, or activity, and source organ or erotogenic zone (otherwise a drive is simply a matter of force, tension or pressure, an unarticulated and unknowable energy). However, the ego is an alienating representation. Something of the subject is barred from this primordial signifier and threatens to displace it: the id. Fundamentally self-different, both libido or life-and-death drives, ego and id, the subject can never be integrated into a unity; no signifer can represent all of its drives. Its aggression therefore is directed against its self as image, which radically excludes a portion of its being, rather than against some other who frustrates its desires—it is the self *as* other that both frustrates and fascinates the subject of the imaginary.

Nevertheless, because the imaginary is characterized by transitivism, in which others function as the ego's counterparts, social situations are a "drama of primordial jealousy" that "tips the whole of human knowledge into mediatization through the desire of the other . . ." (*Ecrits*, 5). The subject's "internal conflictual tension . . . determines the awakening of his desire for the object of the other's desire . . . from which develops the triad of others, the ego, and the object" that precipitates the subject into rivalry, the ambivalence that will structure the oedipal complex, the subject's relations to the parents and siblings (*Ecrits*, 19). In the imaginary, the other as the adored object is everything and the ego is nothing—unless it is that object. Its difference—its splitting (ego, object-as-alter-ego, id)—makes it anxious about its unity and mastery, expressed in fantasies about the body in pieces. The subject of the imaginary expresses an insatiable demand for love, an exchange with the other in which the subject can only see itself as lovable through its identification with an ideal; the object-other "fortifies" it, supplements it, by "giving" the subject that loveable ideal through its love. The subject identifies with the other and so with his desire—which is the subject as what completes him. Yet the other poses a threat to the subject's possession of the object—to its self-possession as the object; the Hegelian struggle for recognition in desire as desire of the other is therefore not only murderous but suicidal, reinforced on both sides by life and death drives, as the former strives to create larger unities (beginning with the ego) and the latter to dissolve them.[42]

In this intersubjective relation, the subject *is* the phallus for the mother as other whose lack generates the desire with which the child identifies in the oedipal complex of the phallic stage. Together they form a closed dyad (or the illusion of one) that is ruptured by the intervention of the third term, the father whose name *(nom)* or law *(non)* prohibits the incestuous couple, dividing them into desiring subject and taboo object, insituting the endless displacements of substitute objects and activities that characterizes desire in the symbolic. In effect, both child and mother are castrated, "cut" from each other, by the recognition that the child is not and does not have just what the mother wants (lacks/desires). The child both accedes to and defends itself from castration through the repression of the representative of the drive whose object is the mother, the phallus as the primoridal signifier that has no signified. While there is a return of the repressed, it is in disguised form, with different (and less satisfying) objects and/or aims as the displaced representatives of the insistent drive (the subject gains phallic pleasure at the expense of nonphallic *jouissance*). The resolution of the castration complex results in the "comedy" of the sexual (non)relation, in which subjects take up gendered "roles" marked by this constitutive lack: each offers the other what she does not have to give and in return receives what she does not desire, even if she has demanded it (there is always something lacking in love—both one's own and the other's).

As Lacan describes it, this relation turns around the phallus and the two positions it makes available, that of "being" or "having" it for the other, both of which are a matter of "seeming" so as "to protect it on one side, and to mask its lack in the other" (*Ecrits*, 289). For Lacan, gender and sexuality is marked by "the function of the mask in so far as it dominates the identifications in which refusals of demand are resolved" (*Ecrits*, 291). The mask is the picture or "gaze" the subject makes of himself so as to lure the Other's desire, a "seeming" that is fetishistic for man and woman. "Paradoxical as it may seem," Lacan writes, "I am saying that it is in order to be the phallus, that is to say, the signifier of the desire of the Other, that a woman will reject an essential part of her femininity, namely, all her attributes in the masquerade. It is for that which she is not that she wishes to be desired as well as loved. But she finds the signifier of her own desire in the body of him to whom she addresses her demand for love. Perhaps it should not be forgotten that the organ that assumes this signifying function takes on the value of a fetish" (*Ecrits*, 289–90). Many feminist theorists have argued that any apparent equality or reciprocity between man and woman is undermined by the sexual hierarchy the phallus constitutes when its difference from the penis is disavowed. As they have noted, Lacan's phallus looks like the penis. If the latter is really only a fetish, it is one that "works" for him too:

> The phallus is the privileged signifier of that mark in which the role of the logos is joined with the advent of desire.
>
> It can be said that this signifier is chosen because it is the most tangible element in the real of sexual copulation, and also the most symbolic in the literal (typographical) sense of the term, since it is equivalent there to the (logical) copula. It might also be said that, by virtue of its turgidity, it is the image of the vital flow as it is transmitted in generation. (*Ecrits*, 281)

How can a signifier without a signified, which has been radically repressed, be tangible or turgid? The phallus that resembles the penis is an imaginary organ, but one whose function is legitimated by the symbolic father, who sanctions the misrecognition. The man's masquerade or "display" behavior therefore is more persuasive than the woman's; he really seems to have what she wants, whereas her obvious lack ensures his depreciation of love and "divergence towards 'another woman'" (*Ecrits*, 290). The phallus sets man on the symbolic's errant path of desire, while it freezes woman in place, somewhere between the imaginary and the symbolic, frigid ("frigidity . . . is relatively well tolerated in women") and narcissistically demanding to be loved as the phallus she strives to be for the man who will never have it by having her (*Ecrits*, 290).

In effect, woman's masquerade sustains man's; she does not seem to see through his deception as he does through hers. His mask is described as a function of her perception, rather than his narcissistic desire to be loved; her mask, however, is fully narcissistic, as she cathects it (her "self") instead of an anaclitic object. She loves to be loved, whereas he loves to love. She sees herself seeing herself (as lovable), while he makes himself seen (as lover)—and catches her in her narcissistic act. By implication, Lacan's woman suffers from everything attributed to her by an apparently "cruder" Freudian biologism, in which the penis is the phallus, including a damaged superego (and moral sense) and a difficulty with sublimation, which, as Sara Kofman observes, seems to justify the cultural repression of women.[43] For Freud and Lacan, the little girl really is castrated, while the little boy is the one who recognizes it because he is not. The little girl never gets over her penis envy, but the little boy resolves his castration complex, erecting the whole of culture as a kind of defense against it, a culture in which the little girl does not participate except as the *mater* (mother/matter) that caused it. What if this mater did not want what the father "had" to offer her? What if she refused to submit to his law, his signifiers? How would we know who we are? How could we stage our desire? What kind of differences and social relations would be possible? These are the questions Irigaray addresses throughout her work, as she emphasizes woman's absence from and resistance to the patriarchal order of things. When masquerade becomes what Irigaray calls "mimicry," a gap is introduced between woman and her image, which signifies her distance from it and, therefore, her humanity. "Only the subject—the human subject, the subject of the desire that is the essence of man—is not, unlike the animal, entirely caught up in this imaginary capture," Lacan writes. "He maps himself in it. How? In so far as he isolates the function of the screen and plays with it. Man, in effect, knows how to play with the mask as that beyond which there is the gaze" and desire of the other (*Concepts*, 107).

If the feminine "look" signifies that woman becomes the object of desire for man, mimicry produces becoming as distinct from being and suggests that woman could be the subject of desire and the scopic and other drives. As Lacan says, only a madman regards himself as absolutely self-identical (*Concepts*, 76). Mimicry allows for a feminine symbolization or representation of the woman's identity as an alternative to identifying with masculinity, entering the symbolic or "cursive" time by "passing" as men. In mimicry, woman "repeats" the imaginary—but *as* imaginary. To do so is to enter the symbolic, which, according to Jane Gallop, "can be reached only by not trying to avoid the imaginary, but knowingly being *in* the imaginary."[44] Irigaray calls into question Lacan's insistence in Seminar XX, *Encore*, that woman's "supplementary" and non-phallic *jouissance* can be reduced to the visible, known only by man through his mastering gaze, and spoken only by man in the language of his symbolic.[45] She wishes to unmask Lacan's sexist phallocentrism even where he seems to be gesturing toward another, non-phallocentric economy, because, as Lacan himself has noted, the phallus plays its role best when veiled (*Ecrits*, 288). Her deconstruction of Lacanian phallo-centrism consists in pointing out how the phallogocentric criteria of visibility and mastery haunt Lacan's feminine, making it an essentially masculinist fem-inine, since woman continues to be looked at, known, and spoken for by man. Mimicry is an important moment in this deconstructive critique because it signifies that the feminine difference is ultimately unknowable except as dif-ference from and through representations of femininity. As Mary Jacobus comments, "There is no 'outside' of discourse, no alternative practice avail-able to the woman writer apart from the process of undoing itself."[46] The deconstruction of the feminine coexists with and indeed depends on its reconstruction, since women must speak their desires or risk having them spoken by patriarchs like Lacan.

However, this reconstruction is for Irigaray a recognition of what always already exists by virtue of the "fact" that women are female (or have female bodies). Her theory, therefore, is essentialist, grounding the feminine differ-ence in the feminine body. Before the advent of what Spivak popularized as "strategic essentialism," any such appeal was critiqued as metaphysical ideal-ism, at odds with the materialist and deconstructive emphasis on the social construction of reality through representation; Toril Moi, for instance, argues that it undermines Irigaray's deconstructive impulse.[47] As Doane explains, essentialism all too often has been used to oppress women. However, like a number of other feminist scholars, she believes that the apparently essential-izing moments in Irigaray are actually strategically essentialist, since they enable the production—or recognition—of a feminine difference, a different language or relation to speech that would somehow construct or reflect woman's specificity by, in Doane's phrase, "leaning on" the body.[48] This body is not a given but a discursive production, as Gallop notes: "If phallomorphic logic is not based in anatomy but, on the contrary, reconstructs anatomy in its own image, then Irigaray's vulvomorphic logic is not predestined by anatomy but is already a symbolic interpretation of that anatomy, a poeisis, or a creat-ing of the body" ("Quand," 78–79). According to both Gallop and Diana Fuss, in her reconstruction of femininity Irigaray privileges not paternal metaphor but maternal metonymy, the touching or contiguity she associates with the feminine body and the feminine psyche that she describes as express-ing the experience of that body. With Irigaray, deconstruction and recon-struction occur together; mimicry cannot be rejected because it provides for nothing but a feminine negativity or because it too simplistically embraces a feminine positivity.

In theory, then, miming the feminine, playfully *repeating* it, produces knowledge about it: that it is a role and not a nature, and an exploitative role at that. To playfully repeat the feminine is to speak it ironically, to italicize it, in Nancy Miller's phrase, to exaggerate it through what Doane describes as the "hyperbolisation of the accoutrements of femininity," or to parody it, as Mary Russo, Judith Butler, and Linda Kauffman suggest.[49] Kauffman asserts that the parodic effect is achieved through assimilating numerous genres and styles of the feminine in a Bakhtinian dialogism: the effect of such a patchwork is a grotesque or carnival of femininity. Her notion of mimicry as an incongruous accumulation of disparate signifiers is not unlike that of Butler, although the disparity the latter privileges is that between masculinity and femininity, whose signifiers are said to be incongruously juxtaposed both in the body of the hermaphrodite and in butch-femme couples (whether gay, lesbian, or straight), where the sexed body contrasts with gender as do ground and figure when the object or other is there to throw the confusion into relief. Russo, like Kauffman, appeals to Mikhail Bakhtin, but aligns the grotesque with Kristevan abjection rather than incongruity; parody reveals the feminine to be "scrupulously fake" not through patchwork but through "overacting" ("Grotesques," 224). Her notion of parody as excess therefore is closer to what Doane calls "hyperbolisation" than to Kauffman's or Butler's idea of an overaccumulation of incompatible signifiers, although it should be noted that Butler, at times, links mimicry to parody (*Gender*, 122, 137–49). What all these theorists share is a notion that mimicry problematizes the naturalness of gender through an excess that creates a perception of incongruity. Its apparent goal, like that of contemporary "performance art," is to subvert the commodification process of the (art) object, which in mimicry is the woman herself.[50] The mimic as performance artist denaturalizes ideology by questioning the terms in which she is produced and circulated as commodity in patriarchal culture, calling attention to the conventions that encode her as woman, re-presenting representation and so unmasking through a conscious masking (mimicry) the masquerade of (woman's) nature, what is supposed to precede cultural construction. She "does" ideology in order to undo it.[51]

MIMICRY, MASQUERADE, OR THE REAL THING?

All theorists of mimicry assume that it can only be disruptive if it is legible as such, distinctly unlike "the real thing." Characterized by irony, hyperbole, parody, italicization, pastiche, and quotation, mimicry is evidently the quintessential postmodern practice, reappropriating a "canonical" text so as to call attention to the gap between the sign and the referent, the signifier and the signified. The problems with reading or "getting" mimicry are similar to the problems with reading other postmodernist texts. How can parody or irony

be distinguished from sincere imitation or the real thing? What makes mimicry different from masquerade or feminine identity if the latter is also an
alienated and alienating relation to an image of the self? Most theorists of
mimicry, like theorists of parody and irony, locate the answer to these questions in the production of "difference," implicitly relying on a model of communication in which the encoding of a message determines its meaning or
decoding. They appeal to a notion of authorial intention when they want to
read parody, irony, or "difference" into what might be a mere repetition of
the same, an instance of imitation or even "plagiarism." After having thus
produced this difference, they find it "in the text itself," just where the author
"intended" it to be.

For instance, in a book on postmodernist parody Linda Hutcheon says the
latter offers "an activation of the past by giving it a new and often ironic context," adding that "quotation or borrowing . . . is not meant to signal only
similarity. . . . It is not a matter of nostalgic imitation of past models; it is a
stylistic confrontation, a modern recoding which establishes difference at the
heart of similarity."[52] This suggests the similarity of parody and mimicry and
would seem to distinguish them from what Fredric Jameson has termed postmodern "pastiche" or nostalgic imitation, which he contrasts with the "genuine" parody of eras before the postmodern:

> Parody capitalizes on the uniqueness of . . . styles and seizes on their
> idiosyncrasies and eccentricities to produce an imitation which mocks the
> original. . . . the general effect of parody is—whether in sympathy or
> with malice—to cast ridicule on the private nature of these stylistic man-
> nerisms and their excessiveness and eccentricity with respect to the way
> people normally speak or write. . . .
>
> Pastiche is, like parody, the imitation of a peculiar or unique style, the
> wearing of a stylistic mask, speech in a dead language: but it is a neutral
> practice of such mimicry, without parody's ulterior motive, without the
> satirical impulse, without laughter, without that still latent feeling that
> there exists something normal compared to which what is being imitated
> is rather comic.[53]

Though Jameson and Hutcheon differ as to whether postmodernism involves
a mocking or sincere imitation, parody or pastiche, both make intention key
for the meaning of a text. Jameson refers to a motive impulse, for example,
while the intending subject latent in Hutcheon's gerunds is manifest at other
moments in her text: "When we speak of parody, we do not just mean two
texts that interrelate in a certain way. We also imply an intention to parody
another work (or set of conventions) and both a recognition of that intent and
an ability to find and interpret the backgrounded text in its relation to the

parody" (*Theory*, 22). She goes on to discuss parody as an "inferential walk" a reader takes, citing Umberto Eco: "[These walks] are not mere whimsical initiatives on the part of the reader, but are elicited by structures and foreseen by the whole textual strategy . . ." (*Theory*, 22). And she describes readers of parody as "decoders of encoded intent" who cannot ignore their "inferences" of parody (*Theory*, 23).

The use of the word *inferences* is telling: if the parody really is in the text, as Hutcheon insists it is, requiring only what she terms "the competence of the reader" for it to be uncovered, then she might more correctly have used the word *implication*. Writing *inferences* is symptomatic of the split in her argument between a notion that readers read parody into a text and that parody is somehow in the text because an author intended to put it there and only incompetent readers could fail to find it. She insists that the self-conscious text, like its self-conscious author, knows what it is up to; each guarantees the other and, therefore, the parodic effect. The unintentional irony of an intentionalist theory of irony by poststructuralists undoubtedly familiar with Roland Barthes's and Michel Foucault's critiques of the privileging of authorial intentions is instructive.[54] Sometimes one produces irony when one hasn't intended it; sometimes, despite one's best intentions, no one gets the joke. Irony is not stable, however much Wayne Booth—or Hutcheon, who derides him for believing it is, or Jameson, who nostalgically longs for its stability— might like it to be.[55]

By the same token, neither is mimicry, however much feminists might like it to be. The instability of mimicry is revealed in Irigaray's attempt to produce a distinction between it and masquerade. Of the latter, she writes, "Psychoanalysts say that masquerading corresponds to woman's desire. That seems wrong to me. I think the masquerade has to be understood as what women do in order to recuperate some element of desire, to participate in man's desire, but at the price of renouncing their own. . . . What do I mean by masquerade? In particular, what Freud calls "femininity." The belief, for example, that it is necessary to *become* a woman, a "normal" one at that, whereas a man is a man from the outset" (*This Sex*, 133–34). Irigaray alludes to psychoanalyst Joan Riviere's essay on femininity as masquerade, in which Riviere states she discovered that a masculinity complex could be the source not of lesbianism, as might be expected, but of a heterosexual hyperfemininity. From this Riviere concludes, "Womanliness therefore could be assumed and worn as a mask, both to hide the possession of masculinity and to avert the reprisals expected if she was found to possess it. . . ."[56] Furthermore, she asserts, there is no difference between "genuine womanliness" and the "masquerade" ("Womanliness," 213). For Riviere—as for Lacan, who borrowed from her—femininity itself is a travesty. Mimicry, as a female transvestism, would be a "travesty of a travesty," to employ Shoshana Felman's phrase, a masquerade of what is already a masquerade, a hyper-hyperfemininity, or what Jean Baudrillard has termed "simulation," a copy without an original.[57]

In simulation, the difference between copy and original, true and false, real and imaginary ceases to be significant. As Baudrillard describes it, simulation is "a liquidation of all referentials . . . no longer a question of imitation, nor of reduplication, nor even of parody. It is rather a question of substituting signs of the real for the real itself . . ." (*Simulations*, 4). Simulation is opposed to representation, even "envelops the whole edifice of representation as itself a simulacrum," according to Baudrillard (*Simulations*, 11). He suggests there have been four successive phases or eras of the image/sign:

> —it is the reflection of a basic reality
> —it masks and perverts a basic reality
> —it masks the absence of a basic reality
> —it bears no relation to any reality whatever: it is its own pure
>   simulacrum. (*Simulations*, 11)

If Brownmiller's feminist critique is part of the second phase (femininity masks and perverts a basic masculinity), Irigaray's is part of the third phase (as masquerade, femininity masks the absence of the feminine). Like Brownmiller, Irigaray still believes femininity is a sign of something. Riviere, however, suggests that femininity is only a sign of itself, a representation of a representation, outside any referentiality except self-referentiality. For Riviere, femininity is not a sign but a simulation.

Because Irigaray fails to follow through on the insight that femininity is a construction, a simulation, rather than a representation of any "genuine womanliness," whether present or absent, she remains committed to a belief in origins and copies and gets caught up in producing an artificial—and impossible—distinction between mimicry and masquerade so as to prevent the real and the imaginary from being confused. Like Jameson, she wants to know parody from pastiche, ironic "quotation" from nostalgic imitation, and she appeals to intention as the guarantor of that distinction. But poststructuralism, especially poststructuralist psychoanalysis (within which Irigaray's work would be located), has compellingly problematized the privileging of conscious intentions as the guarantor of anything. It is not surprising, then, that the distinction between mimicry and masquerade is sometimes rather indistinct in Irigaray's writing and in the writing of those who rely on her theory or who elaborate a similar analysis of mimicry, such as Judith Butler. For instance, Irigaray frequently associates "play" with mimicry, describing it as "playful repetition" and "playing with mimesis" (*This Sex*, 76). Yet she also associates play with masquerade, as is clear when she discusses woman as commodity, noting that "on the [sexual] exchange market . . . woman would also have to preserve and maintain what is called *femininity*. The value of a woman would accrue to her from her maternal role, and, in addition, from her 'femininity.' But in fact that 'femininity' is a role, an image, a value, imposed upon women by male systems of representation. In this masquerade of femininity, the woman loses herself, and loses herself by playing on her femininity . . . this masquerade requires an *effort* on her part for which she is not compensated (*This Sex*, 84). In this quotation, femininity loses the markers of an ironic or distanced attitude toward it (italics, quotes) as it is subsumed under masquerade. Curiously, however, a certain irony remains, signaled by the words "play" and "effort." Despite her best intentions, it would seem Irigaray cannot keep mimicry from slipping into masquerade.

The same thing happens in Doane's piece on the subject, where "masquerade" occludes "mimicry" so that the term never even appears in the essay, though it seems called for by the need to qualify or distinguish masquerade from itself by writing of "foregrounding" it, "flaunting" it, "realigning" it, or "doubling" it.[58] And Doane, like Irigaray, makes ironic distance dependent upon good intentions. Similarly, in an essay on Riviere, Stephen Heath exacerbates the confusion between the two practices not by leaving out one term but by discussing them as if they were interchangeable. "In the masquerade the woman mimics an authentic—genuine—womanliness," he writes, adding, "but then authentic womanliness is such a mimicry, *is* the masquerade"; masquerade is equivalent to mimicry, according to this statement.[59] He too is unwilling to abandon the conscious, intending subject who, for most theorists, grounds mimicry, though his focus shifts between encoding and decoding, the production and perception of mimicry. However, since he is talking about the masquerader herself, the two activities are not clearly distinct. The mimic's act is also an identity, but Heath implies she both produces it and experiences it as an act because it is alienating. Like Heath, Irigaray and Doane also vacillate between locating the intentions that make mimicry on the side of the producer and on the side of the perceiver of the image of womanliness.

All three theorists of mimicry symptomatically reveal that womanliness is always already a distance from womanliness; this generates their anxiety over the threatened indifference between mimicry and masquerade, an indifference they attempt to fix as difference by appealing to the intending subject behind—or in front of—the signs of femininity. They conflate experiencing alienation (being woman) with experiencing it as alienation (knowing woman). For them, femininity is an unwitting masquerade, while mimicry is a witty redoubling of that doubling inherent to femininity. The female mimic

—self-aware, self-conscious—apparently knows what she is up to. She is up to her neck in patriarchy, but her head is clear. Fortunately, this means she will be able to get a grip on herself and haul herself to safety. The female masquerader, equally bogged down in patriarchy—at her wit's end, perhaps without knowing it—flaunts but apparently does not flout her femininity, and so remains mired in masculinism. To Baron von Munchausen, these women may look alike; from the spectator's perspective it is hard to see that one has bought femininity and the other has not—or rather has, but has not bought into it (she wears her commodity fetishes playfully or parodically). The difference between being resigned to femininity and re-signing femininity is not so clearly visible.[60] Perhaps the baron is an incompetent reader; he does not see any irony in the situation. But for the story he is plotting, it does not much matter which woman he rescues, since her intentions and self-consciousness will not figure in it anyway.

The best intentions guarantee nothing. A woman's intending to repeat the feminine with a difference may enable *her* to have a different relationship to femininity but may have no such effect on men—or other women, for that matter. In short, the mimic could find herself in the same old story. The shifting of the intentions that are supposed to make a difference between the encoder and decoder of femininity is symptomatic of this difficulty. The specular subject of femininity is not produced by or inherent in the text, but is also produced by a social context. Feminist film critic Claire Johnston made that point a number of years ago, noting that there is no specific effectivity of a text regardless of context; the subject is not inscribed in a text but in a history.[61] This is a central tenet of British cultural studies. It alerts us to the fact that mimicry is not a strategy that will always and everywhere be subversive because the perception of irony does not depend on the author's intentions or on the text itself. To believe the former is to assume that language is transparently expressive and the subject is fully in control of it. To believe the latter is to accept a formalist reification of the text which anyway most often ends by appealing to an implied author—one "in the text" but in it as or in the manner of that intending author already discussed, who author-izes the text's meaning. Both are phallogocentric notions.

The alternative is to recognize that irony—and mimicry—are produced by reading a difference into what could be mere repetition, mere masquerade. Seeing a difference depends on a different point of view, which may be enabled by a different history; different histories produce differences in what Tony Bennett calls "reading formations." "Texts exist only as always already organized, or as activated to be read in certain ways," Bennett writes, "just as readers exist as always-already activated to read in certain ways."[62] If there are no transcendental authors, there are also no transcendental readers; there are only different reading—and writing—contexts. The appeal to intention to guarantee in advance a reading of mimicry is an attempt to force simulation back into the economy of representation, where not the Platonic original but the simulacrum or copy is "good," and the two can still be distinguished.[63]

If all reality is constructed through representation, as antiessentialism suggests, then femininity—whether mimicry or masquerade—is always an alienating identity, a set of signifiers the gendered subject assumes that refers not to an origin or anterior reality but to the signifying set itself; that alienation is inevitably experienced, but not necessarily consciously. Intentionalist theories of mimicry, however, would make some copies more originary than others in the insistence that mimicry consciously copies with a difference a "genuine womanliness" that functions as the real thing. Masquerade serves as the norm, the zero degree of femininity that mimicry exaggerates or parodies. If masquerade is fetishism, mimicry would be hyperfetishism, "the hyperbolisation of the accoutrements of femininity," in Doane's phrase. But there is no zero degree of fetishism: any little thing can serve as a fetish, even something as insubstantial as a shine on the nose, as Freud notes in his essay on fetishism.[64] Nor is there hyperfetishism; a fetish is either a fetish or it is not, and the multiplication of fetishes is consistent with rather than disruptive of fetishism, as Freud's discussion of the psychic significance of the snakes on the head of Medusa makes clear.[65]

Clothes are and always have been suffused with both psychic and social significance, as fashion historians and theorists have frequently pointed out. In his landmark study, *The Psychology of Clothes*, J. C. Flugel emphasizes the fact, noting that "the primacy of protection as a motive for clothing has few if any advocates."[66] Protection from the elements, like all needs, is thoroughly ideological; the "vital anthropological minimum" is a fiction that, according to Baudrillard, must be deconstructed. "Indeed," he writes, "just as concrete work is abstracted, little by little, into labor power in order to make it homogeneous with the means of production (machines, energy, etc.) and thus to multiply the homogeneous factors into a growing productivity—so desire is abstracted and atomized into needs, in order to make it homogeneous with the means of satisfaction (products, images, sign-objects, etc.) and thus to multiply consummativity."[67] The idealist understanding of clothing needs in terms of a human essence is always complicit with ideological values, as I have argued in my analysis of Brownmiller. For her, masculinity is the origin from which femininity has departed perversely in its concern for the useless tricks or artifices and excessive consumption of ornamentation. Genuine womanliness is middle-class masculinity.

But the woman who mimes the masculine still fails to pass; as Brownmiller herself points out, whatever a woman puts on is likely to be a costume

(*Femininity*, 101). Thus in *The Woman's Dress for Success Book*, John Molloy advises women to avoid what he calls "the imitation man look," which he says makes them appear cute or sexy.[68] Instead, he suggests, women should wear skirted suits, a masculine look with a feminine difference. Voyeur and fetishist, man insists on difference even as he attempts to deny it. A woman is always a female impersonator, even when she is impersonating a man. There is no genuine womanliness; there is only female impersonation. Or, rather, there are female impersonations, a variety of feminine styles of consumption/assumption of signifiers of femininity. These are signifiers of exchange value, not use value, and so participate in a class logic—which is why fetishism is indeed the appropriate concept for understanding impersonation, since it links discourses of representation, economics, and desire. Style is taste, and taste conveys distinction, a matter of cultural capital, according to Pierre Bourdieu. "Charm and charisma in fact designate the power, which certain people have, to impose their own self-image as the objective and collective image of their body and being," he writes.[69] A white, middle-class (and Anglo) look (appearance, and perspective on that appearance) masquerade as masquerade, the real thing, in our culture. The context of mimicry is this hegemonic style, offered for our consumption across the media—literally, through the advertising of commodity fetishes.

Constructing a new theory of irony, one that shifts from a focus on productive intentions alone to perception as a productive activity is crucial. Though feminist critics like Moi have recognized the significance of context for mimicry, they presume that it is avowedly feminist, in which both the encoders and decoders of femininity are prepared to read what may not be legible at first glance: irony or mimicry.[70] Such feminists are prepared to do so because their desires are supposed to be politically correct: they know they want the right thing (resistance to patriarchal femininity) and they unerringly achieve it. As Jacobus says of this feminist quest for a resistant femininity, "We know it must be there because we know ourselves struggling for self-definition in other terms, elsewhere, elsehow. We need it, so we invent it. When such an article of faith doesn't manifest itself as a mere rehearsal of sexual stereotypes, it haunts contemporary feminist criticism in its quest for specificity . . ." ("Question," 208). But if her rhetoric is ringing, her politics is perturbing since she assumes a feminist subject who coincides with her ego as the agency of conscious thought and perception, able to master and act on her intentions and perceptions. The potentially disturbing similarity of mimicry and masquerade is resolved through collapsing them together and bringing them under the sway not of the producer's consciousness, but the perceiver's. Merely relocating the intentions that make a difference from the author to the reader does not take into account the psychic importance of the context I have outlined above, which constitutes the subject as split by her desires and experiences. While cultural studies is right to emphasize the importance of historical context, it must not lose sight of the fact that history, like the subject, is a construct, the product of a narrative which makes experience meaningful after the fact. Its temporality is that of the psyche's, the future anterior tense appropriate for retroactive memory or "deferred action" (*Nachträglichkeit*), in which effects constitute their causes after the fact, rendering past events meaningful in—and for—the present. What Kristeva calls "cursive time," the time of history, is literally the time of writing, of the agency of the letter. Both the subject *in* history and the subject *of* history are desiring beings whose interests and desires may not coincide, as Spivak has stressed. If "history is what hurts," as Jameson has defined it, the trauma, like what Lacan terms the "real," is a force that drives the subject to signification and its unceasing deferrals and displacements of meaning.[71] Neither the subject nor its signifiers can master the real. Conscious intentions are as much an effect as a cause of history; they, too, must be read for their significance. Any privileging of such intentions, even the feminist intentions one might assume are behind the production and perception of mimicry, needs to be examined, because feminists (so often white and middle class) can be complicit in oppression too. As Walter Benjamin notes (in the epigraph to this chapter), "Rather than ask, 'What is the *attitude* of a work to the relations of production of its time?' I should like to ask, 'What is its *position* in them?'"[72] This is the question I address in each of the succeeding chapters. If there can be no clear distinction between being and miming the feminine because there is no genuine womanliness, since all identities are masquerades, then a feminist analysis of the grounds for labeling some masquerades as mimicry is required. What has passed for "passing for" rather than *being* womanly—the "parody" of femininity—may cover up certain unexamined notions of "genuine" or "natural" femininity that are class biased and ethnocentric, securing rather than contesting the identity of the middle-class white woman. The politics of the unconscious that subtends this politics of consciousness needs to be examined.

NOTES

1. Simone de Beauvoir, *The Second Sex*, 1949; trans. H. M. Parshley (New York: Vintage Books, 1952), 301; hereafter cited parenthetically as *Second*.

2. See Frantz Fanon, *Black Skin, White Masks*, 1952; trans. Charles Markmann (New York: Grove Press, 1967), introduction and chaps. 7–8; hereafter cited parenthetically as *Black Skin*.

3. Jacques Lacan, *Ecrits: A Selection*, trans. Alan Sheridan (New York: W. W. Norton, 1977), 6; hereafter cited parenthetically as *Ecrits*. This selection of essays was made by Lacan from the French edition published in 1966, and represents less than half the material of that earlier edition.

4. Julia Kristeva, *The Revolution in Poetic Language*, 1974; trans. Margaret Waller (New York: Columbia University Press, 1984), 22.

5. On the "riddle of femininity," see Sigmund Freud, "Femininity," 1933; *New Introductory Lectures on Psychoanalysis*, ed. and trans. James Strachey (New York: W. W. Nortion, 1965), 100.

6. Julia Kristeva, "Women's Time," 1979; trans. Alice Jardine, *The Kristeva Reader*, ed. Toril Moi (New York: Columbia University Press, 1986), 193; hereafter cited parenthetically as "Women's."

7. Anne Phillips, introduction to *Feminism and Equality*, ed. Anne Phillips (New York: New York University Press, 1987), 3.

8. For example, see Moira Gatens, "A Critique of the Sex/Gender Distinction," in *A Reader in Feminist Knowledge*, ed. Sneja Gunew (New York: Routledge, 1991), 139–57; Judith Butler, *Gender Trouble: Feminism and the Subversion of Identity* (New York: Routledge, 1989), especially 6–27 and 111–20 (hereafter cited parenthetically as *Gender*); Kathleen Jones, "The Trouble with Authority," *differences* 3:1 (1991), 104–27; Shane Phelan, "Specificity: Beyond Equality and Difference," *differences* 3:1 (1991), 128–43; Iris Marion Young, "The Ideal of Community and the Politics of Difference," in *Feminism/Postmodernism*, ed. Linda Nicholson (New York: Routledge, 1990), 300–323; and Linda Alcoff, "Cultural Feminism versus Post-Structuralism: the Identity Crisis in Feminist Theory," *Signs* 13:3 (1988), 405–36.

9. Elizabeth Grosz, "Conclusion: A Note on Essentialism and Difference," *Feminist Knowledge: Critique and Construct*, ed. Sneja Gunew (New York: Routledge, 1990), 338; hereafter cited parenthetically as "Conclusion."

10. Shulamith Firestone, *The Dialectic of Sex* (London: Jonathan Cape, 1971).

11. Gatens persuasively criticizes Firestone's refusal of female procreativity and argues against the neuter body in "A Critique of the Sex/Gender Distinction." The reproductive imperative to which she adheres is also shared by Luce Irigaray and Julia Kristeva, for whom the maternal is a privileged category, as I will argue in Chapter 2.

12. Tania Modleski, *Feminism without Women: Culture and Criticism in a "Postfeminist Age."* (New York: Routledge, 1991), 3–22; hereafter cited parenthetically as *Feminism*.

13. Hortense Spillets, "Mama's Baby, Papa's Maybe: An American Grammar Book," *diacritics* 17:2 (1987) 65-81.

14. Sander Gilman, "The Hottentot and the Prostitute: Toward an Iconography of Female Sexuality," in *Difference and Pathology: Stereotypes of Sexuality, Race, and Madness* (Ithaca: Cornell University Press, 1985), 76–108.

15. Ann Rosalind Jones and Peter Stallybrass, "Fetishizing Gender: Constructing the Hermaphrodite in Renaissance Europe," in *Body Guards: The Cultural Politics of Gender Ambiguity*, ed. Julia Epstein and Kristina Straub (New York: Routledge, 1991), 80–111; Valerie Traub, "The Psychomorphology of the Clitoris," *GLQ* 2:1–2 (1995), 81–113.

16. For example, see Michel Foucault's introduction to Herculine Barbin, *Herculine Barbin: Being the Recently Discovered Memoirs of a Nineteenth Century French Hermaphrodite*, ed. Michel Foucault, 1978; trans. Richard McDougall (New York: Pantheon, 1980), vii–xvii.

17. Elizabeth Spelman, *Inessential Woman: Problems of Exclusion in Feminist Thought* (Boston: Beacon Press, 1988), 13.

18. Susan Brownmiller, *Femininity* (New York: Fawcett Columbine, 1984); hereafter cited parenthetically as *Femininity*.

19. In a more recent analysis of femininity and fashion, Naomi Wolf provides a catch-

phrase for "the feminine look" which conveys the violence she finds in it even more graphically than Brownmiller's "tyranny of Venus"; she calls it "the Iron Maiden," likening it to the medieval German instrument of torture because "[t]he modern hallucination [of the ideal of feminine beauty] in which women are trapped or trap themselves is similarly rigid, cruel, and euphemistically painted." Wolf, *The Beauty Myth: How Images of Beauty Are Used against Women* (New York: Anchor Books, 1991), 17.

20. Naomi Schor, *Reading in Detail: Aesthetics and the Feminine* (New York: Methuen, 1987); see especially chaps. 1 and 3.

21. From "Ornament and Crime," quoted in Peter Wollen, "Fashion/Orientalism/the Body," *New Formations* 1 (1987), 6.

22 Kaja Silverman, "Fragments of a Fashionable Discourse," in *Studies in Entertainment*, ed.Tania Modleski (Bloomington: Indiana University Press, 1986), 139-152.

23. See William Pietz, "The Problem of the Fetish, I," *Res* 9 (1985), 5–17; "The Problem of the Fetish, II," *Res* 13 (1987), 23–45; and "The Problem of the Fetish, IIIa," *Res* 16 (1988), 105–23.

24. Jacqueline Rose, *Sexuality in the Field of Vision* (London: Verso, 1986), 5. The introduction and third chapter, "Femininity and Its Discontents," demonstrate the importance of psychoanalysis to feminism. Rosalind Coward makes a similar argument in "Sexual Politics and Psychoanalysis: Some Notes on Their Relation," in *Feminism, Culture and Politics*, ed. Rosalind Brunt and Caroline Rowan (London: Lawrence and Wishart, 1982). Louis Althusser's now classic discussion of ideology, subjectivity, and the imaginary is *Ideology and Ideological State Apparatuses*, 1968; trans. Ben Brewster (New York: Monthly Review Press, 1971), 127–86. In it, he draws heavily on Lacan to critique the Marxian notion of "false consciousness," which implies ideology is only a surface phenomenon, and therefore easily remedied; see especially 158–77.

25. Laura Mulvey, "Afterthoughts on 'Visual Pleasure and Narrative Cinema' Inspired by *Duel in the Sun*," 1981; in *Feminism and Film Theory*, ed. Constance Penley (New York: Routledge, 1988), 69–79; Claire Johnston, "Femininity and the Masquerade: *Anne of the Indies*," in *Jacques Tourneur*, ed. Claire Johnston and Paul Willemen (London: British Film Institute, 1975), 1–8.

26. For a brief discussion of this issue, see Toril Moi, *Sexual/Textual Politics* (London: Methuen, 1985), 12–13, 95–99, and Ann Rosalind Jones, "Inscribing Femininity: French Theories of the Feminine," *Making A Difference: Feminist Literary Criticism*, eds. Gayle Greene and Coppelia Kahn (London: Methuen, 1985), 92–108. See also Julia Kristeva, "Women's Time," and the essays in *Feminism and Equality*.

27. Peggy Phelan, *Unmarked: The Politics of Performance* (New York: Routledge, 1993), 205.

28. Jonathan Culler, *On Deconstruction: Theory and Criticism after Structuralism* (Ithaca: Cornell University Press, 1982), 49; hereafter cited parenthetically as *On Deconstruction*.

29. Gayatri Chakravorty Spivak, "Can the Subaltern Speak?" in *Marxism and the Interpretation of Culture*, ed. Cary Nelson and Lawrence Grossberg (Urbana and Chicago: University of Illinois Press, 1988), 276–78; hereafter cited parenthetically as "Subaltern."

30. Slavoj Žižek, "'Beyond Discourse-Analysis," in Ernesto Laclau, ed. *New Reflections on the Revolution of Our Time* (London: Verso, 1990), 259.

31. Mary Ann Doane, "Woman's Stake: Filming the Female Body," *October* 17 (1981), 26. Hereafter cited parenthetically as "Woman's."

32. Sigmund Freud, "Fetishism," 1927; trans. Joan Riviere, in *Sexuality and the Psychology*

of Love, ed. Philip Rieff (New York: Collier, 1963), 214–29. See also Freud, "Splitting of the Ego in the Defensive Process," 1938; trans. James Strachey, in *Sexuality and the Psychology of Love*, 220–23.

33. Recounted by Tony Bennett in "Texts in History: The Determinations of Readings and Their Texts," *JMMLA*, 18:1 (1985), 4.

34. Luce Irigaray, *This Sex Which Is Not One*, 1977; trans. Catherine Porter, with Carolyn Burke (Ithaca: Cornell University Press, 1985), 76; emphasis in the original.

35. Judith Butler, *Gender Trouble: Feminism and the Subversion of Identity* (New York: Routledge, 1990), 10–12, 18–19.

36. Luce Irigaray, *Je, Tu, Nous: Toward a Culture of Difference*, 1990; trans. Alison Martin (New York and London: Routledge, 1993), 21.

37. Fanon discusses négritude in (among other places) *Black Skin, White Masks*, chap. 5, and *The Wretched of the Earth*, trans. Constance Farrington (New York: Grove Press, 1963), chap. 4. In a chapter on negritude in his book on Fanon, Jock McCulloch points out that Fanon changes his mind about its value; see *Black Soul White Artifact: Fanon's Clinical Psychology and Social Theory* (Cambridge: Cambridge University Press, 1983), 35–62; see also the discussion of the topic in Irene Gendzier, *Frantz Fanon: A Critical Study* (New York: Pantheon, 1973), 36–44.

38. Freud, "On Narcissism: An Introduction," 1914; trans. Cecil Baines, in *General Psychological Theory: Papers on Metapsychology*, ed. Philip Rieff (New York: Collier, 1963), 70.

39. See, in particular, *Speculum: Of the Other: Woman*, 1974; trans. Gillian Gill (Ithaca: Cornell University Press, 1985), 11–129, and *This Sex*, 34–75, 86–105. See also Sarah Kofman, *The Enigma of Woman: Woman in Freud's Writings*, 1980; trans. Catherine Porter (Ithaca: Cornell University Press, 1985), 50–71, 82–97.

40. Virginia Woolf, *A Room of One's Own* (1929; reprt. New York: Harcourt, Brace, Jovanovich, 1957), 35.

41. Richard Boothby, *Death and Desire: Psychoanalytic Theory in Lacan's Return to Freud* (New York: Routledge, 1991), 26.

42. Mueller and Richardson are therefore mistaken in their effort to "go beyond the explicit text" of Lacan and explain this aggressivity as primarily adaptive, a response to a perceived threat to the unity of the ego. This follows from their misreading of what Lacan calls the "vertigo of the domination of space," which refers to the subject's being mastered by, rather than master of, "his" space. Jacques Lacan, *The Four Fundamental Concepts of Psycho-Analysis* (1973); trans. Alan Sheridan (New York: W. W. Norton, 1978), hereafter cited parenthetically as *Concepts*.

43. Kofman, *Enigma*, 202.

44. Jane Gallop, *Reading Lacan* (Ithaca: Cornell University Press, 1985), 60. For a comment on this, see Phil Barrish's review "Rehearsing a Reading," *Diacritics* 16:4 (1986), 15.

45. The offending passages from *Encore* have been translated by Jacqueline Rose in "God and the Jouissance of The Woman," in *Feminine Sexuality*, 137–48; see especially Lacan's comments on who can know and speak about women (Lacan, of course), 144, and his insistence that one only has to go and look at a statue of a woman (Bernini's Saint Theresa) to know all about woman, 147. Stephen Heath has written about the phallocentrism of *Encore* in "Difference," *Screen* 19:3 (1978), 50–112.

46. Mary Jacobus, "The Question of Language: Men of Maxims and *The Mill on the Floss*," *Critical Inquiry* 8:2 (1981), 210; hereafter, cited parenthetically as "Queston."

47. Spivak discusses the concept in her interview with Elizabeth Grosz, reprinted in *The Post-Colonial Critic: Interviews, Strategies, Dialogues* (New York: Routledge, 1990), 11–12. Since then, she has expressed reservations about it; see "In a Word: *Interview*," with Ellen Rooney, *differences* 1:2 (1989), 124–56. Moi's well-known criticism appears in her *Sexual/Textual Politics: Feminist Literary Theory* (London and New York: Methuen, 1985), 139.

48. Mary Ann Doane, "Woman's Stake: Filming the Female Body," *October* 17 (1981), 31–33. See also Jane Gallop, "Quand Nos Lèvres S'écrivent: Irigaray's Body Politic," *Romanic Review* 74 (1983), 77–83, hereafter cited parenthetically as "Quand"; Diana Fuss, *Essentially Speaking* (New York: Routledge, 1989), 55–72; Naomi Schor, "Introducing Feminism," *Paragraph* 8 (1986), 94–101, and "This Essentialism which Is Not One," *differences* 1:1 (1989), 38–58; Margaret Whitford, "Luce Irigaray and the Female Imaginary: Speaking as a Woman," *Radical Philosophy* 43 (1986), 3–8.

49. Nancy Miller, "Emphasis Added: Plots and Plausibilities in Women's Fictions," *PMLA* 96 (1981), 38; Mary Ann Doane, "Film and the Masquerade—Theorizing the Female Spectator," *Screen* 23:3–4 (1982), 82; Mary Russo, "Female Grotesques," in ed. Terese de Lavetis, Feminist Studies/Critical Studies (Bloomington: Indiana University Press, 1986), 217, hereafter cited parenthetically as "Grotesques"; Judith Butler, *Gender Trouble*, 122, 137–49; Linda Kauffman, *Discourses of Desire: Gender, Genre and Epistolary Fictions* (Ithaca: Cornell University Press, 1986), 294–95, 298.

50. On performance art, see Judith Harrera, "Postmodern Performance, Postmodern Criticism," *Literature in Performance* 7:1 (1987), 13–18. Michel Benamou suggests that performance is the unifying mode of the post-modern; see "Presence and Play," in *Performance in Postmodern Culture*, ed. Michel Benamou and Charles Caramello (Madison, WI: Coda Press, 1977), 3–7. Irigaray discusses woman as commodity in "Women on the Market" and "Commodities among Themselves," in *This Sex Which Is Not One*.

51. The notion of "doing" ideology in order to undo it comes from Judith Williamson, who discusses it in a review of the work of Cindy Sherman, which according to Williamson can be understood in reference to mimicry; see "Images of 'Woman,'" *Screen* 24:6 (1983), 103.

52. Linda Hutcheon, *A Theory of Parody: The Teachings of Twentieth-Century Art Forms* (New York: Methuen, 1985), 5, 8. Hereafter cited parenthetically as *Theory*.

53. Frederic Jameson, "Postmodernism and Consumer Society," in *The Anti-Aesthetic: Essays on Post-Modern Culture*, ed. Hal Foster (Port Townsend, WA: Bay Press, 1983), 113–14.

54. The critique of the author's intentions began with the new critics and W. K. Wimsatt and Monroe C. Beardsley's essay, "The Intentional Fallacy," in *The Verbal Icon* (Lexington: The University Press of Kentucky, 1954), 3–18. It was given a poststructuralist twist in Roland Barthes, "The Death of the Author," in *Image, Music, Text*, trans. Stephen Heath (New York: Hill and Wang, 1977), 142–48, and Michel Foucault, "What Is an Author?" in *Language, Counter-Memory, Practice*, trans. Donald Bouchard and Sherry Simon, ed. Donald Bouchard (Ithaca: Cornell University Press, 1977), 113–38.

55. Hutcheon talks about interpreting irony, 94. Booth's text is *A Rhetoric of Irony* (Chicago: University of Chicago Press, 1974).

56. Joan Riviere, "Womanliness as a Masquerade," (1929); reprt. in *Psychoanalysis and Female Sexuality*, ed. Hendrik M. Ruitenbeek (New Haven: College and University Press, 1966), 213. Hereafter cited parenthetically as "Womanliness."

57. Shoshana Felman, "Rereading Femininity," *Yale French Studies* 62 (1981), 28. Jacobus discusses this essay and the question of masquerade at length in "Reading Woman

(Reading)," in *Reading Woman: Essays in Feminist Criticism* (New York: Columbia University Press, 1986), 3–24. Baudrillard elaborates on postmodernity and simulation in *Simulations*, trans. Paul Foss et al. (New York: Semiotext(e) at Columbia University, 1983); hereafter cited parenthetically as *Simulations*.

58. Doane, "Film and the Masquerade," 81–82. In her reconsideration of masquerade, Doane addresses many of the difficulties I have outlined with her first essay. She mentions as problematic the confusion of producer and perceiver I talk about below, and attributes the linking of masquerade with "exaggeration" to Riviere. Though she does not directly confront the intentionalist assumptions underlying the earlier essay, in this reconsideration she herself strongly emphasizes the antiessentialist force of the notion of masquerade which a reliance on an idea of exaggeration might seem to undermine. Nevertheless, a trace of the difficulty haunting the earlier essay remains in the reference to masquerade as problematic for feminists because it involves socially inappropriate behavior. The issue of class difference as a style difference signifying a possible power differential between women as well as between women and men needs to be confronted. See "Masquerade Reconsidered: Further Thoughts on the Female Spectator," *Discourse* 11:1 (1988–89), 42–54.

59. Stephen Heath, "Joan Riviere and the Masquerade," *Formations of Fantasy*, ed. Victor Burgin et al. (New York: Methuen, 1986), 49.

60 Re-signing or reappropriation has been discussed by Claude Lévi-Strauss as a kind of *bricolage*, where one takes what is at hand and makes it signify differently; John Clarke considers it a strategy for subgroup identity formation; see his "Style," *Working Papers in Cultural Studies* (University of Birmingham, England), 7–8 (1975), 175–91.

61. Claire Johnston, "The Subject of Feminist Film Theory/Practice," *Screen* 21:2 (1980), 27–34.

62. Bennett, "Texts," 7.

63. The allusion to Jacques Derrida's reading of mimicry and writing is deliberate; see *Dissemination*, trans. Barbara Johnson (Chicago: University of Chicago Press, 1981), especially 61–286.

64. Freud, "Fetishism," 214.

65. Sigmund Freud, "Medusa's Head," 1922; trans. James Strachey, in *Sexuality and the Psychology of Love*, ed. Philip Rieff (New York: Collier, 1963), 212–13.

66. J. C. Flugel, *The Psychology of Clothes* (London: Hogarth, 1930), 16.

67. Jean Baudrillard, *For a Critique of the Political Economy of the Sign*, trans. Charles Levin (St. Louis, MO: Telos Press, 1981), 83.

68. John Molloy, *The Woman's Dress for Success Book* (New York: Warner, 1977), 27–42. Of course, the *Annie Hall* "look" also demonstrated as much.

69. Pierre Bourdieu, *Distinction: A Social Critique of the Judgement of Taste*, trans. Richard Nice (Cambridge: Harvard University Press, 1984), 208. Of course, signs convey more than class status; Bourdieu's readings tend to be rather reductive because he privileges only the one signified.

70. Moi, *Politics*, 141.

71. Fredric Jameson, *The Political Unconscious: Narrative as a Socially Symbolic Act* (Ithaca: Cornell University Press, 1981), 143.

72. Walter Benjamin, "The Author as Producer," in *Reflections: Essays, Aphorisms, Autobiographical Writings*, ed. Peter Demetz, trans. Edmund Jephcott (New York: Schocken, 1986), 222. The essay was originally delivered as an address at the Institute for the Study of Fascism in Paris in 1934, and was published in German in 1966.

CHAPTER TWO

FEMALE IMPERSONATION AND FETISHISM

Taste classifies, and it classifies the classifier.
—Pierre Bourdieu, *Distinction*

I
n the autumn of 1987, during the first broadcast of her short-lived weekly TV variety show, Dolly Parton discussed her new look with the audience. Though her corporeal excesses had been trimmed down, as she proudly pointed out, her sartorial excesses were as much in evidence as ever, to which she drew attention with a laugh by announcing that if she had been born a man, she would have been a female impersonator. It would seem that Dolly Parton is a self-confessed female female impersonator, miming or playing the feminine rather than simply being feminine, opening up a space within feminine identity so that it is not quite identical with itself—a space that might just be a critical distance. The buxom blonde bombshell as feminist? Susan Brownmiller would blanch at the very idea! Yet the catachrestical category of the female female impersonator, to which Dolly Parton would seem to belong, is what feminists like Luce Irigaray have in mind when they propose that by practicing mimicry, women can contest femininity through femininity, deconstructing that patriarchal discourse from within rather than

from some transcendental utopia purely outside it.[1] "Utopia" signifies "no place," and many poststructuralist feminists would insist there is indeed no place where there are "real" women who, untainted by patriarchal feminization, could critique femininity's deviance from some true or essential womanliness. Mimicry is the alternative to speaking from "no place" in the name of a feminine essence (utopic—and too often used against women). Furthermore, mimicry does not necessitate an identification with a masculinity that has pretended to be the "no place" from which one could view femininity dispassionately, with a critical eye. As I argue in my discussion of Brownmiller in the introduction, the suggestion that feminism necessitates a transvestic identification consolidates rather than critiques masculinity's hegemony. Mimicry, therefore, is also an alternative to speaking from "no place" in the name of a masculine science (essentialist as well, since in it masculinity functions as the bedrock of human nature, with femininity a deviation in need of explanation).

In theory, the female mimic denaturalizes ideology by calling attention to the conventions that encode her as woman; she repeats femininity with a playful difference that is a critical difference, producing knowledge about it: that it is a role and not a nature. This deliberate repetition in mimicry of what Jacques Lacan has termed the "feminine masquerade" is supposed to disrupt the masculine imaginary—the patriarchal symbolic—by signifying that there might be a nonphallocentric femininity, as Irigaray puts it, "elsewhere."[2] Jane Gallop has said that to repeat the imaginary as imaginary by repeating its images is to enter the symbolic.[3] But whose images are to be repeated, whose imaginary to be raised to the symbolic? In theory, according to Irigaray, women's playing around with the images men have produced "for" them would "cure" not only women but also men. Yet as I have pointed out, women have always been making spectacles of themselves, apparently without disrupting the specular relation (voyeuristic and fetishistic) that subtends the symbolic. What, in practice, makes the difference—the visible difference—between mimicry and masquerade?

As I have argued in the introductory chapter, it is precisely the fear that there is no difference between them that theories of mimicry symptomatically reveal. Once it is recognized that as a simulation, femininity is a signifier without an essential link to a referent, always already an alienated identity, the distinction between irony or mimicry and imitation or masquerade is not self-evident. To insist that masquerade is a representation of genuine womanliness, while mimicry is a representation of that representation, is an indefensible attempt to make some copies more originary than others. Not surprisingly, this metaphysical move to establish an origin relies on the classic—and suspect—strategy of appealing to the author's intentions as determinant of meaning. But if all representations are about representation rather than the real, a new theory of irony is called for, one that focuses not on productive intentions but on perception as a productive activity. However, this does not involve merely relocating the intentions that make a difference from the author to the reader, as I conclude in chapter 1. Conscious intentions can be misleading, even for a feminist. If there can be no clear distinction between being and miming the feminine because all women are, ultimately, female impersonators, then on what grounds have feminists read some masquerades as mimicry? Does mimicry reinscribe differences between women by reproducing as "genuine womanliness" a style of femininity that may be class-biased and ethnocentric? The unintended effects of the mimic's good intentions need to be examined.

THE POLITICS OF IN-DIFFERENCE

Indeed, Irigaray's recourse to good intentions to explain the difference between mimicry and masquerade allows her to effect a slippage between production and perception, and the potential contradiction between them, which veils the fact that the symbolic is really more than the masculine imaginary. The masquerade of femininity involves not only man's but woman's relation to "her" image, even if that image is enunciated by or on behalf of men. In patriarchy, woman serves as a mirror in which man can see himself as whole. Though woman does not really see herself in it, since it reflects only man's lack, she does misrecognize the image as her own, becoming the other that man desires her to be. Mimicry is supposed to shatter the mirror man offers woman, interrupting the masquerade of closeness to the image he desires and producing knowledge effects, teaching both men and women to relate differently to the image of femininity by disrupting both the masculine and the feminine imaginaries. Irigaray assumes that effects resulting from actions in the latter have the same effects in the former: she makes the feminine imaginary equivalent to the masculine. This is a blind spot in her discussion of mimicry, a dream of transitivity that supposes an indifference of the two, which cannot be collapsed together this way. Though a woman may intend to repeat the masquerade with a difference, thus disturbing her imaginary, her mimicry may be consistent with a man's merely repeating his imaginary, which requires women to make spectacles of themselves regardless of their intentions—for him, perhaps, a matter of indifference. (Of course, it cannot be assumed that conscious intentions would necessarily affect anyone's imaginary.) Watching the woman who seems to be the imaginary woman she is only seeming to be may not threaten man's voyeurism and fetishism, which sustain his imaginary.

This is evident in the response to Cindy Sherman's work, which is both art photography and mimicry as performance or body art. Sherman generally poses as woman in her various stereotypical guises, complete with appropriate setting, gesture, and costume (including wigs, dress, and make-up). Usually she herself takes the photographs (by remote, the wire often visible in the picture), but on occasion others have taken them for her (including her father). The scenarios she mimes are drawn from the media, primarily film (her earliest black-and-white photos are collectively referred to as *Untitled Film Stills*), but also magazines (in particular, fashion journals and pornography), and photography itself (portraits and pinups); a typical example is the *Psycho* photo (*Untitled Film Still no. 2*, 1977) in which Sherman, in platinum blonde wig and towel, stands next to a shower, half-turned toward a mirror into which she somewhat fearfully looks.[4] Sherman quotes a range of identities that make up "woman" or "the eternal feminine," and in so doing, theorists of the postmodern argue, she reveals these identities are conventional and not natural, an object position rather than a subject position, even when they pretend to be "for" woman, as in fashion photographs.

Judith Williamson argues that this is the subversive edge of Sherman's practice. She suggests that by presenting all the images of woman at once, Sherman draws attention to the male viewer's production of the photographs. He is required not to deconstruct the image as identity but to reconstruct it, and thereby recognizes that femininity as identity is inseparable from an image, is the image itself. "[T]he way we are forced to supply the femininity 'behind' the photos through *recognition* is part of their power in showing how an ideology works—not by undoing it, but by *doing* it," Williamson writes.[5] This is consistent with mimicry, and in fact one critic, Craig Owens, has explicitly related Sherman's work to it. He asserts that she acts out femininity as masquerade, adding that her photographs function "as mirror-masks that reflect back at the viewer his own desire (and the spectator posited by this work is invariably male)—specifically the masculine desire to fix the woman in a stable and stabilizing identity . . . for while her photographs are always self-portraits, in them the artist never appears to be the same. . . ."[6]

It would seem that simply *doing* ideology is more likely to confirm than contest it; no doubt this is why Williamson italicizes the word, turning *doing* into *overdoing*, and returning masquerade to mimicry by insisting on an ironic distance opened up by "excess." Furthermore, Williamson's italicization of *recognition* ensures it is not what Louis Althusser and Lacan have termed "imaginary misrecognition," which is the function of ideology. The emphasis once more suggests an ironic distance, although in the perceiver rather than the producer. Similarly, Owens resolves the danger that the viewer might not "get" the picture by appealing to the "obviousness" of

Sherman's parodic intentions. He notes that Sherman's work is "the decon-struction of the supposed innocence of the images of women projected by the media, and this Sherman accomplishes by *re*constructing those images so painstakingly, and identifying herself with them so thoroughly, that artist and role appear to have merged into a seamless whole in such a way that it seems impossible to distinguish the dancer from the dance. It is, however, the urgent necessity of making such a distinction that is, in fact, at issue. For in Sherman's images, disguise functions as parody; it works to expose the iden-tification of the self with an image as its dispossession. . . . By implicating the mass media as the false mirror that promotes such alienating identifications, Sherman registers this 'truth' as both ethical and political."[7] Once again, the emphasis added (in the prefix added) to ideological construction moves it outside the ideological (as *re*construction), though the difficulty of access to this emphasis is surely itself emphasized by speaking of Sherman's imperson-ations as "seamless."

Indeed, Peter Schjeldahl, the critic who wrote the introduction to a vol-ume of Sherman's work, reveals he did not see the (supposedly obvious) par-ody. The film stills, he suggests, are "identifiably the extension of an adolescent narcissist's conceits," adding that they are *not* "campy." And as if to make it absolutely clear her work in no way disrupted his male viewing pleasure, he asserts that the photos are "about the film frame" that "snaps desire to attention, whetting our appetite for heightened, carefree satisfac-tions," going on to confess that he finds the pictures very erotic.[8] Schjeldahl's response to Sherman's parody of femininity through the appropriation of media stereotypes is a reminder that the appropriation of media stereotypes is exactly what advertising (and the mass media in general) encourage in women. Star actresses function as commodities for both men and women (images to possess or identify with) despite—or, no doubt, because of—their "exaggerated" femininity. This point was made some twenty years ago by the *Cahiers du Cinéma* collective in an analysis of Josef von Sternberg's *Morocco*, in which they note that though the film attempts to critique fetishism by hyper-bolizing it, it cannot disturb "the power of seduction and fascination that Marlene [Dietrich] exerts."[9] The best of intentions may not make a differ-ence in man's relation to images of woman.

Rather, what makes a difference is differences within those monolithic, biologistic constructions, man and woman. Irigaray's indifference to differ-ences other than gender blinds her to this. Like Laura Mulvey and other the-orists of visual pleasure, she presupposes that sex and text are the only relevant categories for meaning construction, assuming all men relate to all women in the same way, regardless of class, race, ethnicity, or sexual prefer-ence. But all men do not have the same relation to the gaze as the white middle-class man. As Jane Gaines has shown in her analysis of Berry Gordy's film *Mahogany*, racial difference structures a hierarchy of access to the feminine image, with the white photographer monopolizing the controlling look.[10] The gaze of the black or working-class man at the woman may be framed by a white bourgeois gaze—male or female—that perceives it as unnatural and therefore threatening. The narrative can work to punish or castrate the male usurper of the gaze, as it often does the woman who appropriates the look, making the would-be subject of vision its object once again. Manthia Diawara analyzes this dynamic in the D. W. Griffith film *The Birth of a Nation*, in which a black man is lynched for having desired and pursued a white woman; his look is turned into a fearful spectacle.[11] Something similar happens to Aziz in E. M. Forster's *A Passage to India* and Joe Christmas in William Faulkner's *Light in August*; in fact, in the former, it is the woman, Adela, whose hysterical vision (hallucination) literally frames Aziz. Insofar as she is white and bourgeoise, then, the woman could be the bearer of the imperialist and middle-class gaze, as I demonstrate at length in Chapter 3.

If Irigaray's repression of the existence of a feminine imaginary sustains a dream of transitivity, of identity between the masculine and feminine imaginaries, it also sustains a dream of symmetry, of absolute difference between them. Hers is not only a blindness but a vision, a fantasy vision of a feminine imaginary as a utopic "elsewhere" untainted by the aggressiveness and self-aggrandizement of the masculine imaginary, made possible by her indifference to the significance of a range of differences other than that of gender. For Irigaray, mimicry is not only deconstructive, it is also reconstructive, producing a feminine space of reciprocity like that described in "When Our Lips Speak Together."[12] This is the space of the feminine imaginary, in which all relationships are characterized by what might be called an "in-difference," difference neither refused nor embraced, so that subject-object relations, including the subject's relations with herself, her words, and others, would not be predicated on aggressive disidentification from images of lack. The feminine look would not demand a becoming, but it would not impersonate a masculine look, voyeuristic and fetishistic, to distance itself from its object. All women would be equal in this in-difference.

Because Irigaray seems to base this in-difference in the feminine body, she is criticized for being an essentialist by many feminists. Yet hers is a peculiar essentialism, both deconstructing and reconstructing the body to which it appeals as ground, rather than simply assuming it as always already there, a given. For the paternal metaphor of the phallus that subtends the Lacanian symbolic, she substitutes the maternal metaphor of the lips, but a metaphor that signifies metonymy, contiguity, the touching she associates with the feminine and that Lacan has associated with the imaginary. "Woman," she writes, "touches herself all the time . . . for her genitals are formed of two lips in continuous contact. Thus, within herself, she is already two—but not divisible into one(s)—that caress each other."[13] Irigaray deconstructs the opposition between metaphor and metonymy, a necessary operation on a binary opposition that has both a metaphorical and metonymic relation to the binarism of sexual difference, according to Gallop.[14] This deconstruction enables a reconstruction of feminine difference and of a feminine imaginary that, paradoxically, would be a kind of symbolic in that it is characterized by speech or representation—deconstructing, then, the opposition between symbolic and imaginary as well.

In the feminine imaginary, woman speaks, though "in-differently." Her speech is not proper, and it does not name or identify her properly; rather, it subverts itself and herself, disabling any unified subjectivity. The two lips Irigaray refers to/reconstructs are doubly double, of the head and the genitals; woman literally speaks her sex, her sexual difference as in-difference. "This 'style,' or 'writing,' of women tends to put the torch to fetish words, proper terms, well-constructed forms. This 'style,' does not privilege sight; instead, it takes each figure back to its source, which is among other things *tactile*," Irigaray writes. "*Simultaneity* is its "proper" aspect—a proper(ty) that is never fixed in the possible identity-to-self of some form or other. It is always *fluid*. . . . Its 'style' resists and explodes every firmly established form, figure, idea or concept."[15] The feminine remains outside discourse as we know it in patriarchy. It is non-sense representing a non-identity, a space of speech that would not be a writing in the Derridean sense, the violence of classification and difference. This *parler-femme* would disrupt every dichotomizing, according to Irigaray, "including the one between enunciation and utterance."[16] The feminine subject would no longer be split from herself or from her other(s). Her language would produce her relation to "her" self and to "other" women as in-different.

Women's autoaffection and in-difference disrupt not only the "homosexual" libidinal and linguistic economies discussed by Irigiray, based on the exchange of (female) equivalents to facilitate a relation between men that consolidates their self-identities, but also the market economy "proper." Women among themselves cease to function as (masculine) property, in fact cease to have anything to do with property at all, even a proper identity or self-possession, let alone the possession of another. "Commodities among themselves are thus not equal, nor alike, nor different," Irigaray asserts. "They only become so when they are compared by and for man."[17] The differences between women are only their different exchange values for men, "a representation of the needs/desires of [masculine] consumer-exchanger subjects [and] in no way . . . the 'property' of the signs/articles/women themselves."[18] They

are the manifestation of the relations between men and are correlated with the
three social roles women fill: mother, virgin, and prostitute. Among themselves, women maintain what Irigaray describes as another kind of commerce
in which "use and exchange would be indistinguishable. The greatest value
would be at the same time the least kept in reserve. Nature's resources would
be expended without depletion, exchanged without labor, freely given, exempt
from masculine transactions: enjoyment without a fee, well-being without
pain, pleasure without possession."[19] Class or race would cease to be significant, since they are the products of a capitalist exploitation that is not only
analogous to but derivative from patriarchal exploitation—or so Irigaray
implies, writing, "To be sure, the means of production have evolved, new
techniques have been developed, but it does seem that as soon as the father-
man was assured of his reproductive power and had marked his products with
his name, that is, from the very origin of private property and the patriarchal
family, social exploitation occurred. In other words, all the social regimes of
'History' are based upon the exploitation of one 'class' of producers, namely,
women."[20] But this is a reductive understanding of patriarchal capitalism, in
which gender, race, and class are complexly articulated together, their relations overdetermined, even contradictory across discourses. Irigaray ignores
differences of power and privilege between women, does not want to know
anything about them—an active ignorance that reproduces white, middle-
class women's domination not just of feminism but of women. She does so by
appealing to a common biology (symbolically reconstructed, to be sure, but
only in terms of gender—as if there were no negative symbolizations of the
raced and classed body dependent on imaginary representations of real differences) and a common oppression (itself grounded in biology in that it concerns reproduction, which Irigaray does not symbolically reconstruct as she
has the feminine body). This appeal to a bodily sameness constitutes women
as a homogeneous group and covers over the specificities of the oppressions
suffered by particular women in particular times and places—oppressions due
in part, perhaps, to their white, bourgeois "sisters."

"You/I: we are always several at once. And how could one dominate the
other? impose her voice, her tone, her meaning?" Irigaray asks.[21] Yet the history of the relations between women is a history of domination, of the difference differences have made. These differences haunt gender, fracturing what
seems to be a simple binarism, in an uncanny return of what is repressed in
all feminist texts that refer to "the" feminine, texts that are beginning to be
interrogated for their white, heterosexist, and middle-class presumptions and
assumptions. Irigaray's in-difference, too, needs to be interrogated. It is a
blind spot that should be seen, a (symptomatic) dream of symmetry in which
what the feminine imaginary mimicry produces "really" is the inverse of the

masculine, wholly good instead of evil. Absolute identity or disidentity of the masculine and feminine imaginaries, too little or too much difference—this transitivity and symmetry characterize Irigaray's writing on the imaginary and are symptoms of the imaginary itself. Irigaray has, in fact, constituted rival imaginaries locked in an imaginary relationship with one another. How could this imaginary relationship to the imaginary be made symbolic?

PHALLUS/PENIS: IN-DIFFERENCE?

One must begin with the recognition that gender is not the only significant difference in the West. As I suggested above, discourses articulate the relation of class, race, and gender to lack—and illusory wholeness—differently, though there may be an overlap across a culture; the place of lack can be occupied by men as well as women, and cannot simply be correlated with sexual difference. Yet feminists and psychoanalytic critics all too often assume that only gender matters in the symbolic. Even many Marxist feminists have privileged domestic issues at the expense of considering women's wage labor (itself frequently "domestic," part of the low-paying but growing service industry). It is, therefore, not surprising, if still upsetting, that a socialist feminist like Rosalind Coward would suggest that "a gendered distinction . . . is perhaps the most significant distinction by which identities are presupposed."[22] Significant for whom? Black women, for instance, have felt obliged by statements like that to choose between black and feminist activisms which do not really address the specificity of their oppression; this is the poignant irony informing the title of a recent collection edited by Gloria Hull and others, *All the Women Are White, All the Blacks Are Men, But Some of Us Are Brave: Black Women's Studies*.[23]

Coward implies that gender is of paramount importance because it is so visible: "Anatomical women are constantly and continuously recognized as women," she writes.[24] But race too is visible. This, I take it, is what Gayatri Spivak means when she says that class is a totally artificial sign system, in contrast to race and gender (with ethnicity somewhere "in between").[25] In fact, it is the business of discourses to make their epistemic and disciplinary objects visible (literally to make them appear and appear as other) in order to subject them to a knowing, controlling gaze, as I noted in chapter 1. Michel Foucault has very convincingly demonstrated that they do this, and that they view these differences as a nature rather than as a product of their own activity. There is, therefore, nothing natural about the visibility of racial difference any more than there is about the visibility of sexual difference. Both are simulations, artificial sign systems like class. Our very anxieties about "passing," and knowing who is "really" white or "really" male reveal this. These anxieties are evident not only in our obsession with the figure of the tragic mulatto or transvestite but also in the debates about hairstyles and black politics, or high heels, makeup, and feminist politics.

What makes someone black? It is not nappy hair or a dark complexion; these signs are unreliable, despite the nineteenth century's belief in anthropometry and its development of devices for scientifically measuring cranial capacity and thickness of the lips as well as degree of hair curl or skin color. Race is not primarily a biological category, though no doubt work is even now underway to find "black" genes. Rather, as Barbara Fields points out, race is an ideological category. She recounts a probably apocryphal but nevertheless telling story about an American journalist who asked the late Papa Doc Duvalier of Haiti what percentage of the population there was white. When Duvalier answered "ninety-eight percent," the journalist, Fields writes, "was sure he had either misheard or been misunderstood, and put his question again. Duvalier assured him that he had heard and understood the question perfectly well, and had given the correct answer. Struggling to make sense of this incredible piece of information, the American finally asked Duvalier: 'How do you define white?' Duvalier answered the question with a question: 'How do you define black in your country?' Receiving the explanation that in the United States anyone with any black blood was considered black, Duvalier nodded and said, 'Well, that's the way we define white in my country.'"[26] In fact, legislation has frequently specified just what quantity of black blood "made" one black; it has been possible to be black in one state and white in another.

Something similar occurs with respect to sex. Genders, too, can be counterfeited, and as with mulattoes, "nature herself" produces hybrids (usually thought of as monstrous or defective) about whom it is possible to be mistaken at first sight. Such was the case with Herculine "Alexina" Barbin, a nineteenth-century French hermaphrodite whose diary Foucault has published.[27] Though at that time the gender-determining factor was the presence of the male gonads, now, of course, it is genes. Like anthropometry did for race, biology employs all sorts of devices for measuring sex, from anatomical inspection to hormone assays to karyotyping (chromosome testing), but it is the last that is definitive in the eyes of the law, which pierce through superficial appearance (the mere phenotype) to the very nucleus of the cell itself in search of the genotype, the essence of sex. However, even this is sometimes inconclusive: there are "disturbances" in genetic makeup that prevent a determinate karyotyping (for instance, Klinefelter's syndrome, in which the subject "is" 47 XXY and therefore neither male—46 XY—nor female—46 XX).

Still, the law could legislate sex on the basis of chromosomes, but it does not always do so. A transsexual, for instance, gets a new birth certificate after surgery, and usually has no problems obtaining a driver's license or even a passport. Yet the transsexual who is legally female on her driver's license (and, therefore, in the discourse of driving) may not be legally female in a different discourse, that of sports, for example, to which even the general public has been alerted by the notoriety surrounding the Renée Richards case. Initially the U.S. Tennis Association and the Women's Tennis Association would not allow her to compete in the U.S. Open because she was not "really" (genotypically) a woman; she sued for the right to play and won. However, she still could not play in European tennis tournaments: as far as the sport of tennis was concerned, she was female on one continent and male on another. Similarly, in *Corbett v. Corbett* (1970), the husband was granted his petition to have his marriage to a transsexual annulled; the judge decided that the marriage had not been consummated because intercourse involving an artificial cavity did not count as "natural" coitus, and in marriage, the term *woman* referred to "a person who is naturally capable of performing the essential role of a woman in marriage."[28]

The debates about style and politics in the black and women's movements reflect a concern about "real" identities similar to that which anxieties about "passing" reveal. The slogan "Black is Beautiful" was meant to prompt an "acceptance" of a black identity and a refusal to attempt to pass as white. Thus white standards of beauty were to be rejected, including—in fact, especially—"white" hair; to be black was to accept the "nature" of black hair as nappy and, accordingly, to cultivate an Afro hairstyle. Of course, the very fact that it had to be cultivated suggests that the "natural" was already a particular cultural style, an artificial sign and not a nature, its meaning determined by its difference from other signifiers (other hairstyles) and not by its indissociable bond with any referent. As a sign, an Afro meant (black) "nature," an acceptance of and indeed pride in that nature, considered only or primarily as a matter of race, and (at least for a while) a black militantism that seemed to follow from that black pride. Thus, black hair signified racial identity, black consciousness/consciousness of blackness, to black activists and white racists alike; though the political effects were different, the assumptions were not.[29]

Feminist style politics, too, have been concerned with the representation of "natural" identities. Thus the image of the "glamour girl" is said to address men rather than women, to speak to masculine rather than authentic feminine desires (that is, women who evince these desires are said to be victims of a kind of false consciousness or, where a more sophisticated notion of ideology holds sway, products of the implantation of perversions). In the name of nature, even of health and safety, women are urged to throw out their high heels, which are viewed as operating analogously to Chinese foot binding, or their girdles and bras, seen as modern versions of the constrictive and restrictive Victorian corset. This is exactly the argument Alison Lurie makes in *The Language of Clothes*, for instance. She believes that it was only possible in the late sixties and early seventies for women to dress in a way that didn't "handicap" them with respect to men, arguing that women's fashions, in all other times and places, have made women desirable to men at the expense of their comfort. Indeed, she implies throughout that such physical handicapping contributed to their desirability, as when she asserts that "clothes which make a woman's life difficult and handicap her in competition with men are always felt to be sexually attractive."[30]

The same sort of reasoning fuels the feminist rejection of makeup. Powder and paint are thought of as an artifice, covering up a woman's "natural" beauty and/or disguising her imperfections in order to make her conform to some false ideal of beauty. Besides being in the service of dishonesty (makeup meaning "made up" rather than genuine), cosmetics are harmful, damaging to a woman's limited resources of time and money or even to her health itself, as with the use, in earlier times, of lead-based powders to whiten the complexion. "The more a woman risks, the more beautiful she is seen to be—not because the risk enhances the actual beauty itself, so much as because the fact that the woman was prepared to chance so much for the sake of someone else's pleasure or approbation counts for a lot," Robin Lakoff and Raquel Scherr write.[31] Women's dependence on men for their self-esteem also divides them from each other through encouraging competition for men's approval—a theme of Susan Brownmiller's *Femininity*, which takes the argument to extremes in the claim that "every wave of feminism has foundered on the question of dress reform."[32] In fact, as I discuss in chapter 1, Brownmiller seems to advocate something like miming the masculine for the would-be feminist; she not only admires men's clothes, she admires the masculine values that she thinks they embody, and even, perhaps, inculcate. A similar sentiment motivates John Molloy's *The Woman's Dress for Success Book*, in which he advises women to wear suits—but skirted suits, a (middle-class) masculine look with a feminine difference (ensuring that a woman who "mimes" man will will display signs of her difference and so fail to "pass").[33]

For activists, as well as for conservatives, then, the signs of race and gender difference can—indeed, must—be seen and known because they are the guarantees of "real" identity. However, they are not themselves the real; rather, they are the products of the discourses that comprise the symbolic in its mapping or signifying of the real. Nevertheless, they have real, material effects, since differences, in our symbolic, are produced in power relations— imaginary, luring relationships between whites, the middle class, men, and their others. The symbolic is more than a masculine imaginary; it is a bourgeois and imperialist imaginary as well. Though it is necessary for feminists to insist, as do Jane Gallop and Jacqueline Rose, that the phallus can never be disengaged from the penis in a patriarchal symbolic, that such a misrecognition is constitutive, feminists must also insist that the phallus is not the penis, or else they risk reproducing equally constitutive misrecognitions of white, middle-class privilege.[34] This is what Irigaray does. So long as the phallus "really" is the penis, then women have not got it and never had it; therefore, they cannot be guilty of the aggressive acts and oppressive looks characteristic of the masculine imaginary, the result of anxiety about losing the symbolic/imaginary/real organ. As the hole in man's whole, woman is on the side of God for Irigaray in more than one way. She can do no wrong to others if she is the other as other: her hole, apparently, is a halo.

FEMALE FETISHISM AND IN-DIFFERENCE

Lacking is a way of having for Irigaray; woman, as other is assured of her moral rectitude, her propriety—compared to man's, hers is a proper identity (properly nonidentical, in-different). She has her *jouissance*; he has his pleasure—only his pleasure. As Gallop has pointed out, the very fact that *jouissance* cannot be translated into English signals its plenitude with respect to some lack or inadequacy.[35] It would seem English is too manly a language for speaking of feminine eroticism, whereas French is on the side of the woman. But then the French have always been notorious for their effeminacy; it is no surprise so many of them are now busy becoming woman. They know a good thing when they see it, as Lacan has revealed in his discussion of Giovanni Lorenzo Bernini's *Saint Theresa* (or, rather, Lacan knows he doesn't know, which comes to knowing just the same). When jouissance is erected into a principle in this manner, it has "the tendency to stiffen into a strong, muscular image," according to Gallop. It becomes phallic, "an ego-gratifying identity," and "fear or unworthiness are projected outward. . . ."[36] Woman can fetishize her wound (the signs of her lack), just as man does. She can disavow her castration, just as man does. And just like man, she makes use of projection to that end. But the victims of this defense mechanism are not always men but also women—"other" women. The feminine look may not always demand a becoming; it can be instrumental in aggressive disidentification from perceived images of lack—lack projected onto the white, middle-class woman's others. Irigaray's dream of a feminine imaginary veils the nightmare of oppression that often characterizes the relations between First- and Third-World women, and middle- and working-class women, relations symptomatic of an already existing feminine imaginary.

In our symbolic, some women do have what other women lack (and "other" men as well, in certain discourses); some women, that is, do "have" the phallus. Of course, no one *really* has it; rather, the symbolic encourages that misrecognition—because in it the phallus is more than the penis, since the phallus can be signified by all the other signs of power and privilege in our culture, signs that stand not only in a metaphoric and metonymic relation to "penis" but also to "white" and "bourgeois," among other potent identities. This does not mean that gender ceases to be significant even in a discourse that constructs power relations primarily along class or race lines; this primacy of other differences is only relative, and gender will still signify or make a difference in the operation of such a discourse. Because class, race, and gender are complexly articulated, the differences a discourse institutes will have class, racial, and sexual meanings all at once—meanings for narcissistic desire. Relations between members of one class or race and another, like relations between members of different genders, are desiring relations, and can be understood in terms of voyeurism and fetishism.

Female fetishism, as Naomi Schor has noted, is generally thought of as impossible (indeed, any sort of female perversion is considered by psychoanalysts to be rare; women are usually diagnosed as hysterics rather than perverts).[37] Woman is the fetish rather than the fetishist—she must be the phallus in order that man may have it and make good his lack. She therefore masquerades as the phallus so man can parade his phallus: the phallic function necessitates that both mask their lack, according to Lacan, due to "the intervention of an 'appearing' which gets substituted for the 'having' so as to protect it on one side and to mask its lack on the other. . . ."[38] Though Lacan's pronouns are notoriously (indeed, critics argue, purposefully) free-floating, "it" would here seem to refer to the phallus. What he describes is a certain shiftiness about the shifting function of the phallus, since, with regard to it, the child moves from being, to having or not having, to appearing. Appearing masks a lack both for and of the woman. Man not only fetishizes her (masks her lack), he also fetishizes himself (masks his lack). It is not just that he projects his lack onto woman and then disavows it through the fetishistic transfer of phallic value to another part of her body, some item of her clothing, etc., thereby distancing himself from lack. It is also that he maintains a belief that the phallus is the penis—a fetishistic belief of which Lacan is an exemplar—that takes the form of a disavowal which can be phrased in the manner Octave Mannoni has suggested is characteristic of fetishism: "Je sais bien mais quand même . . ."; "I know very well [that the penis is not the phallus], but all the same. . . ."[39] And woman is required to be the support of that belief; she must be maintained in her credulity (this fetishism requires a dupe besides the fetishist himself, which Mannoni might have recognized had he looked more closely into the fetishistic imposture he associates with Casanova).

The significant factor in the fetishism of imposture (of having the phallus) is that the distance between the fetishist and his object collapses. Kaja Silverman has suggested that fetishism involves a shift from the subject and the look (the glance at the nose, in the case of one patient that Sigmund Freud describes in "Fetishism") to the object and the spectacle (the shine on the nose that that same fetishist required of his feminine love object). But the displacement of lack from subject to object is never finally effected, which Silverman also points out, noting that the fetish "never stops speaking to the absolute reversibility of male viewer and female spectacle, and hence to the shared lack of subject and object."[40] This accounts for why fetishism and transvestism tend to slide into one another in practice and in theory (for instance, Otto Fenichel's early and very important article on transvestism describes it as a special case of fetishism).[41] In fact, transvestism is fetishistic imposture; if the transvestite identifies with the phallic mother as well as chooses her as his object, as analyses of transvestism reveal, so too does the fetishist. Lacan and Wladimir Granoff make this quite clear when they write that the fetishist vacillates between anxiety and guilt, the imaginary and the symbolic, "in his object-choice and, by the same token, later, in his identification."[42] Similarly, in the fetishism of the suspensory belt/bathing drawers that Freud describes, it does not seem to matter who wears the fetish. He writes that "this piece of clothing covers the genitals and altogether conceals the difference between them. The analysis showed that it could mean that a woman is castrated, or that she is not castrated, and it even allows of a supposition that a man may be castrated, for all these possibilities could be equally well hidden beneath the belt; its forerunner in childhood had been the fig-leaf seen on a statue."[43] The male fetishist oscillates between accepting and repudiating his own castration through accepting and repudiating that of the woman (the [m]other) with whom he identifies.

Yet it is this undecidability of gender difference that is usually associated with woman. Shoshana Felman and Mary Jacobus, for example, link it to femininity because the latter cannot be dissociated from hysteria as the return of woman's repressed masculinity and an expression of her bisexuality. Sarah Kofman and Elizabeth Berg, on the other hand, link such undecidability not so much to feminine hysteria (in which it is only partially expressed) but to feminine perversion, to what they call "female fetishism."[44] Both male and female fetishism involve the disavowal of lack through the imposture of appearing to have the phallus. Furthermore, because the system of sexual difference is organized around an appearing with respect to one—phallic—term, femininity, as fetishistic masquerade, is of necessity an appearing to have. Woman can only appear to be the phallus by appearing to have the phallus or what signifies having the phallus, its metaphoric and metonymic attributes, in particular, "her" fetishes. Being and having are confused in the phallicizing (virilizing) effect of masquerade. But they are equally confused in masculine parade, as Lacan reveals when he writes that "virile display itself appears as feminine."[45]

There is what might be described as a general incitement to fetishism in our culture. Both masculinity and femininity are signified fetishistically, and love itself, for both sexes, is fetishistic. The fetishistic nature of man's love has been remarked not only by feminists but by Lacan himself, who stresses that there can be no sexual relation because woman does not exist except as a symptom or fantasy of man in his desire for wholeness. Woman's love, too, is fetishistic, at least so far as her phallic jouissance is concerned, since she finds the signifier of her desire in the body of the man, and as Lacan tells us, "the organ actually invested with this signifying function takes on the value of a fetish."[46] Both sexes love to be one, according to Lacan, and the measure of this is perhaps the very tendency for phallic jouissance to slip into nonphallic jouissance, or for the former to be mistaken for the latter. This happens fairly frequently in Lacan's texts, for example, when he writes of "mystical ejaculations," which would seem to be an oxymoron, given his alignment of mysticism with nonphallic jouissance.[47] The effect is to make it possible for him to be both man and woman, mystic and analyst, to know that he does not know (unlike the female mystic herself, who, he insists, knows nothing), as I pointed out in the introduction. The new and jubilant assumption of femininity by male poststructuralist theorists who "become woman" (or feminists) can have the same old oppressive effects, as I argue at length in the fourth chapter.

The in-difference of phallic and nonphallic jouissance also occurs in some feminist texts at those moments when what is supposed to be nonphallic jouissance fixes rather than undoes wholeness. As I suggested above, this happens when woman erects her lack into a principle of identity, fetishizing the signs of her lack just as man does, insisting she is in his imaginary rather than being in one of her own at the same time. She thereby perpetuates the misrecognition of the penis as the phallus, when in fact the penis is not the only substitute for the phallic signifier, as fetishism's displacements only too clearly reveal. The significance of these displacements is apparent if it is recalled that the loss of the mother (she is lacking to and for the subject after the symbolic father's intervention) comes to symbolize all the preceding losses. Desire has to to do with loss; it is a remainder, what has been subtracted from the whole and is excessive in demand. The missing part is symbolized by the *objet a*, which promotes the fetish. Associated with the other, it renders him desirable, allowing the other to be confused with the "Other" (a confusion that analysis sets out to undo, according to Lacan). But it also renders him fearful; it is almost, but not quite, a phobic object (since it is almost, but not quite, lost). The fetish disturbs identity because it is an encounter with castration or lack. Yet it also attracts the subject, exerting the fascination of the primary repressed, which is linked to the mother and the pre-oedipal oral, anal, scopic, and invocatory drives. The fetish threatens the subject with a castration that would be a complete loss of self even while it promises the jouissance that loss of identity as fusion with the [m]other would enable.

But the fetish takes on its significance because it symbolizes more than the lack of the [m]other. Peter Stallybrass and Allon White foreground this in their attempt to theorize the psyche in terms of class.[48] In a productive rereading of Mikhail Bakhtin, they argue that hysteria is not just an expression of bisexuality but also of a repressed (abjected) carnivalesque associated with the lower class. They detail how the middle-class subject is constituted over and against the working-class female in particular, the maids and nannies employed by the Victorian and Edwardian bourgeoisie, who inhabited the middle-class home as an otherness within. These women were an erotic constituent of bourgeois fantasy life because they represented all that had to be repudiated by the middle-class child as she grew up: what Bakhtin calls the "grotesque body." The latter is associated with the regressive decomposition of the partial drives that are unified and hierarchized under the genital drive in the "classic body," all that must be lost—given up—in order to have a proper identity, which I have linked to the fetish and *objet a*. The grotesque body knows little of proper dress, manners, speech, or hygiene; in the way it looks, acts, talks, and smells it reveals its difference or otherness from the classic body—or, rather, the classed body, since it is the proletarian who "lacks" class. This, of course, is just as true today as it was in the Victorian period. (The theory does not depend on the actual presence of servants in the home; a proper upbringing with the right dose of representations of the class other—in school, or on television—would suffice.) Both then and now, to have class is to be at a controlling distance from what signifies its lack.

Homi Bhabha describes a similar psychic mechanism at work in the construction of colonial subjects, and he explicitly labels it *fetishism*.[49] He argues that ethnic subjectification is made possible through stereotyping, which produces points of identification in scenes of fear and desire even as it produces racial difference. The difference of the ethnic other is conceived (projected) as lack and so is misrecognized: the racial imaginary, like the class and gender imaginary, is organized around one term, the *phallus*, and an appearing to have or to lack it. Signs of racial difference, therefore, function fetishistically, enabling the disavowal of lack or difference and the play between narcissistic identification with an image of wholeness (the other as the phallus, the "Other") and aggressive disidentification from an image of lack (the other as lacking the phallus).

Bhabha recounts what he refers to as one of Frantz Fanon's "primal scenes" of (the disavowal) of racial difference in order to underline the violence of the positioning of the raced body. In the scene, a little white girl "fixes Fanon in look and word" as she turns from him to identify with her mother, saying "Look, a Negro . . . Mamma, *see* the Negro! I'm frightened. Frightened." Fanon describes the experience as "an amputation, an excision."[50] Its violence is that of a castration, as in the retrospective understanding of the sexual primal scene. In each primal scene subjects are positioned with respect to signifiers of the phallic signifier; there are only two positions, and they are antithetical: one has or lacks color; one has or lacks the penis. And just as sexual difference can be refused and recognized at the same time in fetishistic disavowal, so too can racial/ethnic difference be disavowed. Signs of it are both feared and sought for in the object, who is both punished and worshipped (or at least romanticized) for the difference these signs display. It is exactly their fetishistic value that have made skin color and hair curl key signifiers in racist and black activist politics, as I suggested above. They mark a lacking and a having at the same time, and the vacillation between these poles is fixed (or the attempt is made to fix it) in order to ground a politics of identity (whether conservative or radical).

It is not surprising, then, that a middle class Victorian gentleman like Arthur Munby should have found his maid, Hannah Cullwick, particularly desirable when she would "do the signs of . . . [her] lowness" and was "dressed in . . . [her] dirt."[51] As Stallybrass and White describe him, Munby was clearly a class fetishist, whose pleasure in his object depended on the fearful/desirable presence of what he had (almost but not quite) repudiated or "lost": the (abject) signifiers of class otherness. His attitude to Cullwick was both sadistic and masochistic. Even after he married her, he would not condone an education for her and still took pleasure in her drudgery, to the extreme of having her lick his boots and wear a slave collar to which he held the key (she called him "Massa," what they took to be the black slave's word for master, which suggests the fascination with racial as well as class and gender difference in their relationship).[52] Yet Munby also admired her "strength" (a common fantasy about the working class), in particular, her work-roughened hands (they both appreciated the fact that her hands were too big to fit in his gloves). And when Cullwick engaged in cross-dressing games, it was to allow Munby to express his admiration for a working class/masculine strength he fancied she embodied. In addition, he liked to sit on her knee or be given a bath by her as if he were a child. There was, then, a certain limited reversibility in their relationship (though it always addressed Munby's fantasies), in which Cullwick functioned as a phallic other whom

Munby both revered and reviled because her difference(s) guaranteed, and at the same time threatened, his "wholeness."

Fetishism maintains the subject on the edge of subjection itself, poised between the imaginary and the symbolic, acceding to phallic and nonphallic jouissance in an in-difference from the phallic other. The point is not that fetishism makes the fetishist passive with respect to the phallic other who threatens castration, as D. N. Rodowick (in a reconsideration of Mulvey on voyeurism and fetishism) or Berkeley Kaite (in an essay on pornography, including transvestic pornography) insist.[53] Rather, the significance of fetishistic disavowal is its doubleness: the fetishist is both active and passive, castrating and castrated—the split in the object is generated by the split in the subject because the [m]other and what she symbolizes have not yet been split off or lost. As far as the psyche is concerned, then, fetishism/transvestism is both conservative and transgressive. This is an obvious point once it is recognized that all subjects engage in imposture (either masquerade or parade) with respect to the "appearing" the relation to the phallus demands. Man and woman dupe each other into a certain credulity about "having" because they are the dupes of a symbolic that they reproduce as it produces them.

The "cure" for the fetishist (male or female) in the phallic imaginary that is misrecognized as a symbolic does not involve a disidentification from images of lack and concomitant identification with phallic images (of having) so as to mitigate aggressivity. This is what Ellie Ragland-Sullivan suggests women should do in order to break with the symbolic as a patriarchal imaginary.[54] However, it is, in effect, to call for positive images of women, a practice that has been thoroughly critiqued by many feminists because it does not reorder the social but merely allows a new group access to the same old suspect values if they engage in the imaginary game (to say nothing of the implication that identification is only a matter of volition rather than a process rooted in the unconscious). And the imaginary game is one in which women are already engaged if the phallus is not just masculine but also white and bourgeois privilege, as I have been arguing.

However, if the cure cannot be disidentification from lack, it cannot simply consist in identification with it, either. Were a "lacking" identity already "assigned" one by the symbolic taken up, this would reinscribe the relations the symbolic has instituted (its values and its imaginary). And to identify with the other whom one is not is impossible from the point of view of the "Other," which is the locus of truth (another way of saying that the symbolic assigns or legislates identity on the basis of its imaginary). Such an identification would, therefore, be an imaginary gesture in its positive form, as I noted in chapter 1. Romantic (when not psychotic), it echoes the fetishist's worship of the wound he has himself inflicted, and still signifies a desire to be whole; it involves a misrecognition of the self as the other who is the "Other." Rather than repeating the imaginary, the cure should effect a break with the imaginary (it must repeat it knowingly, placing it at a distance). This means interrogating what signifies lacking and having and determining what one's position is in the phallic symbolic's imaginary game(s) through recognizing how one is both fetishized and fetishizing at the same time.

Such a cure would necessitate what Jane Gallop calls "dephallicization": assuming the phallus and an identity (including a collective identity) on its basis and critiquing that assumption, unveiling it as fraud.[55] It will require both the risk of sameness (by daring to speak of one's equal right to symbolic privileges because of it) and the risk of difference (by daring to speak of the need to change the symbolic because of it). The strategy will be to multiply resistances, affiliations, and insurrectionary knowledges and modes of knowledge production in order to create new social and desiring relationships (since in the social desire is inescapable). For instance, feminists must speak as women, differently, even hysterically, but also as men, in the name of reason, refusing to give over reason to the conservatives. Women must "take on" their identity, accept it and critique it, and critique it explicitly in the name of the differences within: within the self and the collectivity (which is not an imaginary homogeneous class called "women"). They must see both their differences from and similarity to their others (masculine and feminine), and analyze the effects of this, avoiding a pluralistic celebration of difference as sameness, oneness (a unified body politic), which would be to repeat the jubilation of the imaginary even while engaging in its aggression.

IRIGARAYAN MIMICRY AND FEMALE FETISHISM

It is just such an imaginary jubilation Irigaray engages in when she proposes there is a feminine imaginary that is purely other with respect to the masculine imaginary, untainted by its aggression and self-aggrandizement. This is a misrecognition with oppressive consequences for women who, in their relationships with white, middle-class women, are constructed as lacking. The mimicry Irigaray advocates as a strategy for disrupting the masculine imaginary and producing the utopic community of the feminine imaginary is itself a practice of a dominative imaginary because the unconscious desires subtending it have remained unanalyzed. I have already suggested above that mimicry's effects on the masculine imaginary are equivocal precisely because there is no one masculine imaginary per se; the latter is heterogeneous once class and race, in addition to gender, are considered as factors in phallic fetishism. The look of the white bourgeoise at the classed and raced male other can be controlling and knowing, projecting lack on to him and finding the signs of difference as justification for his exploitation. But if her look can be castrating, it can also be worshipful; both moments are characteristic of the fetishistic gaze, according to Freud.

For instance, the white woman may both denigrate and romanticize the ethnic other, fear and desire him (or her) in the process of disavowing difference and lack. To primitivize the ethnic other is to assimilate him to the West as an alter ego, positioning both at opposite ends of an evolutionary scale. This sanctions the allegorical move in which the West reads in the other all that has been lost in the name of progress, civilization (mistaking the the other for the "Other"). The primitive is seen as being closer to nature— Mother Earth—as well as being able to enjoy a more natural, uninhibited sexuality. Thus advertisements often sell products by representing them in association with lands of exotic adventure, discreetly hinting at exotic sexual adventures as well, as Judith Williamson and Kim Sawchuk have demonstrated.[56] This is particularly true of tourism of itself. The holiday snapshot of picturesque natives in ethnic dress in authentic local haunts not on any of the tourist maps aestheticizes difference. As Christian Metz has explained, the aesthetic look differentiates subject and object by turning the latter into a picture, making it imaginary even in its presence: the picturesque is a picture.[57] Or, rather than aestheticizing and romanticizing, the picture might prove that difference is degradation, even disease, and that the native's so-called uninhibited sexuality is the cancer consuming a degenerate social body. Hence we have Africa as the land of unself-conscious, bare-breasted women, and Africa as the land of AIDS.

The significance of ethnic difference for mimicry is revealed by the reactions of the press to the clothing (in particular, the shoes) of Imelda Marcos when she was arraigned in federal court on charges of embezzlement and bank fraud. As *Time* magazine describes it, "the former Philippine First Lady stunned the waiting throng with her sheer, low-cut turquoise *terno*—the national costume in her homeland. Amid pushing photographers and chanting protesters, the elegant attire seemed inappropriate for the occasion. . . ."[58] The implication, of course, is that the terno is inappropriately feminine, too feminine, for the manly business of legal prosecution by Uncle Sam (underlined as well in the affirmative-action suit brought by an assistant state attorney in Florida, who was fired for her high fashion taste): a three-piece suit, perhaps navy blue with an understated pinstripe, would have been more acceptable, less provocative. Though it might seem Marcos should have read John Molloy's *The Woman's Dress for Success Book*, she knew what she was doing; the dress, she said, was meant to show that she was a Philippine patriot. She has understood the feminization of Third-World countries by the United States or, rather, that their fetishization has a feminizing effect.

The culture of Third-World women (their clothing, their sexuality, their rights and duties) is the object of intense scrutiny by both the First and the Third Worlds in the struggle over the meaning of woman (and her activities) as a sign in discourses about gender and about imperialism, as the fascination with clitoridectomy in particular reveals. Marcos's shoes (the exemplary fetish for Freud) signified a certain lack in the Philippines for the West, what had to be repudiated. Corazon Aquino, more sensibly shod, seemed better able to keep in step with the march toward (Western) progress. What is required of her is a mimicry of middle-class Western woman, who, in turn, is expected to mime middle-class Western man. It is not so much that there is a displacement of questions of gender into questions of race and class or the reverse; rather, gender is never thought outside race and class. This is the point Sander Gilman makes in his discussion of nineteenth-century discourses about the Hottentot and the prostitute, which fetishize the female genitals themselves (as in pornography) as a sign of fearful/desirable differences of class, race, and gender differences—and power/pleasure relations—these discourses help (re)produce.[59]

I would argue that class difference in particular is the support—and unintended effect—of mimicry in its conception by Irigaray and others as a strategy open to white, middle-class feminists to disrupt "the" imaginary. As I have noted above in my discussion of Stallybrass and White, the classy or "classic" body is one that is at a controlling distance from the classless or "grotesque" body. But because this voyeurism is fetishistic, it involves a romanticization as well as a denigration of the class other (as "Other") and a pleasurable/threatening in-difference that fetishism keeps in play through an oscillation between disidentification and identification. It is just this in-difference that mimicry calls for—mimicry is not so much a strategy leading to the feminine imaginary Irigaray dreams about as it is a practice deeply embedded in "the" feminine imaginary that already exists. This becomes clear once it is recognized that class fetishism does not operate only in heterosexuality, which is how Stallybrass and White describe it, but also in homosexuality and, therefore, at least potentially in lesbianism, including the sort of lesbianism associated with the imaginary of Irigaray's "When Our Lips Speak Together."

In fact, Jeffrey Weeks points out that there was a "widely recognized upper-middle-class fascination with crossing the class divide, a fascination that shows a direct continuity between male heterosexual and male homosexual mores."[60] He goes on to say that this was perhaps due to a feeling that sex could not be "natural" with a member of one's own class, and that a working-class man was considered more desirable because he was a "real man"—

inherently heterosexual (that is, he "really had" the phallus)—by comparison with the homosexual's middle-class and aristocratic counterpart. This would seem to suggest that if the working-class male was the man's man, the middle- or upper-class male was only a partially successful male impersonator, something like John Molloy's skirted businesswoman, whose phallic imposture dupes no one (it is a masculine look with a—telling—feminine difference). Of course, it is exactly class difference that becomes a desirable difference in E. M. Forster's *Maurice*; as in D. H. Lawrence's *Lady Chatterley's Lover* it is the working-class gamekeeper whose "natural" sexuality incites and fulfills the desires of his "superior," symptomatic of a fetishistic bourgeois fantasmatic.

This has obvious implications for a potentially utopic lesbian look. Feminist theorists generally discuss women's pleasures as unmotivated by voyeurism or fetishism, but once class and ethnic difference is seen as productive of (fetishistic) desire, then forms of otherness between women assume an erotic significance that all too often has been overlooked. To the extent that both men and women are subject to symbolic castration, both wish to find an object of the drive to close up the lack; both love to be one and conflate the other (as bearer of the *objet a*, the abject remainder) with the "Other." Gallop usefully draws attention to this in an essay on Annie LeClerc's letter to her lesbian lover, who Gallop suggests is aligned with the maidservant in the Jan Vermeer painting *Lady Writing a Letter, with her Maid* to which LeClerc frequently refers.[61] Gallop points out that LeClerc romanticizes the servant as an all-knowing plenitude, making her function as the narcissistic and desirable woman for the lady, as the lady does for her lover. The maid is, therefore, a kind of woman's woman. If she plays the phallus for her lady, as Gallop seems to be suggesting, then the mistress can be said to disavow lack by projecting it onto her maid in order to find the signs of it there, an imaginary misrecognition like that Stallybrass and White suggest generally occurs between the middle class and its working-class other. Just as the lady is the phallus for her male lover, so the maid is the phallus for the lady (in a repressed lesbian desire). The feminine look is here fetishistic.

It may be premature, then, to celebrate a film like Susan Seidelman's *Desperately Seeking Susan*, as Jackie Stacey does, for constructing a lesbian subject through narrativizing a woman's investigation of the enigma of femininity and aligning the gaze of the camera with the female detective protagonist.[62] In fact, Susan, played by Madonna, strikes bourgeois housewife Roberta as an exciting and desirable mystery woman precisely because she is not middle class. Furthermore, Roberta is confused as to whether she wants Susan or wants to be Susan, a confusion characteristic of fetishism, which I have described as an oscillation between being and having the phallus played out in the realm of appearance (not having/having). This confusion is particularly evident when Roberta goes "slumming," attempting to pass as Susan, at which point her fetishism of Susan's leather jacket is quite marked. Of course, Roberta's fetishism of Susan/Madonna, her clothes and her gestures (smoking, for instance) is not unlike the fetishism of any other Madonna wanna-be —or even Madonna herself, who seems to have experienced a similar confusion over Marilyn Monroe.

Confusion—or female impersonation, mimicry? Along with Mae West, Phyllis Diller, and Dolly Parton, Marilyn Monroe is one of the most often mimed characters in female impersonator shows. Perhaps the only way to appear to mimic rather than masquerade as the feminine is to impersonate a man impersonating a woman. This is evidently what Dolly Parton thinks she is doing and is how Karen Newman accounts for what she argues is Kate's female transvestism in her reading of William Shakespeare's *The Taming of the Shrew*.[63] According to Newman, what supports her interpretation is the fact that the role of Kate was filled by a male transvestite, which calls attention to the representation of femininity as a representation. Similarly, Mary Russo wonders if women "putting on" the feminine risk reinscribing themselves as objects of contempt in a way that men who put on the feminine do not, while Toril Moi suggests that there is nothing revolutionary about Jane Gallop's conscious strategy of writing from the position of castration, since women have always had to do so.[64] When woman mimes woman, the illusion could succeed too well. The representation might fail to reveal itself as a fictional construct, an imposture or simulation that does not reflect "the real thing." What could ensure a difference between masquerade and mimicry, "woman" and woman?

I have already made it clear that the answer to that question has to do with class, race, and ethnicity, which figure significantly for mimicry. As Dolly Parton opened this chapter on the gender act, it is only fitting that she should close it. From what perspective can she be seen as a mimic, a female impersonator, as she herself has suggested she is? How can her illusion of femininity be said to fail when she seems to love to "do" it, from her platinum blonde wigs down to her stiletto heels? No doubt it is because from a middle-class point of view she overdoes it; she does not quite get femininity right; her style is too tacky, her taste for the excessive in excessively bad taste. Of course, good taste, as Susan Brownmiller and John Molloy have demonstrated, is always that of the middle class (man), understated, even conservative, a classic suit or its feminine facsimile, the skirted suit. In this regard, likening mimicry to female impersonation because it exaggerates "the real thing," as feminists generally do, is revealing, since it is exactly the exaggeration of femininity that feminists object to in men's female impersonations.

Many feminists regard the latter as aggressive burlesques on the grounds of the bad taste they exhibit. For instance, in her book on fashion, Alison Lurie writes, "Although women in male clothes usually look like gentlemen, men who wear women's clothes, unless they are genuine transsexuals, seem to imitate the most vulgar and unattractive sort of female dress, as if in a spirit of deliberate and hostile parody." The transsexual, she adds, "usually prefers the sort of clothes a woman of his own age and social position would choose."[65] The class anxiety here is transparent: if boys will be girls they had better be ladies. The same maxim would apply equally to girls: a real woman is a real lady; otherwise, she is a female impersonator.

A woman passes for the real thing when she masquerades as a middle-class man, an imposture always seen through because of the feminine difference: the suit with a skirt. A woman passes for "passing" for the real thing, miming it, when she masquerades as a working-class woman, an imposture always seen as such because of her "unnaturally" bad taste: the skirt with the sequins and the slit up to the navel. The implication is that only middle-class women are real women. Mimicry can be distinguished from masquerade because there are significant—that is, signifying—differences between women. From a middle-class perspective, Dolly Parton may indeed look like a female impersonator; from a working-class perspective, she may be the epitome of genuine womanliness. Nor does what she says she intends matter as far as the effects of her public appearance are concerned; what counts is the positioning within multiple differences of her audience.

The feminists in the audience all too often see her only through middle-class eyes. Female fetishists, they distance themselves from working-class women even as they assimilate the latter by romanticizing them as the locus of a critical knowledge about femininity, critical because of its presumed distance from what counts as natural femininity: bourgeois style. Miming the feminine, then, means impersonating a middle-class impersonation of a working-class ideal of femininity. It calls for "flaunting" lack by projecting it onto the class other, from whom the mimic distances herself though an apparent identification that is in fact a disidentification: it is implicit that the feminine look at "the" feminine look precludes a becoming when the latter is in bad taste. Judith Williamson suggests that "the appropriation of other people's dress is fashionable provided it is perfectly clear that you are, in fact, *different* from whoever would normally wear such clothes."[66] Feminist theorists of mimicry merely seem to substitute "critical" for "fashionable"; the indifference to the politics of such an appropriation is the same, a politics based on a disavowal of the multiplicity of differences that signify lack. As disavowal, the disidentification from the other in mimicry also includes identification; mimicry—female fetishism—maintains the subject on the edge and threatens the subject's self-identity even as it seems to consolidate it. This accounts for both the feminist desire for positive images of women with which to identify, and its corollary, the fear of being identified with negative images of women (as evinced by Russo and Moi, for instance). But there is a world of significance in the difference between identifying with and being identified with or as some other—the world of the symbolic. The symbolic legislates the imaginary dyad(s) in which the subject finds herself locked in identification/disidentification with (phallic fantasies of) the other: as the "third term" it both produces them and intervenes in them in the name of truth, the truth about the subject's "real" identities. A subject's imaginary is, then, always already part of the symbolic's imaginary and its misrecognitions, the effect of which is domination. It is these effects that must be analyzed if the mirrors of the imaginary are to be shattered. For in the fetishistic scene, if the subject is on the edge, the object/other is only a phallic fantasy. She does not exist as such.

This is a statement with a double meaning: the other does not exist for the subject (who is only concerned about her wholeness) and the other is a subject in his own right, with desires, an unconscious and also an imaginary that may break against the (phallic) fantasy the subject has about her otherness. What might the other have to say about mimicry? This is a question that takes its significance from the fact that white, bourgeois, heterosexual femininity has been the standard against which deviancy has been measured, even if it is itself measured against white, bourgeois, heterosexual masculinity and found wanting. It is precisely her relation to the feminine "norm" that Dolly Parton understands when she says she is a female impersonator, which reveals something about the constitution of her subjectivity, as well as about the potentially oppressive effects of mimicry. The black or working-class woman's mimicry could only be "passing," which by definition is the opposite of mimicry; the strategy, therefore, puts her in a double bind. However, theories of mimicry have not concerned themselves with the other's problems or subjectivity; the other is constituted as what must be repudiated (a symptom) or what can make one whole (the Other who knows, who can guarantee one's full knowledge and self-presence). If there is an irony in mimicry, as feminists have insisted, it is at the expense of the "other" woman, unconscious and unconscionable. Feminists must be sensitive to their positioning in a number of discourses beside those of gender in order to redress this insensitivity to their class and ethnic others. We must begin to recognize the articulation of our own imaginary fixations with those of the symbolic in all of our practices and relationships, or our feminism will be part of the problem rather than the solution.

NOTES

1. Irigaray discusses mimicry (and masquerade) in a number of places, most prominently in *This Sex Which Is Not One*, trans. Catherine Porter (Ithaca: Cornell University Press), 76–77, 133–34.
2. Ibid., 76.
3. Jane Gallop, *Reading Lacan* (Ithaca: Cornell University Press, 1985), 60.
4. Cindy Sherman, *Cindy Sherman* (New York: Pantheon Books, 1984); the photo described is plate no. 1.
5. Judith Williamson, "Images of 'Woman,'" *Screen*, 24:6 (1983), 103.
6. Craig Owens, "The Discourse of Others: Feminists and Postmodernism," *The Anti-Aesthetic: Essays on Postmodern Culture*, ed. Hal Foster (Port Townsend, WA: Bay Press, 1983), 75.
7. Craig Owens, "The Allegorical Impulse: Toward A Theory of Postmodernism," *Art After Modernism: Rethinking Representation*, ed. Brian Wallis (New York: New Museum of Contemporary Art, 1984), 233–35.
8. Peter Schjeldahl, "The Oracle of Images," introduction to *Cindy Sherman*, 8–9. Many other passages from the essay would have served to make this point. The supposed foregrounding of masculine voyeurism and fetishism through the obvious framing of the picture (to which even he refers) made no difference in his pleasure.
9. Cahiers du Cinema collective, "Morocco," trans. Diana Matias, in *Sternberg*, ed. Peter Baxter (London: British Film Institute, 1980), 92.
10. Jane Gaines, "White Privilege and Looking Relations: Race and Gender in Feminist Film Theory," Patricia Erens, ed. *Feminist Film Theory*. (Bloomington: Indiana University Press, 1990), 197–214.
11. Manthia Diawara, "Black Spectatorship—Problems of Identification and Resistance," *Screen* 29:4 (1988), 67–70 and 73–74.
12. Irigaray, *This Sex*, 205–18.
13. Ibid., 24.
14. See the chapter entitled "Metaphor and Metonymy" in Jane Gallop, *Reading Lacan*, 114–32.
15. Irigaray, *This Sex*, 79; emphasis in the original.
16. Ibid., 79.
17. Ibid., 177.
18. Ibid., 180.
19. Ibid., 197.
20. Ibid., 173.
21. Ibid., 209.
22. Rosalind Coward, *Gay Left* 10 (1980), 9.
23. Old Westbury, NY: *The Feminist Press*, 1981.
24. Coward, 9.
25. Gayatri Chakravorty Spivak, seminar conducted at the Pembroke Center for Teaching and Research on Women, Brown University, November 12, 1987.
26. Barbara Fields, "Ideology and Race in American History," in *Region, Race, and Reconstruction: Essays in Honor of C. Vann Woodward*, eds. J. Morgan Kousser and James McPherson (New York: Oxford University Press, 1982), 146.
27. Herculine Barbin, *Herculine Barbin: Being the Recently Discovered Memoirs of a Nineteenth Century French Hermaphrodite*, intro. Michel Foucault, trans. Richard McDougall (New York: Pantheon Books, 1980).

28. The case (British) is discussed by Beverley Brown and Parveen Adams in "The Feminine Body and Feminist Politics," *m/f* 3 (1979), 48.

29. A very astute article on this topic is Kobena Mercer, "Black Hair/Style Politics," *New Formations* 3 (1987), 33–54. For an opposing opinion, see Derrick McClintock, "Colour," *Ten. 8*, no. 22 (1986), 26–29.

30. Alison Lurie, *The Language of Clothes* (New York: Vintage, 1983), 220.

31. Robin Lakoff and Raquel Scherr, *Face Value: The Politics of Beauty* (Boston: Routledge and Kegan Paul, 1984), 282.

32. Susan Brownmiller, *Femininity* (New York: Fawcett Columbine, 1984), 79.

33. John Molloy, *The Woman's Dress for Success Book* (New York: Warner, 1977).

34. Jane Gallop, "Phallus/Penis: Same Difference," in *Men by Women*, ed. Janet Todd (New York: Holmes and Meier, 1981), 243–51; my section title deliberately echoes the title of this essay; Jacqueline Rose, "Introduction: II," in *Feminine Sexuality*, eds. Jacqueline Rose and Juliet Mitchell (New York: W. W. Norton, 1982), 56.

35. Jane Gallop, "Beyond the Jouissance Principle," *Representations* 7 (1984), 112.

36. Ibid., 114.

37. Naomi Schor, "Female Fetishism: The Case of George Sand," in *The Female Body in Western Culture*, ed. Susan Suleiman (Cambridge, MA: Harvard University Press, 1986), 363–72.

38. Jacques Lacan, "The Meaning of the Phallus," in Rose and Mitchell, eds., *Feminine Sexuality*, 84.

39. He meditates on fetishism in "Je sais bien, mais quand même . . ." in *Clefs pour l'imaginaire ou l'autre scène* (Paris: Editions du Seuil, 1969), 9–33.

40. Kaja Silverman, *The Acoustic Mirror: The Female Voice in Psychoanalysis and Cinema* (Bloomington: Indiana University Press, 1988), 20.

41. Otto Fenichel, "The Psychology of Transvestism" (1930); reprt. in *Psychoanalysis and Male Sexuality*, ed. Hendrik M. Ruitenbeek (New Haven: College and University Press, 1966), 203–20.

42. Jacques Lacan and Wladimir Granoff, "Fetishism: The Symbolic, the Imaginary and the Real," in *Perversions: Psychodynamics and Therapy*, ed. Sandor Lorand (New York: Gramercy Publishing Co., 1956), 273.

43. Sigmund Freud, "Fetishism," in *Sexuality and the Psychology of Love*, ed. Philip Rieff (1927; reprt. New York: Collier, 1963), 218–19. When Silverman discusses the case (*Acoustic Mirror*, 21), she assumes that the woman wears the belt, but I think Freud is equivocal on this point. The possibility of wearing the clothes of the same sex for transvestic purposes has been outlined by the psychoanalyst George Zavitzianos, who considers this a "perversion" he named "homeovestism." He says the subject engages in it in order to deny castration and reinforce an identification with the parent of the same sex (which are, I am arguing, the reasons behind fetishistic imposture as well); see "Homeovestism: Perverse Form of Behaviour Involving Wearing Clothes of the Same Sex," *International Journal of Psycho-Analysis* 53 (1972), 471–77.

44. Shoshana Felman, "Rereading Femininity," *Yale French Studies* 62 (1981), 19–44; Mary Jacobus, "Reading Woman (Reading)," in *Reading Woman: Essays in Feminist Criticism* (New York: Columbia University Press, 1986); Sarah Kofman, *The Enigma of Woman: Woman in Freud's Writings*, trans. Catherine Porter (Ithaca: Cornell University Press, 1985), esp. 202–10; Sarah Kofman, "Ça cloche," in *Les Fins de L'homme: A partir de Jacques Derrida*, ed. Philippe Lacoue-Labarthe and Jean-Luc Nancy (Paris: Galilée, 1981), 83–116; Elizabeth Berg, "The Third Woman," *Diacritics* 12 (1982), 11–20.

45. Lacan, "The Meaning of the Phallus," 85. Female fetishism in particular is linked to the confusion of being and having in two Lacanian analyses of it: George Bonnet, "Fétichisme et exhibitionnisme chez un sujet féminin," in *Psychanalyse à l'université*, vol. 2 (Paris: Editions Replique, 1976), 231–57, and François Sirois, "Fétiche de femme," *Revue française de psychanalyse* 47 (1983), 409–11.

46. Lacan, "The Meaning of the Phallus," 84.

47. Lacan, "God and the Jouissance of The Woman," in Rose and Mitchell, eds., *Feminine Sexuality*, 147.

48. Peter Stallybrass and Allon White, *The Politics and Poetics of Transgression* (Ithaca: Cornell University Press, 1986).

49. Homi K. Bhabha, "The Other Question: Difference, Discrimination, and the Discourse of Colonialism," in *Literature, Politics, and Theory: Papers from the Essex Conference, 1976–84*, eds. Francis Barker et al. (New York and London: Methuen, 1985), 148–72.

50. Bhabha, "Queston," 163. Of course, the fact that it is a little girl who figures in the scene is not without significance, though Bhabha does not remark on it; as I suggest below, because women are made to signify race or nation, their purity guarantees the purity of the group and a certain vigilance over it is maintained. Thus both the fear of the dilution of "the blood" through miscegenation and the fear of the loss of indigenous or native practices seem to redound on women more than men.

51. Stallybrass and White, *Politics*, 155.

52. For the first four years of their marriage, Cullwick lived with Munby as his maid. I am indebted to Lenore Davidoff's essay for some of the details of their relationship; see her "Class and Gender in Victorian England," in *Sex and Class in Women's History*, eds. Judith Newton et al. (Boston: Routledge and Kegan Paul, 1983), 16–71.

53. D. N. Rodowick, "The Difficulty of Difference," *Wide Angle* 5 (1982), 4–15; Berkeley Kaite, "The Pornographer's Body Double: Transgression Is the Law," in *Body Invaders: Panic Sex in America*, eds. Arthur and Marilouise Kroker (New York: St. Martin's Press, 1987), 150–68.

54. Ellie Ragland-Sullivan, *Jacques Lacan and the Philosophy of Psychoanalysis* (Urbana: University of Illinois Press, 1986), 302–3.

55. Jane Gallop, *The Daughter's Seduction: Feminism and Psychoanalysis* (Ithaca: Cornell University Press, 1982), 121–23.

56. Judith Williamson, "Woman Is an Island: Femininity and Colonization," in *Studies in Entertainment: Critical Approaches to Mass Culture*, ed. Tania Modleski (Bloomington: Indiana University Press, 1986), 99–118; Kim Sawchuk, "A Tale of Inscription/ Fashion Statements," in Kroker and Kroker, eds., *Body Invaders*, 61–77.

57. Christian Metz, *The Imaginary Signifier*, trans. Ben Brewster (Bloomington: Indiana University Press, 1977), 62–63.

58. Jacob Lamar, "From Ally to Pariah," *Time*, November 14, 1988, 24. I have no wish to defend Marcos; the intent here is to point out the fetishistic fantasmatic of the press. The story about the assistant state attorney (Brenda Taylor) bringing an affirmative action suit appears in the same issue, 98. It is perhaps not surprising, given the recent fascination with "sex scandals," that Taylor was told she looked like a "bimbo." Her case would seem to be exactly that of the masquerade that veils masculinity, as described by Joan Riviere in "Womanliness as a Masquerade," Ruitenbeek, ed., *Psychoanalysis and Female Sexuality*, 213–29. Ironically, the story about Taylor mentions the affirmative action suit being brought by another woman (Ann Hopkins,

against Price Waterhouse in Washington, D.C.), who says she lost her job because she wasn't feminine enough for her employers, who had advised her to "wear makeup, have her hair styled and wear jewelry."

59. Sander Gilman, "The Hottentot and the Prostitute: Toward an Iconography of Female Sexuality," in *Difference and Pathology: Stereotypes of Sexuality, Race, and Madness* (Ithaca: Cornell University Press, 1985), 76–108.

60. Jeffrey Weeks, "Inverts, Perverts, and Mary-Annes: Male Prostitution and the Regulation of Homosexuality in England in the Nineteenth and Early Twentieth Centuries," *Journal of Homosexuality* 6:1–2 (1980/81), 121.

61. Jane Gallop, "Annie Leclerc Writing a Letter, with Vermeer," in *The Poetics of Gender,* ed. Nancy Miller (New York: Columbia University Press, 1986), 137–56. Interestingly, the cover of this book repeats the shoe fetishism I have described above; gender differences are inscribed in terms of class differences: a work boot such as a construction worker might wear touches the toe of a "sensible" black pump (plain, with no spike heel) that a career woman might wear. Once again, the working-class man signifies the real man. There may also be a suggestion here that he is the one whose gender politics especially are in need of change—the classic feminist (indeed, feminine) complaint is about the catcall or whistle from the construction worker.

62. Jackie Stacey, "Desperately Seeking Difference," *Screen* 28:1 (1987), 48–61.

63. Karen Newman, "Renaissance Family Politics and Shakespeare's *The Taming of the Shrew*," *English Literary Renaissance* 26 (1986), esp. 98–100.

64. Mary Russo, "Female Grotesques: Carnival and Theory," in *Feminist Studies/Critical Studies*, ed. Teresa de Lauretis (Bloomington: Indiana University Press, 1986), 216; unfortunately, Russo, who chides Bakhtin for having failed to address gender (219), herself fails to address class, a significant oversight, given that Bakhtin's theory of carnival is explicitly about "class" relations in precapitalist society; Toril Moi, "Feminism, Postmodernism, and Style: Recent feminist Criticism in the United States," *Cultural Critique* 9 (1988), esp. 14–15.

65. Lurie, *Language*, 258; 259.

66. Williamson, "Woman Is an Island," 115.

FEMINISM, RACISM, AND IMPERSONATION

We need more feminist work that interrogates sexual ideologies for their racial specificity and acknowledges whiteness, not just blackness, as a racial categorization.

—HAZEL CARBY, *RECONSTRUCTING WOMANHOOD*

F eminists have been troubled by the pleasure so many representations of femininity provide because that pleasure is complicit with patriarchy, helping to reproduce oppressive gender identities. As long as women give pleasure to men by identifying with "woman," that image of femininity in which man takes pleasure, they will confirm rather than contest patriarchal sexual relations. For according to feminists, man quite literally takes pleasure from woman. His pleasure is at her expense: he is the subject of the knowing, desiring gaze because she is its object. As voyeuristic and fetishistic spectacle, she confirms his identity by conceding the specificity of her own, including the desires that would sustain it. Anxious to take back woman's pleasure, feminists have attempted to recover it by uncovering it in representations of femininity, troubling the troping of woman's submission to masculine desire through the sacrifice of her own desire and, therefore, of her subjectivity itself. They take pleasure in representations of woman as the subject and not the object of speech and desire.

As I have suggested throughout, feminists must interrogate their pleasure in the representation of feminine subjectivity, since this pleasure may be regressive. Any feminine identity is necessarily produced at the site of the intersection of a number of competing and even contradictory discourses, perhaps most importantly those of race and class. Attempts to isolate a feminine specificity that fail to take into account differences within as well as between the sexes may reproduce the hegemony of the white middle class, in which white middle-class women participate. The man who is the representative of the "universally human" is not just any man—he is white, bourgeois, and heterosexual; to a limited extent (some) women can operate his values because they are able to identify with him (and be identified with him) on the basis of their share in that proper identity. Though a certain feminist rhetoric would insist we are all sisters, women can and do oppress "other" women.

FEMINISM AND RACISM

Gayatri Spivak explains this in terms of woman's transvestic identification with (bourgeois) man. The project to make the subaltern woman the subject of discourse runs the same risk as Sigmund Freud's project to make woman the subject of hysteria: domination. The desires attributed to the other reveal more about the self constructing them than about the other; they may be narcissistic, consolidating the subject through constituting an object for it. "As a product of these considerations," Spivak writes, "I have put together the sentence 'White men are saving brown women from brown men' in a spirit not unlike the one to be encountered in Freud's investigations of the sentence 'A child is being beaten.'" And she goes on to say, "White women— from the nineteenth-century British Missionary Registers to Mary Daly— have not produced an alternative understanding."[1] That is, both white men and women have racist rescue fantasies about brown women that disguise the disciplinary function of the civilizing mission. The allusion to Freud's essay on the beating fantasy not only reminds us of the secret sadistic and masochistic pleasures of discipline but also suggests the complexity of latent identifications and desires the manifest form of a fantasy may disguise.

An analysis of the beating fantasy reveals that the same, enounced—a child is being beaten—has different enunciations, offering both feminine and masculine subject positions.[2] What is crucial for the analogy Spivak makes between this fantasy and the racist fantasy is the masculine identification of the little girl in what Freud labels phase three of her fantasy: in it (the conscious phase), the little girl is watching a father figure beat a male child with whom she identifies. That is, though the fantasy takes a sadistic form (she is watching a scene of violence), the girl's pleasure is masochistic (she identifies with the object, not the subject, of the violence). In short, the girl wants to be loved like a boy who wants to be loved like a girl by the father. The manifest form disguises her latent incestuous desire by regression to the anal-sadistic phase (the boy is being beaten, not loved, by the father) and by "transvestism" (it is apparently a boy, rather than a girl, who is being beaten). The transvestism suggests the girl's desire must be deeply repressed, so that she is removed from the erotic act itself and made a spectator; in the corresponding phase of the boy's fantasy, he is a participant (though the homosexual nature of his wish is disguised because it seems to be the mother who beats him). Nevertheless, Freud points out, the girl derives pleasure from the scene because she can identify with the boy.

Therefore, even though the white woman appears to be absent from the racist fantasy expressed in "White men are saving brown women from brown men" she is offered two subject positions in it: that of spectator and that of savior, the latter effected through a transvestic identification she can make with white men. She, too, takes on the white man's fantastic burden of civilizing the savages, in particular by "bettering" the lot of native women, to whom she attributes her own desires and goals (the same femininity, even feminist femininity) in a strategy of assimilation that nevertheless marks a difference (the brown woman is other; she needs to be enlightened, to understand her femininity as the product of oppression by brown men). The white civilizing/rescue mission is fantastic because it is motivated by imperialist desire and because its goal—what Homi Bhabha describes as the production of mimic men (and women)—is contradictory, since it would constitute a sameness that is also an alterity.

The mimic man is a partial imitation of the white man, almost the same but not quite. Because mimicry, as Bhabha suggests, is both resemblance and menacing difference, the reforming, civilizing mission is inextricable from its "disciplinary double."[3] The mimic man's difference from the white man ensures the proliferation of panoptic strategies: racial otherness is at once sighted, incited, and corrected. Brown women become the terrain on which is fought the battle between colonizer and colonized over the production of and resistance to a colonial subjectivity and the values it sustains. Brown women are, in effect, reduced to signs in a violent homoerotic exchange between white and brown men, in which they signify capitulation or resistance. This battle is the sadistic version of the exchange founding tribal society that Claude Lévi-Strauss has discussed and feminists like Luce Irigaray have critiqued.[4]

Society, according to Lévi-Strauss, is based on an exogamy regulated by the incest taboo, in which men exchange their sisters not so much for wives as for brothers-in-law. As Irigaray points out, society is, therefore, "hom(m)osexual" (what Eve Kosofsky Sedgwick calls "homosocial"), since men do not desire women but other men, though that desire must always be mediated by women (homosexuality itself is outlawed).[5] However, society is not only exogamous; it is also endogamous. If sexual relations within the family are ruled out, sexual relations outside the tribe are just as frequently ruled out, as the taboo on miscegenation (or on marriages across class or caste lines) makes clear. The brother-in-law a man wants is his like, his narcissistic double. And the son he wants, in whom he would see himself reproduced, must also be his like. In this way, the tribe reproduces itself by repudiating both ethnic and sexual otherness.

Woman is that difference between father and son (or brother-in-law) that does not signify and yet disrupts the perfect mirroring of men in society. Because she threatens the tribe (its men) with the failure to coincide with itself and to secure its patrimony for itself, a strict vigilance must be maintained over her sexual relations and, indeed, all her activities. The fear of bastardy, the fear of the dilution of "the blood" through miscegenation, and the fear of the loss of indigenous or native practices redound on women more than men. Thus the fantasy Homi Bhabha locates at the center of racism, which I briefly discussed in the last chapter, is the "primal scene" he attributes to Frantz Fanon, a scenario in which the little white girl bonds with her mother through the fear she experiences when she sees the black man. The fact that Bhabha genders the subjects of this drama is significant, since Fanon himself does not mark the sex of the child who speaks of being afraid of him. What Bhabha suggests, and what Fanon himself later discusses, is that the white man fantasizes that his women are "at the mercy of the Negroes."[6]

I would argue that this rape fantasy is the correlative of the fantasy Spivak associates with racism and takes the form of the sentence "White men are saving white women from brown men." It is a fantasy that offers subject positions not only to white men but also to white women. For example, Joan Riviere's masquerading patient, whom I discussed in the first chapter, used to imagine herself being attacked by black men, against whom she "defended" herself by seducing them so that she could turn them over to the authorities.[7] Her recurrent daydream is one complicit with the legitimation of the lynching of black men for suspected rape, and haunts the white imaginary, from D. W. Griffith's film *The Birth of a Nation*, in which it is played out as actuality, to Nicholas Roeg's *Walkabout*, in which it is rendered as feminine hysteria (the white girl is made responsible for the aborigine's death because she persists in seeing what the film suggests is their mutual desire as his threat to her virginity). If Riviere's explanation of the fantasy effaces the racial imaginary by discussing its significance only in terms of gender, Roeg's effaces the sexual: the movie makes no attempt to account for the framing of the girl's fearful gaze by the patriarchal endogamy I have discussed above and instead celebrates as "natural" a sexuality associated with men and condemns as unnatural the prudery of (white) women.

The violence the racist rape fantasy described by Bhabha ascribes to the brown man is similar to the violence ascribed to him by the racist fantasy Spivak mentions. In fact, these fantasies might be seen as permutations of one another, which is why I have attempted to think them together here. That their logic is the same is suggested by Bhabha's statement that the little girl turns to her mother and not her father for comfort when she sees the fearful black man; the mother can take the father's place as savior in the fantasy. Thus the fantasy could be rewritten as "The white person (male or female) is saving the woman (white or brown) from the (violent) brown man." White women are offered two positions in this racist imaginary: that of victim (the classic, passive place) and that of rescuer (active, but still suspect; as Spivak makes clear, the bourgeois feminist is as much an imperialist missionary as her Victorian forebear). White women, like white men, participate in the struggle with brown men over the meaning of brown women, who are reduced to tokens in an imperialist exchange.

Spivak discusses this dynamic in discourses about widow sacrifice, or suttee, but it also animates debates about female circumcision or clitoridectomy, veiling, and female sequestration (e.g.,purdah) all of which are viewed by the first world as sexist, even dangerous, practices in which Third-World men victimize "their" women. As Spivak notes, Hindu suttee, which initially was seen by the British as an uncivilized religious ritual, was redefined as a crime in the nineteenth century, a move she suggests has a clear, if complex, relationship to the change in the British presence in India at that time. Part of the British project of determining the "good society" involved protecting the brown woman from her own kind, a tactic Spivak describes as "the dissimulation of patriarchal strategy, which apparently grants the woman free choice as *subject*."[8] The brown woman is caught between two paternalisms, two inscriptions of desire on her body: the white colonizer's and the brown man's.

The white patriarch (or matriarch) insists she does not really want to die, while the brown patriarch insists she does. Thus, for Third-World men suttee becomes a signifier of Hindu society's resistance to imperialism and the production of mimic men: so long as women refuse to give up indigenous customs and desires like suttee the society has not been assimilated. Inversely, for First-World men and women, Westernization becomes a sign of resistance to native patriarchy and the woman's accession to subjectivity and desire despite her family's attempt to deny her any status other than that of object. Both are fantasies of the woman's "free choice," since she is constrained by paternalism in either case, her subject constitution equally manipulated. "Between patriarchy and imperialism, subject-constitution and object-formation, the figure of the [brown] woman disappears," Spivak writes, "not into a pristine nothingness, but into a violent shuttling which is the displaced figuration of the 'third-world woman' caught between tradition and modernization."[9] She is the "subject" of desires that are spoken for her, what white men and women or brown men desire her to desire as the good object. Reduced to being a sign, the brown woman is the bearer rather than the maker of meaning. "There is no space from which the sexed subaltern subject can speak," Spivak states emphatically.[10]

The white woman's relationship to the "other" woman is, therefore, necessarily suspect. Our representations of her, despite our best intentions, may reproduce our own racist imaginary, consolidating our subjectivity at her expense. To claim that racial difference does not matter between "sisters" is to further rather than to contest the oppression of women by women. Because she is blind to that fact, Luce Irigaray constructs a feminine imaginary that is wholly utopic, as I demonstrated in the last chapter, ignoring (in the active sense Shoshana Felman gives the term) the oppressive feminine imaginary that already exists, in which white middle-class women affirm their identity at the expense of those women who have come to signify only their difference or deviation from the hegemonic feminine ideal.[11] Thus, as Henry Louis Gates points out, Irigaray's feminine imaginary is racist; there are "shades that are not reflected in her mirror."[12]

"There is no danger that one or the other may be a darker double," Irigaray writes of the women in her feminine imaginary, having collapsed black into white as the universal term in what is a characteristic racist gesture. "White and red at once, we give birth to all the colors...," she notes. "For this whiteness is no sham. It is not dead blood, black blood. Sham is black. It absorbs everything, closed in on itself, trying to come back to life. Trying in vain.... Whereas red's whiteness takes nothing away... it gives back as much as it receives."[13] Irigaray fails to attend to the specificity of feminine oppressions and so never questions her own position in them, which is treated as a nonposition, since all women are assumed to be the same, "indifferent" (to follow her terminology). But some women have what other women lack, a "proper" class and racial identity; therefore, they can be signatories to the symbolic's sacrificial contract. Feminists must consider on what terms women accede to a desiring subjectivity, since, as I have been arguing, the latter may be predicated on a fetishistic gaze at the feminine "other" that functions like the fetishistic gaze of man, thereby confirming rather than contesting a bourgeois and racist symbolic. Feminists must not lose sight of this in their pleasure at representations of feminine subjectivity—their own and the other's.

WRITING PROPER IDENTITIES

That pleasure is almost foreclosed in Jean Rhys, making any pleasure in her texts problematic for feminists—indeed, for all readers in an age in which feminist questions have been central, as her critical reception demonstrates. From contemporary reviews of her books to analyses being written today, critics have praised her technique but have been troubled by her theme: the suffering to which women passively submit for love. Her heroines, like Anna Morgan in *Voyage in the Dark* or Antoinette Cosway in *Wide Sargasso Sea*, virtually lose themselves in their desire to be desired.[14] They seem to have no active desires of their own, and even their speech is so spare as to suggest only a very limited interiority. They are not proper characters, not even for modernist bildungsromans, because they lack character. Weak, passive, desireless, almost speechless, they appear to be subject to rather than subjects of the symbolic. Variations on an archetype of the feminine, according to Elgin Mellown, they represent the "figure of degraded womanhood."[15]

Feminists must be suspicious of this assessment, since they do not want to reproduce patriarchal values informing definitions of "proper" identities, including feminine identities. Proper identities are dependent on mastery of the self-other boundary, on a proper distance from what is improper in the other, from what, in fact, has been projected from the self onto the other. The self is a fictional unity, the continual retelling of stories about an otherness that his majesty the ego can never finally banish from his citadel. Naming the ego king is a reminder of the gender of the proper identity in patriarchy, which feminists have asserted is masculine, signified by the proper name, the patronymic. Man effects his identification with his ideal self and inherits his proper name when he renounces (being) the mother, losing her in the name of the law, which is the name of the father. The feminine is that difference—that otherness—that patriarchal man refuses in order to be properly self-identical.

His illusion of unified subjectivity is predicated on the misrecognition of woman, whom he sees as a negative alter ego. In patriarchy woman's images do not reflect her desire but man's: she returns to him a vision of his imaginary wholeness by representing the lack in his being that he has disavowed and projected on to her in fetishistic fashion. I noted in chapter 1 that both Virginia Woolf and Luce Irigaray have employed the metaphor of the mirror to explain this. Woolf says that in the female looking glass, man sees himself larger than life-size.[16] Woman, on the other hand, does not see herself in patriarchy at all. As Irigaray points out, she is not represented in it except as a male fantasy, a fetish object.[17] This suggests that the patriarchal symbolic is actually a masculine imaginary, since in it woman's real difference goes unsymbolized, misrecognized as a lack that is in turn disavowed because the castration man has assigned woman threatens him with the possibility of his own castration.

Caught in the masculine imaginary woman could only make a negative entry into the symbolic, as object, not subject, unable to represent lack for herself because she must represent it for man. In patriarchy, man alone is subject of the knowing, desiring gaze; since woman cannot accede to it, she must identify with its object. Rather like Charlie McCarthy in a skirt, it would seem she could do no more than assume the postures and mouth the words of the puppet master. Thus Abigail Solomon-Godeau accounts for the dozens of photos the nineteenth century countess di Castiglione had taken of herself in various costumes or disguises by suggesting they construct femininity as a pose—but a pose the countess lived, having fully identified with a male gaze she internalized. The photos, Solomon-Godeau asserts, can only signify the impossibility of the countess's attempts to represent herself, her inability to resist masculine domination.[18]

As Spivak points out, it is necessary to clear a subject position in order to be able to speak or write.[19] Apparently the Rhys heroine, like the countess—like all women in patriarchy—has so attenuated a subjectivity she has difficulty representing herself. What we are invited to experience in Rhys through her solicitation of an identification with the heroine is the female protagonist's struggle to become a subject both of speech and desire. We witness her attempted production of a subject position, the birth of an identity. *Voyage in the Dark* alludes to this theme of the bildungsroman in its very title, since the journey is a classic metaphor for spiritual growth. Yet because the title suggests traveling in the dark, or perhaps into the dark, its promise of rebirth is qualified, ironized. It hints at the difficulty Anna Morgan will have in her self-production, a difficulty the novel does, in fact, bear out. Antoinette Cosway's story in *Wide Sargasso Sea* is also of a journey from the West Indies to England, from childhood to adulthood, but it is a journey into someone else's story, Jane Eyre's, in which she will be reborn as a minor character, with a new and alienating name and identity, figuring her role not as heroic self but as mad other. The trouble woman has representing herself as a subject rather than an object in her story is the very substance of both novels.

This trouble is not surprising, since in patriarchy narratives of identity—biographies and autobiographies, bildungsromans—are centered on men; their very function is to produce better men, building character by providing exemplary characters. Franco Moretti notes of bildungsromans that they constitute the ego that psychoanalysis, as an analysis, deconstitutes; they legitimate society's norms by ensuring that the individual "freely" chooses them as his own.[20] Of course, these norms are patriarchal in a patriarchal society.

Autobiography came into being with Augustine's *Confessions*, originating in the *Imitatio Christi*, the specular relation between God and the (male) self which authorized the self-reflection (and concomitant self-construction) the early autobiographers undertook.[21] Both biographies and autobiographies chronicle the lives of important public figures, who are generally men— women having been consigned to the private—representing (and reproducing) the scenarios of a masculine selfhood secure in a self-possession originally founded on its supposed likeness to God, a likeness not readily assumed for woman but, rather, open to dispute. The paradigms of identity these forms offer are, therefore, inconsistent with a "proper" feminine identity.

The woman who would have a proper feminine identity must instead insert herself into the narrative of heterosexual romance as the object of male desire, becoming a good subject by becoming a good object. Paradigmatic in this regard is that moment in Jane Austen's *Pride and Prejudice* when Elizabeth Bennet ceases to resist Darcy's attractions and apparently quite consciously aligns herself with his gaze.[22] That event signals the end of the story and Elizabeth's maturity, since in the love story, the woman's apprehension and acceptance of social values coincides with her marriage to the right man. In the logic of patriarchy, there can be no more significant decision for a woman; the story of her life leads to that moment, and after it nothing further occurs which is worth the telling. The self-possession that the plot of the bildungsroman builds becomes in the romance a self-loss, since in marriage the woman allows herself to be possessed by another, sacrificing her identity and her right to make choices, as Rosalind Coward notes.[23]

If the romance has been updated, it is chiefly through the substitution of sex for marriage; woman's identity remains primarily (hetero)sexual, though "her" story may climax not so much with marriage as with climax itself—she finds herself in what Dr. Ruth Westheimer would call "good sex."[24] But good sex continues to be defined within masculine parameters as heterosexual orgasm (the desirable woman is one who is satisfied by the penis) and it is generally arrived at through a "good relationship," so that sex is not entirely divorced from love and monogamy even today. Peter Brooks has suggested that desire is the motor of all narrative, and that the drive toward the ending is a drive toward death, the absolute reduction of the tension associated with desire (orgasm as "the little death" and the end of the story).[25] The closure in marriage (or a good relationship) of the woman's story, the sentimental romance, would indeed seem to figure the death of the desiring subject, who as woman must give up her desire in order to be what her lover desires. Her story ends with her birth as a nonidentity, as somebody's wife.

Only a very contradictory text could result from appropriating romance for a female bildungsroman, one troubled by symptoms of its incompatible drives: toward a desiring female identity and toward a desirable female non-identity. Such a story—like its heroine—would be neurotic. Roland Barthes associates narrative neuroses with what he calls the text of bliss, which he contrasts with the text of pleasure. The text of pleasure reconfirms the reader's cultural identity through an oedipal narrative that unveils the name of the father. The text of bliss or *jouissance* undoes identity because it "imposes a state of loss . . . unsettles the reader's historical, cultural, psychological assumptions, the consistency of his tastes, values, memories, brings to a crisis his relations with language."[26] Barthes, like Julia Kristeva, links this jouissance to an encounter with the mother, which he describes as fetishistic. "The writer," he says, "is someone who plays with his mother's body . . . in order to glorify it, to embellish it, or in order to dismember it, to take it to the limit of what can be known about the body. . . ."[27]

As a fetishist, the artist both worships and castrates the fetish object, identifies with it and disidentifies from it, attempting to produce and master difference—the difference from the mother the child requires in order to be a subject at all. The text of bliss centers and decenters the subject, constructs and deconstructs identity, including its own identity as one kind of text and not another. As Barthes's reading of Honoré de Balzac's *Sarrasine* in *S/Z* demonstrates, all texts are neurotic, and potentially texts of bliss. Identity, whether that of the fetishist or that of the classic text, is never finally fixed because the symbolic, as I pointed out above, is really an imaginary, produced by and productive of subjects anxious about in-difference and castration. This anxiety translates into fetishism, and the solution to the anxieties of fetishism is more fetishism. Fetishizing the other, man fetishizes himself; disavowing the other's castration, man disavows his own. There is no real movement into the symbolic through an acceptance of castration. Instead, man passes himself off as a desiring subject, engaging in phallic imposture by surrounding himself with the signs of what he has to lose so he can signify he has something to lose —and, therefore, something to desire. Chief among man's fetishes, of course, is the penis, whose equivalency with the phallus patriarchy insists upon by naturalizing it, making both man and woman dupes of that fetishistic misrecognition. Man appears to have the phallus by having what signifies having the phallus: its fetish substitutes—the penis, but also all the signs of patriarchal power and privilege, including the fetishized woman.

PHALLIC IMPOSTURE IN RHYS

Textual neuroses are instances of fetishistic excess, signs of anxiety about such phallic imposture. They are excessive with respect to some sexual/textual norm, an imposture that does not appear as such because it passes as the real thing. Moments of breakdown in the story, they are also symptoms of the breakdown in the writing and reading subject, whose identity they call into question, revealing it to be an unstable fiction. In *Wide Sargasso Sea*, the coherency of Rochester's first-person narrative—and, therefore, of his rational, masculine, British identity—is threatened by the return of what he has repressed, which he associates not only with Antoinette, but also with black women and the West Indian landscape. He says uneasily, "Everything is too much . . . too much blue, too much purple, too much green. The flowers too red, the mountains too high, the hills too near" (*Sargasso*, 70). His equation of the West Indies and those who figure it, like Antoinette and the ex-slaves, with the overpowering or excessive recurs symptomatically throughout his sections of the novel.

For example, smells overwhelm him, especially the smell of tropical flowers, which, he notes, make him "giddy" and which he connects explicitly with Antoinette (83, 99). He is also frightened by night, which he sees as his enemy (146). Night is linked to lunacy, the kind of madness to which sleeping in the moonlight leads, according to Antoinette—and to which she does, finally, succumb (83). It is also linked to "moonflowers," whose scent signifies the madness of sexual passion. Rochester feels keenly the need to master his desire for Antoinette, since he is not convinced she is the proper wife for him, the wife who will subordinate her identity and desires to his. He renames her Bertha in an effort to confer upon her a proper English woman's identity, but Antoinette resists, calling his attempt "obeah" or voodoo and practicing a little of her own by having Christophine, her black, childhood nursemaid, mix a love potion that is supposed to restore Rochester's feeling for her (113). When, after a night of passion, he awakens out of a dream that he was buried alive, he still feels suffocated. Evidently Antoinette's hair, which is lying across his mouth, has precipitated his hysteric inability to breathe because of its weight—or, more likely, because of its "sweet heavy smell" (137). Earlier, Antoinette has imagined her mother's hair as a protective cloak that could cover her (22). For Rochester, however, the woman's body is over present, menacing rather than preserving life.

Significantly, he also associates night with blacks, in particular Christophine, whose voice is "dark" like the darkness itself (156). This strengthens the connection of night to desire, since for Rochester blacks figure an improper sexuality, as his affair with the mulatto maid Amelie bears out. In fact, it is Antoinette's desire for him that makes her so disturbing, and his comment that Creoles like Antoinette are not English suggests he confounds the two meanings of "creole," sharing Antoinette's confusion about her racial identity, a confusion that also signifies doubts about proper feminine sexuality (67). When he glimpses Antoinette and Amelie together in the looking glass, he sees them as mirror doubles, as his later statement that they look alike makes clear (99, 129). The degree of Rochester's fetishistic fear of and fascination with blacks is revealed in his insistence that he could not hug or kiss them as Antoinette does; it suggests a fear that his identity will some-how be undermined if he comes in close contact with blackness, just as he feels Antoinette's closeness at night is suffocating (91). Nevertheless, he finds Amelie very attractive and eventually sleeps with her (after the love potion episode) in order to demonstrate to Antoinette that he is master of her hap-piness and of his own desire—that he is, in fact, a "proper" masculine subject.

Rochester's desire to master feminine and racial difference in order to master his own self-difference is not only fetishistic but paranoid. Both fetishism and paranoia signify the breakdown of identity and the loss of ego boundaries. Fetishism is associated with spectacle—the spectacle of differ-ence that the subject projects on to an object he worships and fears. The fetishist's masochistic fantasy of submitting to a phallicised dominatrix can develop into a full-blown paranoid narrative, a Gothic horror story of perse-cution by her. As a number of feminists including Mary Ann Doane and Claire Kahane have pointed out, paranoia is a pre-oedipal or imaginary anxi-ety about the fact that self and other, child and mother, are terrifyingly indis-tinct.[28] Rochester's comments on Antoinette's "disconcerting" and "challenging" eyes and on Christophine's troubling ability to stare him down allude to a mildly masochistic fantasy about the two, but by the the time he is ready to leave the honeymoon house toward the end of the novel, he not only imagines Antoinette has tried to poison and suffocate him, he insists she will try to kill him again and that there is a long line of others to take her place as murderer if she should somehow disappear (67, 103, 73, 172). This obviously paranoid fantasy occurs in a scene of extreme imaginary aggression, in which Rochester's emotions swing wildly from love to hate as he gazes sadistically at Antoinette in order to reduce her own look to the blankness of a doll's (170). Just a few pages earlier, however, he has, himself, been reduced to echoing Christophine's words about Antoinette, caught in a psychotic imaginary in which he becomes the marionette or puppet whose speech and desires have been mastered by the other (153–54).

There are also moments of fetishistic excess in Antoinette's sections of *Wide Sargasso Sea*, and in *Voyage in the Dark*, which is entirely focalized through the heroine. They take the form of disturbing memories or dreams of childhood that irrupt into the plot and disrupt the speech of the first per-son female narrators, impeding the flow and sense of their narratives. As I have already suggested, these are about their accession to proper feminine identities and so are structured as love stories—but love stories which go awry. In *Voyage in the Dark*, Anna Morgan's tale does not close with a good, middle-class marriage, but with a botched abortion; in *Wide Sargasso Sea*, Antoinette's story ends with her suicide. Both narrators repeatedly attempt to position the heroines within femininity, staging and restaging the scenarios of a passive and masochistic desire. But the narrative these scenes construct is continually interrupted by moments of fetishistic excess, which enable Anna and Antoinette to postpone proper femininity and pass themselves off as desiring subjects so as to keep writing or speaking.

There are a number of signs in *Voyage in the Dark* of Anna's desperation to solicit the male gaze and confirm her femininity. Her movement from mistress to one man, Walter Jeffries, to prostitute for several when she cannot win back Walter could be read as a measure of her desire to be found desirable, even if it is also a sign of her economic plight as a woman without friends or skills in the modern city. Her belief in the importance of having the right clothes, which she shares with other Rhys heroines (including Antoinette) suggests a narcissistic identification with desirable images of femininity. However, since that narcissism commodifies the woman for man, rendering her consumable, it is linked in the text to woman's economic situation: she exchanges love and sex for financial support, including the money with which to buy the clothes that make her desirable. Anna's friend, Maudie, makes this quite explicit when she says that a man once asked her if she had ever thought that a girl's clothes cost more than the girl inside them (*Voyage*, 45). Finally, Anna makes Walter's wishes her own, surrendering her will to his by allowing him to determine not only where and when they will meet and what they will do but what sort of relationship they will have, however different his vision of it may be from hers, indicative of just how much she wants him to want her—and needs him to want her, since he becomes her sole source of income. She abdicates control on their very first night of lovemaking when she accepts the money he puts in her purse, though initially she has protested against taking it. "All right," she says to him, "if you like—anything you like, any way you like" (38). As Arnold Davidson points out, Walter turns Anna into a prostitute without himself having to become a john.[29] Later, after he has ended their affair, she thinks she will die of love—the ultimate masochistic gesture—and imagines telling Walter, "I only want to see you sometimes, but if I never see you again, I'll die" (97).

Antoinette's desire to be what Rochester desires is also quite marked. She tells him he is so important to her he could easily destroy her happiness; it is just the fear of losing it that leads to her disastrous decision to use the love potion on him (92). She is anxious to please him—to wear the dresses that he likes and, as Christophine notices, to submit to the violent sex that he likes (151). Like Anna, Antoinette seems to surrender her will, perhaps most disturbingly in her dreams, in which she passively follows someone of whom she

is very afraid into a walled garden. As Spivak points out, this garden is a romantic topos, the garden of love, but in Antoinette's dream it figures as the prison
of marriage.[30] "I was glad to be like an English girl," Antoinette remarks early
in the novel, after her mother has remarried and she is no longer growing up as
what both black and white West Indians in the novel call a "white nigger."
Clearly, part of being an English girl means making someone a good wife,
which is why it seems to her unthinkable to leave Rochester, as Christophine
insists she should (110). She would rather suffer than part from him.

   I have already suggested that in *Voyage in the Dark* Anna resists being nothing more than the object of Walter's desire, which would mean sacrificing
her own. She makes this quite explicit when she says to him, "I don't like
your looking glass," adding, "Have you ever noticed how different some
looking-glasses make you look?" (37–38). In Walter's looking glass, as in his
look, Anna does not see herself represented; she does not exist for him as
anything other than a fantasy. But her resistance is also figured less explicitly
in what I have described as textual neuroses, the return of her repressed
childhood memories and the different fantasy of femininity they represent.
The story of proper femininity is associated with England and Anna's British
stepmother, Hester, who brings her to England at the opening of the novel in
a voyage that Anna imagines as a rebirth. The new identity she is supposed to
achieve—but does not—stresses her class and racial difference from other
women, in particular the black women she grew up with in the West Indies.
Hester has been careful to point out their differences to Anna, differences
that bleed over into the landscape for her, so that a series of oppositions is
mapped out: white/black, proper/improper, especially proper/improper sexuality, class/no class, civilized/wild, English/West Indian. But Anna has difficulty mastering these differences, identifying with the proper and
disidentifying from the improper. She cannot lose the lack—and the fullness
of being—that blackness has come to signify for her.

   This is true as well of Antoinette in *Wide Sargasso Sea*, who, as I suggested
earlier, is confused about her identity. After Amelie tells her she is a white
cockroach (something Anna, too, has been called), Antoinette says to
Rochester, "That's what they [blacks] call all of us who were here before their
own people in Africa sold them to the slave traders. And I've heard English
women call us white niggers. So between you, I often wonder who I am and
where is my country and where do I belong. . . ." (*Sargasso*, 102). She experiences her identity as split between white and black femininity, passivity and
activity, Bertha and Antoinette, a split the many mirror scenes in the the
book convey.

   Anna and Antoinette are divided within themselves because like so many of
Freud's patients, they had more than one mother and are split along class—

and in their cases, racial—lines: the biological mother (and stepmother) and the servant(s) who performed the real work of child care. As Peter Stallybrass and Allon White have convincingly demonstrated in *The Politics and Poetics of Transgression*, this split is productive of a hysteria comprising a confusion about class identity, since the middle class subject must repress a maternal marked for class or in Rhys, for race.[31] Its return in hysteria—or what I have called moments of fetishistic excess—is a reminder of what the subject has given up: imaginary wholeness, thought in terms of gender, race, and class. I have underlined the fetishistic aspect of what Barthes and Stallybrass and White call neurosis because like other feminists, I wished to stress that the patriarchal symbolic is really a masculine imaginary. But gender is not the only relevant category for identity construction, and the symbolic is more than patriarchal—it is also imperialist and capitalist. If the phallus is not the penis, as Lacanians are always insisting, then, I would argue, the symbolic is also a white, bourgeois imaginary, in which the class and racial other is not represented except as a fetishistic fantasy of lack or wholeness.

This implies that white, middle-class women can engage in phallic imposture on the basis of what they have: signs of a proper class and ethnic identity. Like men, they can be subjects of and not just subject to oppression: they can be oppressors. Psychoanalytic feminist theory has had difficulty recognizing this. It has focused almost exclusively on sexual difference, and so has only been able to account for female subjectivity by postulating a transvestic identification with man, sustained by woman's incomplete repression of the masculinity associated with her childhood bisexuality. As I discussed in the last chapter, however, recently feminists have suggested that what Luce Irigaray terms mimicry is an alternative, and nonphallic, way for women to disidentify from images of femininity as lack.[32] By deliberately repeating in mimicry what Jacques Lacan calls the masquerade of femininity, woman sees her image for what it is: a pose—imposed—and not a nature. Mimicry, unlike transvestism, does not seem to involve woman in an identification with phallic having as the corollary to a disidentification from lack; its politics, therefore, have not appeared suspect to most feminists.

But feminists have not asked what sustains such a disidentification. The answer, I believe, has to do with those differences white, middle-class feminists have too often failed to address—differences that come back to haunt the body of feminist theoretical work. Mimicry has been theorized only as a politics of consciousness: woman's ironic intentions are assumed to ensure the parodic excess that distinguishes mimicry from masquerade. But it is exactly a politics of consciousness feminists have called into question by revealing the unconscious fears and desires structuring phallocentrism. I would argue that the unintended effects of mimicry, the politics of its unconscious, have to do with class and race. The mimic distances herself from feminine lack by flaunting it, projecting it onto a style of femininity she assumes as excessive, unnatural, in an apparent identification that is in fact a disidentification. Style is the mark of difference within "the" feminine, fracturing that supposed unity along lines of class, race, and ethnicity in particular, all of which can signify lack and otherness. The mimic constitutes herself as a subject by constructing her feminine other as a lacking object, a female looking glass in whom she can at last see herself, and see herself excessively, unnaturally large, larger than life-size; the other does not see herself there at all. No Charlie McCarthy, then, the countess di Castiglione reveals her will to domination rather than her submission to it in the class anxiety her photos of herself as other document.

It is the fetishistic fantasmatic Anna and Antoinette share that poses a threat to their subjection to femininity and the death of desire it seems to entail. As most Rhys critics note, for these heroines blacks and the West Indies represent what has to be sacrificed to be a "proper" English woman. But it is a sacrifice they cannot quite make, as revealed by the moments of fetishistic excess that disrupt their stories, moments that figure their identification with blackness and in-difference from the black, maternal other. For example, when Anna falls ill with the fever that precipitates her affair with Walter, who comes to take care of her, she remembers a fever she had as a child during which Francine, one of the family's black maids, looked after her. In the middle of the memory, she suddenly announces, "I wanted to be black, I always wanted to be black. . . . Being black is warm and gay, being white is cold and sad" (*Voyage*, 31). It is impossible to tell whether this thought belongs to the diegetic past (the narrated character's memory), or to the diegetic present (the narrator's "memory"), though it seems likely it belongs to both, disturbing the narrative temporality. Her friends encourage Anna's misrecognition (and perhaps their own, with regard to her) by calling her "Hottentot" (13), while Hester hints that her mother may really have had black blood (53, 65).

Antoinette's imaginary confusion is represented most clearly when she recalls her meeting with the black girl Tia during the burning of Coulibri estate, the Cosway home, which was set afire by ex-slaves. As the daughter of the only friend of Christophine, Tia had been something of a sister until the day she called Antoinette a white cockroach and stole her dress. Seeing her in the crowd at the fire, Anna imagines they could be sisters again, the differences between them effaced. "Then, not so far off, I saw Tia and her mother and I ran to her, for she was all that was left of my life as it had been. . . ," she tells the reader, "As I ran, I thought, I will live with Tia and I will be like her. . . . When I was close I saw the jagged stone in her hand, but I did not see her throw it. I did not feel it either, only something wet, running down my face. I looked at her and I saw her face crumple as she began to cry. We stared at each other, blood on my face, tears on hers. It was as if I saw myself. Like in a looking-glass" (*Sargasso*, 45). Antoinette wants to resolve this split and reunify her two selves, as the passage in the last section of the book about her attempt to kiss her reflection in the mirror suggests (180). It is, therefore, significant that she thinks she sees Tia beckoning to her when she leaps from the flaming battlements of Thornfield in her final dream, in which she dreams the end of the dream in her own end.

As I have already indicated, both novels link being black to the improper, especially improper desire, which is in turn related to the intense colors and smells of tropical flora. There is a long iconographic tradition of associating female sexuality with flowers, as Griselda Pollock observes in a discussion of Pre-Raphaelite painting.[33] Francine, who symbolizes a "natural" sexuality, is explicitly connected with the hibiscus at one point in *Voyage in the Dark* (56). It is this and other West Indian flowers that Hester, the representative of British womanhood, finds particularly disturbing, signifying her repression of sexuality, a repression foregrounded in Anna's memory of her first menstrual period. As Anna tells it, Francine's explanation made menstruation seem perfectly natural, "all in the day's work, like eating or drinking" (*Voyage*, 68). Hester's explanation, on the other hand, induces in Anna the hysteric inability to breathe that Hester, herself, experiences around flowers—perhaps a sign of Anna's hysteric identification with her. It is also clearly Anna's sexuality that Hester disapproves of when they are in England, and Walter, too, feels there is something not quite ladylike about Anna's desire for him. Similarly, Rochester finds Antoinette's sexuality improper, which he sees as akin to the sexuality of the blacks in the book, especially to Amelie's. Like Anna, Antoinette is linked to flowers and "excessive" or overpowering smells and sights in general; thus, after Rochester gets the letter from Daniel Cosway suggesting Antoinette is black and licentious (the two seem to go together) he tramples into the mud the orchids to which he has compared her (*Sargasso*, 99).

Both novels also associate blackness with the breakdown of proper speech. Hester, Anna observes, has "an English lady's voice with a sharp, cutting edge to it," the cut suggesting its castrating and divisive quality (*Voyage*, 57). But when Francine and Anna speak in patois, Hester cannot tell them apart—or so Anna says (65). Patois is "sing-song" and meaningless "jabbering," according to Hester (65). It is connected to the imaginary or the prelinguistic realm that Kristeva calls the semiotic, and it signals a breakdown in subjectivity Anna's encounter with the maternal precipitates, as Deborah Kelly Kloepfer points out.[34] I would add, however, that it is racially as well as maternally connoted, and functions as a less alienating language only in its difference from English, a difference English itself legislates in the novel. This breakdown in meaning, therefore, can be symbolized by a difference within English, as occurs especially in the final section of the book, when Anna is suffering the effects of her botched abortion and her discourse becomes almost unintelligible in the dream about carnival in the West Indies. But all the memories and the dreams in the book retard the heroine's "progress" into proper femininity and so function as breakdowns in narrative logic that signify the breakdown and resistance of the narrating subject.

Antoinette's language and self break down in the final, "mad" section of the novel, when she dreams her dream to its conclusion and then enacts it, suturing her story into Jane Eyre's. Though she must kill herself so that Jane can become a feminist individualist, as Spivak points out, Rhys sees to it that Antoinette is not sacrificed solely for her proper sister's self-consolidation.[35] The whole of Antoinette's text is like a dream or a memory that disrupts Jane's process of identity building through construction of a dark double by foregrounding the cost of Jane's enterprise: the oppressive othering of another woman. But as Spivak quite rightly notes, Jane's story is rewritten by Rhys in the interest of the white Creole and not of black women.[36] Antoinette's memories and dreams of closeness to Christophine and Tia disrupt her achievement of a proper feminine identity and make possible feminist resistance, but at the expense of black women's specificity, which is effaced so that they can serve as representations of rage and sexuality for her as she does (according to Sandra Gilbert, Susan Gubar, and Elaine Showalter) for Jane Eyre.[37] The dark double here has her dark doubles against or through whom she accedes to a vision of herself as whole, empowered. Thus the red dress in Antoinette's closet at Thornfield, "the color of fires and sunset . . . [and] flamboyant flowers," symbolizes her West Indian identity, the "otherness" that she must let out of the closet in order to get out of Jane Eyre's story (185). Seeing the dress, she is reminded of what she desires to do. Setting Thornfield afire allows her to repeat the loss or splitting of the self that resulted from the burning of Coulibri; that is why she dreams Christophine and Tia are there with her as she does it. Her breakdown is in fact a breaking out.

For both Anna and Antoinette, fetishism of the racial other is what makes resistance possible. If Hester and Rochester engage in a violent and castrating fetishism, Anna and Antoinette practice one that seems to be benign, like the romantic antiethnocentrism of Lévi-Strauss, which Jacques Derrida critiques as ethnocentrism in *Of Grammatology*. But their fetishism is fetishism nonetheless, since the other is only a fantasy for them, a fantasy of wholeness that allows them to accede to subjectivity and desire. Their stories are of the inscription of raced subjects, the ideological work the books perform only too well, if we are to judge by what critics have written about them. Invariably, they repeat rather than analyze the fetishism of the heroines, often fetishizing Jean Rhys herself in the process, since they tend to regard all her writing as autobiographical, an expression of her own fascinating otherness.

For example, Rhys's earliest critic, and her mentor and lover, Ford Madox Ford, projects his fascination with the class and racial other on to Rhys, attributing it both to her and of her: for him her origin in the West Indies accounts for her "bias of admiration" for the characters on the fringe she not only wrote about but knew personally. "Coming from the Antilles," he writes in the introduction to her first book, *The Left Bank and Other Stories*, Rhys has "a terrifying and a terrific—an almost lurid!—passion for stating the case of the underdog. . . . "[38] If she knows what he calls "the quarter of the Apache" it is because she is something of an Apache herself or, rather, like Anna Morgan, a "Hottentot"; Ford, I would argue, confuses the meaning of *Creole* just as Rochester does, reading Rhys as Rochester "reads" Antoinette. His fetishism of the Creole woman, white or black, is echoed by later critics. Kloepfer's reference to the "lush, forbidden power of island women" is clearly fetishistic, as is Thomas Staley's association of the island with "vital qualities" and "natural impulses," and Mary Lou Emery's description of it as a place where, unlike England, both the climate and the people are warm and colorful.[39] Similarly, Arnold Davidson's suggestion that Anna undergoes a fall into European womanhood romanticizes black femininity as the Eden from which she has been expelled, as does Helen Nebeker's equation of blackness with a "primal nature" that is sexual, the "world of the id opposed to the white world of the ego-superego."[40]

Rhys critics oscillate between recognizing these as the fetishistic fantasies of the heroines and endorsing them as the truth about black women. They do not distance themselves from the fetishism of the heroines but repeat it, romanticizing racial otherness as the place of wholeness, of that nature that has been lost in the name of culture, including a less alienating, more "natural" sexuality and language, inviting their readers to identify with Anna and Antoinette and their desires rather than to analyze Anna and Antoinette and their desires so as to open up a space between the reader and the fantasy the texts offer. Such a gap or distance is necessary for knowledge, which, as Spivak notes, "is made possible and is sustained by irreducible difference, not identity."[41] The task of criticism must be to produce a knowing distance from a text's pleasurable narcissistic fixations and the phallic impostures they sustain, since it is into these that readers are lured by pleasure. Feminist critics take pleasure in troubling pleasure, disrupting the regressive effect of a pleasure that interpellates woman as object rather than subject of speech and desire. But the pleasure of representing feminine subjects needs to be troubled, too, since it may be at the expense of the "other" woman when she is constructed as an object for that subject, as what must be repudiated (a symptom) or what could make the subject hole (a full self-presence to supplement lack). Such fetishistic representations reproduce relations of oppression between women, confirming rather than contesting a bourgeois and racist symbolic in which the other woman does not exist except as a fantasy, the bearer rather than the maker of meaning. As Hazel Carby suggests in the epigraph to this chapter, we must interrogate sexual ideologies—including feminist ideology—for their racial specificity.[42] Just as feminists have uncovered the man behind supposedly genderless discourses about humankind, revealing them to be sexually marked, so, too, must we reveal the classed and racially marked body enunciating discourses about the universally human, even—perhaps especially—about that feminist abstraction, "the" woman and her desires. Feminists must not lose sight of the complex articulation of gender, race, and class in discourses, which are the site of the reproduction of all these differences. We must be wary of taking pleasure from the other woman rather than with her.

NOTES

1. Gayatri Chakravorty Spivak, "Can the Subaltern Speak?" in *Marxism and the Interpretation of Culture*, ed. Cary Nelson and Lawrence Grossberg (Urbana and Chicago: University of Illinois Press, 1988), 296; 297.

2. Sigmund Freud, "A Child Is Being Beaten," trans. James Strachey, in *Sexuality and the Psychology of Love*, ed. Philip Rieff (New York: Collier, 1963), 107–32.

3. Homi K. Bhabha, "The Ambivalence of Colonial Discourse," *October* 28 (1984), 127.

4. Claude Lévi-Strauss, *The Elementary Stuctures of Kinship*, trans. James Harle Bell et al. (Boston: Beacon Press, 1969); Luce Irigaray, "Commodities among Themselves," in *This Sex Which Is Not One*, trans. Catherine Porter.

5. Eve Sedgwick, *Between Men: English Literature and Male Homosocial Desire* (New York: Columbia University Press, 1985).

6. Frantz Fanon, *Black Skin, White Masks* (New York: Grove Press, Inc., 1967), 157. The child's fear of the black man is described on 112.

7. Joan Riviere, "Womanliness as a Masquerade" (1929); reprt. in *Psychoanalysis and Female Sexuality*, ed. Hendrik M. Ruitenbeek (New Haven, CT: College and University Press, 1966), 212–13.

8. Spivak, "Can the Subaltern Speak?" 299.

9. Ibid., 306.

10. Ibid., 307.

11. Shoshana Felman, *Jacques Lacan and the Adventure of Insight: Psychoanalysis in Contemporary Culture* (Cambridge, MA: Harvard University Press, 1987), 78. Felman sees ignorance as symptomatic, a resistance to knowledge.

12. Henry Louis Gates Jr., "Significant Others," *Contemporary Literature* 29:4 (1988), 609.

13. Luce Irigaray, "When Our Lips Speak Together," in *This Sex Which Is Not One*, 217; 207.

14. Jean Rhys, *Voyage in the Dark* (1934; reprt. New York: W. W. Norton, 1982), hereafter cited parenthetically as *Voyage*; *Wide Sargasso Sea* (1966; reprt. New York: W. W. Norton, 1982), hereafter cited parenthetically as *Sargasso*.

15. Elgin Mellown, "Character and Themes in the Novels of Jean Rhys," *Contemporary Literature* 13:4 (1972), 463.

16. Virginia Woolf, *A Room of One's Own* (1929; rpt. New York: Harcourt, Brace, Jovanovich, 1957), 35.

17. Luce Irigaray, *Speculum: Of the Other: Woman*, trans. Gillian Gill (Ithaca: Cornell University Press, 1985), especially 133–46.

18. Abigail Solomon-Godeau, "The Legs of the Countess," *October* 39 (1987), 67–108. John Berger makes a similar argument about women's relation to images of themselves in *Ways of Seeing* (London: British Broadcasting Corporation and Penguin, 1972), 45–64.

19. Gayatri Spivak, "Imperialism and Sexual Difference," *Oxford Literary Review* 8 (1986), 229.

20. Franco Moretti, *The Way of the World: The Bildungsroman in European Culture* (London: Verso, 1987); see especially 10–16.

21. Bella Brodzki and Celeste Schenck point this out in the introduction to the volume they have edited, *Life/Lines: Theorizing Women's Autobiography* (Ithaca: Cornell University Press, 1988), 2. I am also indebted to the Derridean discussion of naming, self-possession, and identity in Mark Taylor, "The Disappearing Self," in *Notebooks in Cultural Analysis: An Annual Review*, ed. Norman Cantor (Durham: Duke University Press, 1984), 126–43.

22. Jane Austen, *Pride and Prejudice* (1813; reprt. London: Penguin, 1985), 272, where she situates herself as the object of the gaze of his portrait during her visit to his family estate.

23. Rosalind Coward, *Female Desires: How They Are Sought, Bought, and Packaged* (New York: Grove Press, 1985), 176.

24. This is brought out by Coward, *Desires*, 179, and by Stephen Heath in *The Sexual Fix* (New York: Schocken, 1982); see especially 85–110. Both critics have been influenced by Michel Foucault's *The History of Sexuality: An Introduction*, vol. 1 of *The History of Sexuality*, trans. Robert Hurley (New York: Random House, 1978), in which it is argued that modern subjectivity is produced and regulated through discourses of sexuality. Foucault does suggest that this involved a strategic hysterization of women's bodies, saturating them with sexuality (104), but in general, he does not pursue a feminist line of questioning, which would involve greater attention to the issue of power relations between men and women in the production and surveillance of sexual difference—to which Coward and Heath are sensitive.

25. Peter Brooks, *Reading for the Plot: Design and Intention in Narrative* (New York: Vintage, 1985), especially chap. 4, "Freud's Masterplot: A Model for Narrative."

26. Barthes, *The Pleasure of the Text*, trans. Richard Miller (New York: Hill and Wang, 1975), 14.

27. Ibid., 37. Julia Kristeva talks about artistic production similarly in *Desire in Language: A Semiotic Approach to Literature and Art*, ed. Leon Roudiez, trans. Roudiez et al. (New York: Columbia University Press, 1980).

28. Mary Ann Doane, "Paranoia and the Specular," in *The Desire to Desire: The Woman's Film of the 1940s* (Bloomington: Indiana University Press, 1987), 123–54; Claire Kahane, "Gothic Mirrors and Feminine Identity," *The Centennial Review* 24:1 (1980), 43–64.

29. Arnold Davidson, *Jean Rhys* (New York: Frederick Unger, 1985), 54.

30. Gayatri Chakravorty Spivak, "Three Women's Texts and a Critique of Imperialism," in *"Race," Writing and Difference*, ed. Henry Louis Gates Jr. (Chicago: University of Chicago Press, 1985), 269.

31. Peter Stallybrass and Allon White, *The Politics and Poetics of Transgression* (Ithaca: Cornell University Press, 1986).

32. Irigaray discusses mimcry at length in *This Sex Which Is Not One*, 76–77 and 133–34.

33. Griselda Pollock, *Vision and Difference: Femininity, Feminism, and the Histories of Art* (New York: Routledge, Chapman and Hall, 1988), 135.

34. Deborah Kelly Kloepfer links the breakdown of speech to the breakdown of subjectivity due to the encounter with the maternal in *"Voyage in the Dark:* Jean Rhys's Masquerade for the Mother," *Contemporary Literature* 26:4 (1985), 451; she draws on the essays in Kristeva's *Desire in Language.*

35. Spivak, "Three Women's Texts," 270.

36. Ibid., 272.

37. Sandra M. Gilbert and Susan Gubar, *The Madwoman in the Attic: The Woman Writer and the Nineteenth Century Literary Imagination* (New Haven: Yale University Press, 1979), 336–71; Elaine Showalter, *A Literature of Their Own: British Women Novelists from Bronte to Lessing* (Princeton: Princeton University Press, 1977), 100–32.

38. Ford Madox Ford, introduction to Jean Rhys, *The Left Bank and Other Stories* (1927; rept. New York: Arno Press, 1970), 24; the reference in the next line to the "quarter of the Apache" occurs on 14.

39. Kloepfer, "Voyage," 449; Thomas Staley, *Jean Rhys: A Critical Study* (Austin: University of Texas Press, 1979), 61; Mary Lou Emery, "The Politics of Form: Jean Rhys's Social Vision in *Voyage in the Dark* and *Wide Sargasso Sea*," *Twentieth Century Literature* 28:4 (1982), 418–30.

40. Davidson, *Jean Rhys*, 60; Helen Nebeker, *Jean Rhys, Woman in Passage: A Critical Study of the Novels of Jean Rhys* (Montreal: Eden Press Women's Publications, 1981), 59; 62.

41. Gayatri Chakravorty Spivak, *In Other Worlds: Essays in Cultural Politics* (New York: Methuen, 1987), 254.

42. Hazel Carby, *Reconstructing Womanhood: The Emergence of the Afro-American Woman Novelist* (Oxford: Oxford University Press, 1987), 18.

CHAPTER FOUR

BOYS WILL BE GIRLS

DRAG AND TRANSVESTIC FETISHISM

"Girls will be boys and boys will be girls / It's a mixed up muddled up shook up world except for Lola," the Kinks sang in 1970, asserting that the gay man in drag was the only sane person in a crazy world.[1] That rock group's revaluation of camp and masquerade is currently shared by many theorists on the left, who advocate it as a postmodern strategy for the subversion of phallocentric identities and desires. Their now radical chic has made the likes of Dolly Parton and Madonna (and their satin queen or wanna-be parodies or imitations) more than chicks with cheek. They have become draped crusaders for the social constructionist cause, catching gender in the act, as an act, so as to demonstrate there is no natural, essential, biological basis to gender or heterosexuality. Postmodern critics argue that because both gender and sexuality are organized around the phallus in our culture, there can be no escaping phallic effects. Any appeal to identities or desires beyond or before the phallus and its signifiers is both too utopic and essentialist. According to this logic, drag is just postmodern pragmatism, deconstructing identity from within so as not to sacrifice desire to an outmoded, purist, and puritan essentialism.

Not so long ago, camp languished, theorized as the shameful sign of an unreconstructed, self-hating, and even woman-hating, homosexual. Now not only femininity, but even macho masculinity, is read as drag and, therefore, radical. Such a literal rehabilitation of sexual difference seems almost too camp to be sincere. The stories we tell about the gender acts of others tell something about our own as they position subjects and objects with respect to symbolic castration and what signifies lack. If there is a desire for camp, expressed in drag fantasies, there is no camping up desire, which we cannot "put on" or put off with the masquerades that are its symptoms. What is revealed—or concealed—by the desire for drag, whether to perceive or perform it? In whose eyes is what chic radical when all gender is an act and not an expression of an essence? Does a camp relation to identity subvert or support phallocentric hierarchies of difference?

CAMP, HOMOPHOBIA, AND MISOGYNY

Andrew Ross suggests that after the 1969 Stonewall Riots camp was an embarrasment to the gay community, the sign of a pre-political gay identity.[2] But other historians of drag have argued that gay and lesbian activists were uncomfortable with it long before then, at least since the 1950s. Both the Daughters of Bilitis and the Mattachine Society disapproved of it and participated in the consolidation of a distinction between gender and sexual "deviance" that resulted in the separation of transvestism and transsexualism from homosexuality, according to Dave King.[3] The impulse behind the devaluation of camp was the apparent complicity of the latter with the sexual inversion model of homosexuality. Inversion theory, and most "third sex" theories, assert that the "invert" or "uranian" has the psyche of one gender (or perhaps both) and the body of the other, so that what looks like a homosexual object choice is in effect heterosexual. Thus, if men desire men, they do so as a women, as Sigmund Freud explains: "[T]hey identify themselves with a woman and take *themselves* as their sexual object. That is to say, they proceed from a narcissistic basis, and look for a young man who resembles themselves and whom *they* may love as their mother loved *them*." Similarly, among women, "the active inverts exhibit masculine characteristics, both physical and mental, with peculiar frequency and look for femininity in their sexual objects. . . ."[4]

This model reinscribes heterosexuality within homosexuality itself, as Judith Butler, among others, has argued.[5] However, in doing so, it is unable to account for the apparently "normally" gendered partner in homosexual object choices. Freud recognized there was a certain amount of "ambiguity" about masculine inversion (if not about lesbianism), writing, "There can be no doubt that a large proportion of male inverts retain the mental quality of masculinity, that they possess relatively few of the secondary characteristics of the opposite sex and that what they look for in their sexual object are in fact feminine mental traits. . . . A strict conceptual distinction should be drawn according to whether the sexual character of the object or that of the subject has been inverted."[6] He sometimes describes the subject of homosexual desire as feminine in search of a masculine object, and sometimes as masculine in search of a feminine object. In both cases he explains desire heterosexually; his inversion cannot account for the butch gay man or the lesbian femme. Confronting the theoretical impossibility of their existence, gay men and lesbians affirmed both their desire and their gender, refusing to assimilate homosexuality to heterosexuality but repudiating drag and butch/ femme roles as deviations from gender norms. For the Daughters of Bilitis and the Mattachine Society, gay men and lesbians, despite their object choices, were really just like heterosexual men and women. Even more recent theorists have also been wary of drag, asserting that embracing gender norms is not assimilationist but radical, given the public's commonsense model of homosexuality, which is still indebted to the inversion model; for example, Martin Humphries writes, "By creating amongst ourselves [gay men] apparently masculine men who desire other men we are refuting the idea that we are really feminine souls in male bodies."[7] If the logical conclusion of inversion theory is the claim that homosexuality is really transsexualism, the extreme form of the reaction against it, the inverse of inversion theory, is the belief that transsexualism is only a defense against homosexuality. To reject either is to court charges of homophobia or "transphobia," but it is the former that accounts for the gay community's rejection of camp and butch/ femme roles (though it is important to recognize that there was never a feminization of lesbian culture as a counter to charges of masculine inversion comparable to the rise of gay machismo in the 1960s and 1970s).

Transphobia takes the very specific form of misogyny when femininity is devalued, which may be why even drag queens often insist they should not be mistaken for women. The emphasis on gay masculinity might be a defense against the feminization our culture has persistently linked to homosexuality, and not just a counter to heterosexist inversion theory. Hypermasculinity can allay the castration anxiety evoked by man objectified as spectacle, as film theorists have argued.[8] John Marshall is thus right to underline that the association of gender inversion with homosexuality has been used to police masculine and feminine roles, for example, through homophobic questions like, "What are you, a fag?"[9] However, because he privileges sexuality rather than

gender when defining gay identity, he does not discuss the common misogynist corollary, "What are you, a girl?"

Being called a fag or queer, a sissy, and a girl are closely linked in Western
culture, but as Craig Owens indicates, homophobia and misogyny are not the
same thing—which Owens emphasizes by arguing that it is possible for feminists, like Luce Irigaray, to be homophobic. He therefore contradicts himself when he cites Jacques Derrida as authority for the assertion that gay men
are not gynephobic because they do not suffer from castration anxiety.[10] It
does not follow that because gay men are unafraid of being seen as gay, they
are unafraid of being seen as feminine (or castrated, in a patriarchal fantasmatic) unless they "really" are already feminine or castrated, ruled out from
the moment homophobia and misogyny—or homosexuality and gender
inversion—are made disjunct. The fear that homosexuality robs a man of his
virility and feminizes him, which Freud saw in Leonardo da Vinci, conjoins
homophobia and misogyny and impacts on both straight and gay culture.[11]
Denigration of drag queens in gay culture may be a rejection of the heterosexist stereotype of the effeminate invert, who is contrasted with the "real
thing," the gay-identified masculine man, but it also may be a misogynist
rejection of the feminine. The queens in literature or film are often tragic or
abject, as in John Rechy's *City of Night* or Hubert Selby Jr.'s *Last Exit to
Brooklyn*.[12] Those interviewed in *Men in Frocks* are defensive—like Harvey
Fierstein's Arnold in the film *Torch Song Trilogy* (1987; dir. Paul Bogart), who
announces that he is a female impersonator to his soon-to-be-lover Alan with
a bravado that suggests he believes he is being provocative if not downright
offensive.[13] The major premise of the cult hit *Outrageous!* (1977; dir. Richard
Benner), starring Craig Russell, is that his character's drag is just that—outrageous. "It's one thing to be gay, but drag—" his gay boss tells him at one
point, and later fires him for refusing to give it up. Even one of Robin's lovers
says, "I don't usually make it with drag queens—none of the guys do."

Some gay theory's affirmation of the "properly" gay man as a masculine
man may also coincide with a misogynist critique of drag and camp
effeminacy:

> The gay male parody of a certain femininity . . . is both a way of giving
> vent to the hostility toward women that probably afflicts every male . . .
> *and* could also paradoxically be thought of as helping to deconstruct that
> image for women themselves. A certain type of homosexual camp speaks
> the truth of that femininity as mindless, asexual, and hysterically bitchy,
> thereby provoking, it would seem to me, a violently antimimetic reaction
> in any female spectator. The gay male bitch desublimates and desexual-
> izes a type of femininity glamorized by movie stars, whom he then lov-

ingly assassinates with his style, even though the campy parodist may himself be quite stimulated by the hateful impulses inevitably included in his performance. The gay-macho style, on the other hand, is intended to excite others sexually, and the only reason that it continues to be adopted is that it frequently succeeds in doing so.[14]

Leo Bersani here assigns women the place of lack as bitches, actual and potential, in need of the rather violent "help" that drag queens are best equipped to offer them. But drag queens themselves are also the victims of a misogyny for which Bersani would make them responsible, represented as just as bitchy and narcissistic as the "real thing," too self-involved to be stimulating anybody else, unlike the altruistic macho man.[15] Asserting that neither the "glamorized" movie star nor the queen are desirable (they are "asexual," despite the evidence of star fan clubs and "chicks-with-dicks" phone-sex numbers, he condemns them to/for masturbation).

However, Bersani rehabiliates drag when it is dressed up as "feminine masochism" rather than bitchy sadism:

> It is possible to think of the sexual as, precisely, moving between a hyperbolic sense of self and a loss of all consciousness of self. But sex as self-hyperbole is perhaps a repression of sex as self-abolition. It inaccurately replicates self-shattering as self-swelling, as psychic tumescence. If . . . men are especially apt to "choose" this version of sexual pleasure, because their sexual equipment appears to invite by analogy, or at least to facilitate, the phallicizing of the ego, neither sex has exclusive rights to the practice of sex as self-hyperbole. For it is perhaps primarily *the degeneration of the sexual into a relationship that condemns sexuality to becoming a struggle for power.* As soon as persons are posited, the war begins. It is the self that swells with excitement at the idea of being on top . . . .[16]

Bersani argues that promiscuousness best realizes self-shattering *jouissance.* What could be more threatening to the heterosexist media, he asks, than "the sexual act that is associated with women but performed by men and . . . has the terrifying appeal of a loss of the ego, of a self-debasement?"[17] His conclusion implicitly answers what is only a rhetorical question: "[I]f the rectum is the grave in which the masculine ideal (an ideal shared—differently—by men *and* women) of proud subjectivity is buried, then it should be celebrated for its very potential for death."[18]

Though Bersani admits that the ways in which sex politicizes are "highly problematical," he nevertheless reifies one kind of sex as politically progressive because dephallicizing. But do all attenuated intersubjective engagements necessarily fail to function as "relationships"? Freud stressed the relative stability of the fantasies that structure a subject's psyche and characteristic defenses; promiscuity might be defensive and as much a part of that fantasy life as any other type of object choice. Furthermore, in a persuasive analysis of T. E. Lawrence's writings, Kaja Silverman demonstrates that masochism is not inconsistent with phallic naricissism and may even be a crucial component of masculinity and leadership in general.[19] Being the bottom can be a means to being on top. If Bersani is right to insist that women, like men, can experience a phallicizing of the ego, despite what some feminist theorists assert, he is surely wrong to imagine that promiscuous anal sex is a greater guarantee of the self-shattering death of the subject than another kind of sex, including the vaginal sex he has asserted it recalls by association.[20] In this essay, a "feminizing" promiscuous anal sex has a phallicizing function, swelling the ego of the theoretical impersonator (as "feminine masochist") at the expense of women. Gay men are the better women, represented as better equipped to undo identity. When the rectum is a grave, the vagina is evidently a dead end.

THE PHALLIC WOMAN

The gay man in drag in Bersani's essay is sometimes misogynist and sometimes a victim of misogyny, a self-swelling phallic sadist and a shattered and castrated masochist. Too often, feminists have been unable to see that the penis is not the phallus—perhaps not surprising, given that patriarchal culture promotes such a misrecognition. Though no one has the phallus and the omniscience, omnipotence, and wholeness that it signifies, in patriarchy woman often figures as the mirror in which man sees himself whole, through the regressive defense mechanisms of projection, sadism, voyeurism, and fetishism. For many feminists the gay man in drag is just another misogynistic representation of woman. Radical lesbian feminist Marilyn Frye argues that gay camp effeminacy "is a casual and cynical mockery of women, for whom femininity is the trappings of oppression, but it is also a kind of play, a toying with that which is taboo. It is a naughtiness indulged in . . . more by those who believe in their immunity to contamination than by those with any doubts or fears."[21] Judith Williamson writes that men in drag undermine "female characteristics" and satirize women, while Erika Munk argues that female impersonators are like whites in blackface, "hostile and patronizing," and Alison Lurie asserts that "men who wear women's clothes, unless they are genuine transsexuals, seem to imitate the most vulgar and unattractive sort of female dress, as if in a spirit of deliberate and hostile parody."[22] They believe drag is a defense against femininity and the lack it signifies. The femininity of the female impersonation is a put-on, not the real thing, signaling that the impersonator has what women lack: the phallus.

Psychoanalysis offers the same explanation of most cross-dressing, which is labelled "transvestic fetishism."[23] The transvestite feminizes himself only in order to "masculinize" or phallicize himself through the erection the cross-dressing causes. Masquerading as the phallic woman, he is able to have (the illusion of having) the phallus. "I was in Toronto once, and the only female impersonator they had was a woman," the star of a drag act in *Outrageous!* jokes, which is why so many feminists have found drag outrageous, though no laughing matter. By insisting on their difference from "real girls" ("RGs," in transvestic slang) impersonators can defend themselves against the castration the latter are made to signify. Like other men in a patriarchal symbolic, the female impersonator may feel whole at woman's expense, misrecognizing her difference as lack and fetishistically disavowing even that.

Andrew Ross has argued that camp is radical because it defetishizes the erotic scenario of woman as spectacle.[24] But as Freud points out, the fetishist both worships and castrates the fetish object, romanticizing and reviling it for its differences—differences the fetishist himself makes meaningful or invents, like the "shine on the nose" one of Freud's patients could see in certain women even when others could not.[25] The details that mark an impersonation as such function fetishistically, signs of the ambiguous difference between phallic women and RGs. Drag routines generally reveal the body beneath the clothes, which is made to serve as the ground of identity.[26] Joking in double entendres, dropping the voice, removing the wig and falsies, exposing the penis all work to resecure masculine identity by effecting a slide along a chain of signifiers that are in a metaphoric and metonymic relationship with one another and with the transcendental signfier, the phallus.

The pleasure of transvestism is like the pleasure of the Western, in which we see men mutilated, castrated, and restored, rendered whole again.[27] It is exhibitionistic as well as voyeuristic, and may invite identification with, rather than disidentifcation from, the hero/victim. On television, powerful female characters like *Dynasty*'s Alexis Carrington Colby Dexter, serve as a conduit for a gay look, according to Mark Finch.[28] Such phallic women solicit not only a transvestic gaze but a transvestic identification, as they are both the subjects and the objects of the gaze and phallic mastery, as transvestite pornography makes clear. Lola, "tall, dark and hung," and Pasha, "The Polynesian Bombshell," are consistently described and imaged as phallic women in *Drag Queens*.[29] Lola has "the right equipment for either sex . . . [she] loves to play it both ways, and she knows she's got what it takes to make it work," the magazine claims and verifies that with photos drawing attention to Lola's breasts and erect nipples and to her partially erect penis.[30] Both shots and writing emphasize fetishism: "Lola loves to show it all off. The slow striptease is her favorite. Wearing lace, nylons, and high heeled shoes, she hides her meaty truth. At the right moment, she unveils her cock. The shock is erotic and irresistable. Lola is unique!"[31] Phallic narcissism is suggested by the many photos of Lola masturbating and by captions which describe her as "the seducer of herself, a woman capable of turning herself in to [sic] a rigid and throbbing man!"[32] The text makes clear the queen's penis is king, continually reinscibing patriarchal gender hierarchies, describing Lola's feminine half as "turning on the man below," "desir[ing] to please," "giv[ing] way to the long thick cock," etc.[33] And although Lola is never shown having sex with anyone, she is frequently represented masturbating to pornography in which another black man in drag is seen anally penetrating a white man. If Lola is a woman, she is one with a very special difference; after all, "she can take her man where no woman has taken him before."[34] Represented as active, masterful, and complete, Lola is obviously the phallic woman.

John Waters's film *Pink Flamingos* (1972) also plays with the power of the queen. In one sequence, the voyeuristic pleasure of Raymond in a beautiful woman is suddenly disrupted when she lifts her skirt to reveal a penis. The spectator, aligned by the camera with Raymond, can only laugh by disidentifying from him; otherwise, she is the butte of the joke, too. The transvestite's gesture in this sequence is almost literally a punch line, as the look at a shocked and visibly displeased Raymond in the reverse shot reveals. The laughter of the viewer is a defensive response to the castration anxiety suddenly evoked and evaded by making what is literally a transvestic identification with the phallic woman. Such scenes point to the presence of a desire Freud never discusses when he elaborates on the negative oedipus: the boy's acitve, sadistic, and masculine wish to penetrate the father, rather than his passive, masochistic, and feminine wish to be penetrated by him, a desire that undermines the father's alignment with the phallus.

I am not suggesting that spectators are always encouraged to identify with the man in drag, only that such an identification is possible and may not subvert phallic identities. Of course, it is far more common for distancing effects to be maintained by representing the transvestite as mastered and lacking object, rather than potent subject of the gaze, which suggests that Frye's critique of what she calls the "phallophilia" of gay men and drag is neither fair nor accurate.[35] For example, *The Queens*, a "photographic essay" by George Alpert, tells a story of pathos and horror. It incorporates many photos of older comic and ugly "dames" whose failure of femininity is suggested by contrast with the young "glam" queens included, who are usually not seen in extreme close-up or in unflattering lights or poses, and are sometimes even photographed in romantic soft focus, as women often are. But they are also often photographed against or behind doors and windows, sometimes barred, or in corners, suggesting they are tragically trapped by their "perverse" inclinations. The opening and closing series in particular convey this effect. The first ends with a close-up of "Baby" looking pensive; on his cheek glistens what appears to be a tear, though it could just be a drop of water left after washing off makeup. The final picture of the last sequence is of "the twins" sadly trying to peer out over the sill or through the frame of what could be a window that partially obstructs their faces. The photo suggests the pain of being caught in "their" world, barred definitively from "ours." This book does not confuse the queen's penis with the phallus. It envisions the female impersonator as symbolically castrated, tragically—even horribly—lacking, a point of view not necessarily (or only) heterosexist, since it is also available to homosexuals.

MASOCHISM

When *Torch Song*'s "Virginia Ham" (Arnold/Harvey Fierstein) drops her voice to tell her gay audience, "You can't become a dame until you've knelt before a queen," she constitutes herself as a phallic woman, invested with an erotic power denied by Bersani and others. Though spectators might identify with her, her punning address to us invites us to pay her homage in an act that both feminizes and ennobles. The spectacle of the queen makes a lady of her supplicant; she is the phallic woman who offers the ambiguous pleasures of masochism. As D. N. Rodowick has pointed out, Laura Mulvey's almost biologizing insistence on aligning the cinematic gaze with masculinity and an active and controlling voyeurism and fetishism blinds her to the possiblity of a passive component of vision, one in which fetishism coincides with masochism rather than sadism.[36] Interested in theorizing a feminine pleasure in films Mulvey seems to rule out, Rodowick considers Freud's essay on the beating fantasy to extend to film its notion of multiple enunciations for a single utterance. He does not discuss what we can infer, that the gaze directed toward the heroine at those moments when she is most fetishized could be masochistic rather than sadistic. Nor does Rodowick discuss whether the masochistic spectator might fetishize the male hero, who he argues can be viewed as an erotic object by women and men (though Rodowick does not elaborate a homoerotic gaze, his theory, unlike Mulvey's, implicitly includes it).[37] Bound by the Freudian logic he used to question Mulvey, Rodowick does not theorize the significance of difference other than gender for the gaze, desire, and subjectivity, differences that may well come into play in fetishism.

Some recent feminist work shares Rodowick's conviction that the phallus can solicit a masochistic, rather than sadistic, gaze. Griselda Pollock argues that one of Dante Gabriel Rossetti's paintings of women, *Astarte Syriaca*

(1877), transcends the "repetitive obsessive fetishization" of most of his art in order to represent "a figure before which the masculine viewer can comfortably stand subjected . . . a fantasy image of the imaginary, maternal plentitude and phallic mother."[38] Berkeley Kaite arrives at a similar conclusion about pornographic images, asserting that the look at the fetishized woman who looks back—whether that woman's investment with the phallus is "literal" (the transvestite, or "TV") or vestiary (the RG)—provides the pleasure of the surrender to the penetrating "cut," the moment when the subject is severed from the phallic (m)other and accedes to difference and a fantasy of self-possession.[39] And in a series of essays devoted to the topic of masochism itself, Kaja Silverman explores at length the eroticization of lack and subordination for men. She notes that the conscious heterosexuality of the male maoschists Freud discusses in "A Child Is Being Beaten" constitutes a 'feminine' yet heterosexual male subject, one whose identification with the phallus is disrupted by installing the mother in the dominant place. (Freud himself subordinates that fantasy to the unconsious and homosexual desire to be beaten by the father).[40] Like Kaite and Pollock, she privileges the relation to the phallic (m)other who "precedes" the symbolic, which subordinates her, and the child, to the father. She does to make the radical claim that the male masochist "cannot be reconciled to the symbolic order or to his social identity" because his sexuality is "devoid of any possible productivity or use value."[41]

Whereas Silverman's emphasis is on the male masochist, just a few years earlier Jane Gallop and others focused on the subversive force of the phallic woman or mother who undoes the logic of ideological solidarity between phallus, father, power, and man.[42] Yet when Freud discusses the phallic woman, for example in the "Wolf Man" case or the essay on the taboo on virginity in "primitive cultures," he suggests she is phallic on the same terms as the man, having acquired a penis or what stands for it, perhaps from a man with whom she has had intercourse.[43] It is therefore revealing that the marquis de Sade's archetypal phallic woman, the eponymous heroine of *Juliette*, explains her desire as a reactive copy of masculine desire: "My lubricity, always modeled after men's whims, never is lit except by fire of their passion; I am only really inflamed by their desires, and the only sensual pleasure I know is that of satisfying all their deviations."[44] When the active, desiring woman still reflects man's desire, the mirrors of the patriarchal imaginary are not shattered.

The fantasy of the phallic mother is the topic of a great deal of feminist writing on mother-daughter relations.[45] This work has focused on the difficulty of difference for the daughter, who cannot quite distinguish herself from her mother in a symbolic that requires that confusion. Woman is theorized as unable to represent lack for herself because she must represent it for men by becoming, through identification, their lost object of desire. She cannot enter the symbolic, too close to the mother whom she is unable to give up or give up being, because for her, having nothing to lose, castration poses no "real" threat. The daughter's response to this lack of a lack and difference is paranoia, a defense associated with psychosis and foreclosure of symbolic castration. The mother is phallic because she is invested with the power to free her little girl, to divest herself of her phallus-child.

This paranoid fantasy about the phallic mother is a cornerstone of object-relations theory, for which the boy's accession to masculinity is a problem, rather than the girl's to femininity, as in the Freudian/Lacanian paradigm. Object-relations theorists assume masculinity and femininity are there from the start, rather than produced through the resolution of the castration complex and the separation from the mother. They suppose a boy is destined for masculinity even though he begins in a "feminine" dependence on and identification with the mother. She is presumed phallic in that she is blamed for men's "gender identity disorders," like transsexualism, which according to well-known expert Dr. Robert Stoller results from too much mother and too little father.[46] The phallic mother will not let boys be boys.

This phallic mother is at once castrating and castrated. When the fantasy is paranoid and the lack of difference figured as fearful, it cannot be progressive for women; it contributes to the repudiation of femininity that patriarchy already engenders and realigns women with the maternal as a role they can never adequately perform. However, when the fantasy is also fascinating and pleasurable, it maintains the subject on the edge of subjection and self-(dis)possession. Kaite argues that transvestism does just that, providing the pleasure of self-dispossession as castration and the death of desire through the death of the subject, who lacks a lack in or difference from the phallic (m)other. Yet Kaite criticizes Francette Pacteau for associating androgyny with just such a death of desire, which follows from Pacteau's assertion that androgyny represents the narcissistic desire for wholeness in the phallic (m)other, beyond the lack that motivates desire and so beyond difference itself, including sexual difference. According to Kaite, the TV or androgyne expresses a desire for repression rather than a repression (or, more properly, foreclosure) of desire.[47] Kaite wants to retain for transvestism and fetishism the radicality of a refusal of the symbolic and its hierarchies of difference without giving up the recognition of castration, difference, and lack accession to the symbolic is supposed to generate. Kaite's beliefs about fetishism are as contradictory as the fetishist's about the mother's phallus: fetishistic disavowal will (not) make him/her whole. The fetishist at once knows and refuses to acknowledge his lack or castration, his self-difference. The perversion has a defensive function, even if it also has a subversive impulse. In this, fetishism is like what Julia Kristeva has called abjection, which can refashion "his majesty the ego" by storming the fortress in which he reigns, described by Lacan as the "orthopaedic . . . armour of an alienating identity."[48] But the emperor's new clothes threaten to expose him utterly, leaving him defenseless against the phallic (m)other, prey to the psychotic failure of subjectivity itself. For Kristeva, the loss of the subject that abjection threatens is not without its liabilities, even if a rigidly defensive ego is also a liability.

Gendering as feminine such a tantalizing/terrifying loss reveals the defensive nature of masculinity itself. Silverman says that the beating fantasy Freud discusses, and masochistic fantasies in general, attest to the need to be boys to be girls, so that even the female "feminine masochist" has a masculinity complex, albeit one in which she makes an identification with the homoerotic man, wishing to be passive and masochistic rather than active and sadistic. Castration or divestiture, Silverman argues, "can only be realized at the site of male subjectivity because it is there that the paternal legacy is stored."[49] The woman has nothing to lose; it is the male subject's self-fetishizing phallic imposture that provides him with the signifiers of lack: the penis and all that signals the power and privilege accruing to man in a patriarchal culture. Man appears to have the phallus by exhibiting what signifies having the phallus, that which is metaphorically or metonymically linked to it. One such substitute is the woman herself, the fetishized (m)other, who "masquerades" as the phallus so that man can "parade" his phallus, the woman whose lack he needs to feel complete. In the Lacanian paradigm man, like woman, only comes into being when "photo-graphed," (Lacan's term) fixed by the look of the phallic (m)other, who reflects for him an image of wholeness with which he jubilantly identifies.[50] Both man and woman literally appear to be subjects. Their relations revolve around having or being the phallus for one another, which is never more than *appearing* to have or be the phallus for the other who can be duped by the performance.[51]

However, man's fetishistic misrecognition of the organ upon which his identity hangs is legislated by the patriarchal symbolic, so that it seems to be the real thing. The subject who desires to take up the position of being the phallus for the phallic (m)other, the hole in her whole, must be castrated, feminized. This leads to the curious conclusion that only men can become real women (in fact, Moustapha Safouan asserts just that about transsexuals, and it is implicit in Bersani's and Silverman's work on masochism).[52] Masochists—and even theorists of masochism—have been duped by the penis fetish when they fail to distinguish between it and the phallus, even if such a misrecognition apparently does not serve man's phallic narcissism. Masochistic fantasies may include "scenes" in which the male genitals, the symbol of man's identification with the father as bearer of the phallus, are beaten or cut off, but this does not preclude the belief that the phallic mother is phallic because she has castrated the father and retained his penis.

In a classic essay on transvestism that ties it to masochism, Otto Fenichel notes that the little boy can desire to have the mother's baby just as a little girl might desire to have the father's baby.[53] Freud emphasizes that the wish for a child points to an unconscious equation made between the penis and the baby. The daughter's desire to be a mother, expressed in playing with dolls, is motivated by penis envy.[54] The same might be said of the expectant son, who anticaptes the gift of the phallus in sexual relations, even masochistic relations, because they are are all structured around phallic exchange. If a world with such sexual relations would be an inversion of those current in Western patriarchy, the meaning of the phallus and its "privileged" signifiers would nevertheless remain unanalyzed.

DRAGGING IN DIFFERENCES

Luce Irigaray reads the little girl's interest in dolls differently, seeing in it not an expression of penis envy but a desire for a "feminine" mastery of the mother-and-child relationship by playing with an image of the self.[55] Playing with dolls is a variant of what Irigaray calls "mimicry," in which the woman masters "her" image, the fetishistic masquerade, putting it on so as to signify it is a put on and can easily be taken off.[56] Irigaray suggests that mimicry signifies a distance between woman and her image that is necessary for knowledge and hinges on disidentification and difference. Woman cannot know "woman" if she is too close to her image to see it with a critical eye. Transvestism also may express such mimicry, in which the son plays with his image like a doll, dressing it up to signal his distance—and difference, then from lack. If femininity, like masculinity, can be a defense, a phallic imposture, then a literal castration, as in transsexualism, may not effect a symbolic castration. The fact that men can assume femininity (and castration) in order to disidentify from it (as lack) has distressed feminists who have discussed drag. Yet the possibility of assuming it to disidentify from it has excited feminists who theorize a female female impersonation or mimicry. The mimic can know "woman" because she does not have to *be* her and does not have to make a transvestic identification with man in order to have some perspective on her image. Mimicry provides an alternative to adopting a masculine point of view, without necessitating a naive idealist or essentialist belief in the ability to access a "genuine" femininity beyond patriarchy.

Paradoxically, feminists praise in female female impersonation or mimicry what they condemn in female impersonation or drag: its distancing effects.

This contradiction is symptomatic, but not necessarily of homophobia. Rather, it points to the significance of differences other than those of gender or sexual orientation, which have to be "dragged" into drag and its theories. Though feminist theorists of mimicry, and lesbian and gay theorists of drag, generally do not comment on the work of the other camp, both privilege the tactic of assuming an identity as a false identity. For both any identity is "assumed" or false and alienated, unreal, fictional—what Lacan terms "masquerade" or "parade." There is no authentic, "real" self beyond or before the process of its social construction, so our identitites must be subverted from within them.

As Judith Butler explains, drag promotes "a subversive laugher in the pastiche-effect of parodic practices in which the original, the authentic, and the real are themselves constituted as effects. The loss of gender norms would have the effect of proliferating gender configurations, destabilizing substantive identity and depriving the naturalizing narratives of compulsory heterosexuality of their central protagonists: 'man' and 'woman.'"[57] Sue-Ellen Case suggests that butch/femme lesbians camp up the fiction of castration, ironizing it, while Jack Babuscio, Richard Dyer, Jeffrey Escoffier, Andrew Ross, and Vito Russo all discuss drag as a parodic or ironic exaggeration or hyperbolization of gender.[58] These are the very terms and phrases which feminist theorists use when they write about mimicry. To be a mimic, according to Irigaray, is to "assume the feminine role deliberately . . . so as to make 'visible,' by an effect of playful repetition, what was supposed to remain invisible. . . ."[59] To play the feminine is to "speak" it ironically, to italicize it, in Nancy Miller's words, to hyperbolize it, in Mary Ann Doane's words, or to parody it, according to Mary Russo and Linda Kauffman.[60] The mimic and the drag queen "camp up" ideology in order to undo it, producing knowledge about it: that gender and the heterosexual orientation that are presumed to anchor it are unnatural and even oppressive.

For theorists of drag and mimicry, irony and parody set them off from the masquerade or parade of those who play gender straight. But if all identities are alienated and fictional, what makes one credible and the other incredible, an obvious fake? The answer, it seems, is the author's intention: parody is legible in the drama of gender performance if someone meant to script it, intending it to be there. Any potential confusion of the two is eliminated by a focus in the theories on production rather than reception or perception. Sometimes, however, one is ironic without having intended it, and sometimes, despite one's best intentions, no one gets the joke. When, as Lacan points out, the "real thing" is already a comedy, what passes for "passing" for or impersonating a gender must be analyzed.[61]

In theories of camp, butch/femme drag is visible as such because of an essential "gay sensibility" invoked to keep clear the difference between gay and heterosexual gender impersonation. Some theorists, like Babuscio and Russo, explicitly refer to it as the ground of camp, explaining that "passing" sensitizes gays and lesbians to both the oppressiveness and artificiality of gender roles.[62] But as Andrew Britton suggests, such gay essentialism is problematic because it is obvious that the experience of homophobic oppression does not necessarily lead to an understanding of it.[63] Gayatri Spivak has made a similar point about oppression in general, arguing that theorists like Michel Foucault are too ready to credit the oppressed with the power to know and articulate their oppression directly when the very fact of oppression can make that impossible, since consciousness itself may be dominated and, indeed, constituted by hegemonic ideology.[64]

Other theorists of drag only implicitly invoke a "gay sensibility," which manifests itself in the difficulty they have in demonstrating the difference between butch/femme and inversion, on the one hand, and butch/femme and straight gender roles on the other. It is a difficulty apparent in Freudian theory, too, which cannot explain the desire of the femme for the butch lesbian or, conversely, of the butch gay man for the queen—they are "too gay" to be straight inversions.[65] Camp theory has difficulty with the same two roles, which are "too straight" to be gay parodies or drag. Butler, Babuscio, and Oscar Montero suggest that butches and queens mark their impersonations as such through the use of incongruous contrasts, signs of a double gender identity, as well as through what they and other theorists of camp describe as parodic excess (for example, Ross says the queen dresses "over the top").[66] "Excess" is what prevents drag from being mere inversion or a heterosexual role when there are no incongruous contrasts and confused gender signs, as with lesbian femmes and butch gay men. When Butler discusses the play of difference and desire in lesbian camp she argues that the butch does not assimilate lesbianism into heterosexuality as inversion because being a woman recontextualizes masculinity through the confusion of gender signs. She says it is exactly this confusion the femme finds desirable, "she likes her boys to be girls."[67] Butler discusses the butch as the subject of gender play but the object of desire, which enables the lesbian to be consistently associated with transvestic subversion. The femme's being a woman does not obviously recontextualize femininity, nor does it sound particularly radical to suggest the butch likes her girls to be girls. Yet just a few lines later Butler insists the femme displaces the heterosexual scene as if she embodied the same shifting of sexed body as ground and gender identity as figure that the butch does. Similarly, when Case writes that the femme "aims her desirability" at the butch, she inscribes as active a potentially passive femininity so that it can appear as distinct from straight femininity.[68]

What ultimately makes the femme different from the RG for both theorists is that she plays her role for another woman, which they claim makes it excessive and incongruous by "recontextualizing" or "reinterpreting" it (an argument that provides an additional safeguard against butch roles as mere inversion by asserting the legibility of the butch's womanliness despite the confusion of gender signs). This is an essentialist tautology: butch-femme or drag is gender play because it is gay; it is gay because it is gender play. An implicit "gay sensibility" determines in advance what counts as gender play, keeping straight the difference between enlightened drag and unenlightened masquerade or parade. It is not surprising that the tautology fails, as Lisa Duggan reveals in an article tellingly titled "The Anguished Cry of an 80s Fem: 'I Want to Be a Drag Queen'": "When lesbians sponsor strip shows, or other fem erotic performances, it is very difficult to 'code' it as lesbian, to make it feel queer. The result looks just like a heterosexual performance, and lesbian audiences don't respond to it as subversively sexual, specifically ours."[69] In fact, the photo of two women in corsets illustrating this article is by Annie Sprinkle, who has appeared in similar transvestite pornography that has a straight audience. The picture or fantasy has two different enunciations, one that is heterosexual and masculine, and one that is lesbian.[70] Teresa de Lauretis underlines this dilemma when she writes that the femme cannot appear in most contexts "[u]nless . . . she enter [sic] the frame of vision *as* or *with* a lesbian in male drag."[71] Clearly only something like a gay sensibility would enable one to recognize a femme in butch drag.

Perhaps the most troubling consequence of such essentialism is its paradoxical reinforcement of the idea that the "authentic" or "natural" self is heterosexual, even as it inverts the hierarchy by proclaiming the "fake" or artificial gay self to be the "better," smarter—more smartly dressed—self, which deconstructs itself by knowing its difference from itself and the gender role it only assumes like a costume. This erects the gay self as the upright self, properly nonidentical in comparison to the straight self, which also, therefore, lacks gay jouissance. Such uses of jouissance make it "stiffen into a strong, muscular image," according to Jane Gallop; it becomes phallic, a sign of "an ego-gratifying identity" in which "fear or unworthiness is projected outward. . . ."[72] Gays and lesbians are no more free from castration anxiety than anyone else, as this defensive maneuver suggests. Like straight men—and women—they can disavow castration through projection and fetishism, including the self-fetishism of phallic imposture that may not be inconsistent with camp. For when roles are already alienated and unreal, the problem is not how one holds them at a distance but how one responds to that distance. In transvestic drag, it is fetishized: the impersonator assumes a phallic identity through an apparent identifcation that is, in fact, a disidentification, signified by the incongruous contrasts and ironic excess she sees—and those who share that point of view see—in that gender act, which constitute it as camp.

It is also fetishized in mimicry, as I have argued in this book.[73] Theories of mimicry reinscribe white, middle-class femininity as the real thing, the (quint)essence of femininity. This is implicit in the feminist critiques of drag I have discussed, which define its style as a sign of a hostile burlesque by contrasting it with that of a "natural" femininty, whose understated good taste is a sign of the genuine article. If boys will be girls, they had better be ladies. A real woman is a real lady; otherwise, she is a female impersonator, whose "unnaturally bad" taste—like that attributed to working-class women or women of color—marks the impersonation as such. The mimic flaunts or camps up lack by fetishistically projecting it onto some "other" woman, from whom she distances herself through a disidentification that takes the form of an apparent identification, as with the impersonator.

Feminist theorists of mimicry distinguish themselves from "other" women even as they assimilate the latter by romanticizing them, assuming the "other" has a critical knowledge about femininity because of her difference from what counts as natural femininity: white, Anglo, bourgeois style. It is only from a middle-class point of view that Dolly Parton looks like a female impersonator (see chapter 2); from a Southern working-class point of view she could be the epitome of genuine womanliness. Something similar can be said of Divine in the John Waters film *Polyester* (1981), whose polyester marks his impersonation as such for those who find it in unnaturally bad taste, since Divine never gives any (other) indication he is "really" a man.[74] Mimicry is distinguished from masquerade on the basis of differences between women which white, middle-class feminists fetishistically disavow whenever they talk of "the" feminine, as if it were only one thing.

Some women can "have" the phallus in our culture because it is not just the penis but all the other signs of power and privilege, which stand in a metaphoric and metonymic relation not only to "penis" but also to "white" and "bourgeois," the signs of a "proper" racial and class identity. Relations between members of different races and classes, like those between genders, can be structured by the imaginary and characterized by fetishism, in which the signs of difference signify phallic lack or wholeness. The symbolic is more than a masculine imaginary; it is also a white and bourgeois imaginary, which explains the potentially oppressive effects of mimicry and drag when they constitute the other as what must be repudiated (the inverse complement, a symptom of lack and ignorance) or what can make one whole (the supplement, the phallic (m)other who guarantees full self-presence and knowledge). Feminists have shown that talk of a "common humanity" is only a masculinist ruse disguising oppression. The utopic vision of a common femininity and of women free from the effects of symbolic castration and the unconscious it produces, the source of the desires and fears that motivate us, has been made possible by an indifference to the significance of differences other than gender. The same can be said of relations between gay men, which may not be characterized by the perfect reciprocity and equality that Harold Beaver, Craig Owens, and other gay theorists imagine they are.[75]

Homosexuality, like femininity, is marked by the effects of castration anxiety. Gay men, like women (including lesbians), are in the symbolic as much as heterosexual men are by virtue of a phallic imposture they can use to defend themselves from the psychosis with which both homosexuality and femininity have been associated in psychoanalysis since Freud's analysis of Schreber.[76] As Eve Kosofsky Sedgwick points out, gay theorists must acknowledge the significance of differences within the gay community—differences that can be activated defensively and oppressively in gay relationships and identities, including camp.[77] Race and class fetishism can operate in homosexual as well as heterosexual eros, since forms of otherness between men or women can have a phallic significance that all too often has been overlooked. Sunil Gupta, Kobena Mercer, Isaac Julien, and Thomas Yingling, among others, have written about the potential for the replication of racism in gay relationships through fantasies about the black or Asian man's sex, while Jane Gallop has described a lesbian relationship in which the working-class woman functioned as the phallus for her middle-class lover just as women in general function as the phallus for men.[78] If they are at stake in fetishistic masochism, race and class differences can give the fantasy a symbolic productivity or use value even when the subject subverts phallic gender norms.

The fantasy Homi Bhabha locates at the heart of racism, the "primal scene" he claims to derive from Frantz Fanon, centers on a fascinating and fearful interracial rape that could be a permutation of the fetishistic/ masochistic beating fantasy analyzed by Freud. In the scene, a little white girl "fixes Fanon in look and word" as she turns from him to identify with her mother, saying, "Look, a negro . . . Mamma, see the Negro! I'm frightened. Frightened." Fanon describes the experience as "an amputation, an excision."[79] Its violence is that of a castration, as in the retrospective understanding of the sexual primal scene. In each, subjects take up one of two antithetical positions. One has or lacks color; one has or lacks the penis. In the racial primal scene's confluence with the sexual primal scene, however, the other is figured as frighteningly different not because he lacks but because he has the organ, though one that is monstrous.

While Bhabha genders the subject of this drama, Fanon himself does not explicitly mark the sex of the child who speaks of being afraid of him (though later he implicitly does by discussing as the white man's fantasy the fear that "his" women are "at the mercy of the Negroes").[80] The fantasy, therefore, could have a white masculine as well as feminine enunciation, just as the beating fantasy has two gendered enunciations. Freud's exploration of the effects of the primal scene in his analysis of the "Wolf Man" implies just this possibility because in it differences besides gender figure importantly. What the Wolf Man is afraid of is the big, bad dick, symbolized by the well-endowed dream wolves with their overgrown tails.[81] The Wolf Man wants to be loved like a woman by his father, but he is afraid it means he will be castrated.[82] He also wants to be a gentleman like his father and, therefore, different from the maids and male estate workers he might imagine are castrated (because they too seem to have a passive, feminine attitude toward his father).[83] Paradoxically, his very identifcation with his father also means he will be castrated, since he believes his mother retains his father's penis after intercourse.[84] This fetishistic circuit of pleasure, displeasure, identification, and disidentification is condensed in the image of the wolves, who represent both the father and the Wolf Man as at once phallic (their tails are big) and castrated (their tales are too big, are obvious fakes or prostheses disguising their lack).

At stake in the Wolf Man's castration anxiety fantasies are not only his gender but also his class identity. Peter Stallybrass and Allon White make this clear when they discuss the Wolf Man's predilection for "debased" women like Grusha, his nursery maid, as typical for the bourgeois man of his time. They write, "The opposition of working-class maid and upper-class male . . . depended upon a physical and social separation which was constitutive of desire. But it was a desire which was traversed by contradictions. On the one hand, the 'lowness' of the maid reinforced antithetically the status of the gentlemen. . . . But on the other hand . . . she was a figure of comfort and power."[85]

These women represent what has to be repudiated by the middle-class child as she grows up: improper dress, manners, speech, and hygiene, all the signs of someone with no class. At the same time, they threaten the bourgeois subject with the return of the lack he has lost, which accounts for their fearful fascination. Though Stallybrass and White discuss this as abjection, Bhabha terms the similar psychic mechanism at work in the racial primal scene and stereotyping "fetishism."[86] Fetishism also seems to characterize the gay bourgeois "sexual colonialism" Jeffrey Weeks documents, in which "'working class' equals 'masculine' equals 'closeness to nature'"—for better or worse, as with the racial "primitive other."[87] Such fetishism helps reproduce race and class differences, as well as gender differences, in all their ambivalence.

The fetishistic gaze at the "other" may be masochistic, and not just sadistic; Fanon's primal scene offers both enunciations. Race and class differences regularly figure in masochistic fantasies. Riviere discusses a case that seems to anticipate Fanon, in which a (southern) white woman fantasizes being attacked by a black man from whom she defends herself by having him make love to her so she can—eventually—turn him over to justice (a scenario remarkably like that in the many popular film versions of *King Kong*).[88] Silverman describes one in which a man imagines himself a Portuguese prisoner of the Aztecs who is eventually skinned alive, another in which a middle-class woman is beaten by "rough" and "ignorant" working-class women, and yet another in which she is beaten and loved as a male "savage" by a domineering Robinson Crusoe figure.[89] Transvestite pornography often includes stories, sketches, and photos of both men and women who serve a dominatrix as a slave or a maid does a mistress.[90] Even the Kinks' domineering queen Lola has "a dark brown voice," a synethesia suggesting that she is black.

What is remarkable about these fantasies is their subjects' fluid shifting not only of gender but also of racial and class identities in ways that simultaneously subvert and sustain phallic identifications complexly articulated through differences in gender, race, and class. It is not always necessary for the masochist (whether male or female) to fantasize being a man in order to be beaten and loved "like a woman" and thereby symbolically castrated. There are a number of ways to be divested of the phallus in our symbolic that do not center on the penis as the mark of power and privilege. Phallic divestiture by one means can even be congruent with phallic investiture by another, functioning defensively so as to distinguish the subject from the phallic other (mother or father) whose (mis)recognition is solicited and shared in order to be a subject at all.

Furthermore, the fantasy of the other as phallic "Other" is not necessarily radical, since she may be phallic in exactly those terms a sexist, racist, and classist symbolic legitimates, and the fantasizing subject may identify with that position of omnipotence and omniscience, rather than imagine she is excluded from it, as occurs in theories of camp and mimicry. Finally, even when the subject does feel excluded from that place, and her fetishism is an anxious response to a sense of lack, the object/other still remains only a phallic fantasy. She does not exist as such: she does not exist for the subject (who wants to be whole through him/her), and she is not what she seems to be for the subject (since she has desires the subject cannot know). Theorists of camp and mimicry have not concerned themselves with the subjectivity of their "others" except as it seems to guarantee their own status as phallic "Others" who know what they are about. The irony in mimicry and camp is all too often at the other's expense, a defense against castration anxiety. Thus, while it is perfectly possible to imagine a white male transvestic and camp identification with the heroine in *King Kong*, for example, it would not be particularly progressive for black men, made once again the bearers of the big, bad dick that has figured so prominently in the history of race relations structured by fantasies of miscegenation and all too real lynchings.

CONCLUSION

Camp (like mimicry) functions complexly by dragging in many differences at once that are all too easily articulated with phallic narcissism in a symbolic that functions as a white, bourgeois, and masculine fetishistic imaginary. This narcissism needs to be analyzed, its phallic impostures unveiled as such. Gay theorists—like feminist theorists—must recognize their positioning in a number of discourses beside those of gender and sexuality and accept difference, including self-difference and lack. While camp may not always facilitate such recognition and acceptance, it is not essentially at odds with it. Indeed, though Zora Neale Hurston's character Janie Mae Crawford says, "You got tuh *go* there *tuh* know there," Gayatri Spivak points out that "knowledge is made possible and is sustained by irreducible difference, not identity."[91] The play of identification and disidentification in drag could be the very condition of autocritique.

I would argue that it does make possible self-criticism for one very fragile moment in Rechy's *City of Night*, when the first-person narrator, a hustler, briefly accepts his castration by identifying with the beautiful queen Kathy, whom he understands to be castrated, paradoxically, because she has (rather than lacks) a penis; it is what prevents her from being a whole (and phallic) woman. His self-knowledge (which promotes our self-knowledge, since we have been asked to identify with him) is revealed in his response to a scene he witnesses in New Orleans during Carnival, when Kathy directs one of the heterosexual male tourists who has come on to her to grope her crotch:

> The man's hand explores eagerly. Kathy smiles fiercely. The man pulled his hand away violently, stumbling back in astonishment. Kathy follows him with the fading eyes. Now Jocko [a hustler friend] smiles too.
> I turn away quickly from the sign. I feel gigantically sad for Kathy, for the dropped mask—sad for Jocko—for myself—sad for the man who kissed Kathy and discovered he was kissing a man.
> Sad for whole rotten spectacle of the world wearing cold, cold masks.

"Minutes later," the narrator says, "my own mask began to crumble." He tells two johns he is not what they think he is—"tough," "the opposite from them."[92] In effect, he acknowledges his virile "parade" as a masquerade, a charade of having something valuable to give (the penis as phallus) to those others who can afford to pay for it, who can "afford" to be castrated for him,

as the Wolf Man could not for his father. The narrator understands that like
Kathy he is only a man, and not what he must seem to be in the comedy of
sexual relations. At that moment, he recognizes that sex could be something
other than an exchange of the phallus, though he is not quite sure how. But as
the rest of the novel reveals, he resumes hustling and refuses the painful
knowledge of castration that nevertheless returns to haunt him as the feeling
that heaven is unfairly barred to some. The "solution" to anxiety about
fetishistic phallic imposture proves to be more fetishism—not surprising,
since the symbolic itself legislates the repudiation of lack. Disrupted by
camp, the camp moment does not last; misrecognition follows upon recognition, and incredible acts, unfortunately, begin to seem credible once more.

NOTES

1. The Kinks, "Lola," on *Lola versus Powerman, and the Moneygoround, Part One*
    (Burbank: Warner Bros. Records, R56423, 1970).
2. Andrew Ross, *No Respect: Intellectuals and Popular Culture* (New York: Routledge,
    1989), 144.
3. Dave King, "Gender Confusion: Psychological and Psychiatric Conceptions of
    Transvestism and Transsexualism," in *The Making of the Modern Homosexual*, ed.
    Kenneth Plummer (Totowa, N.J.: Barnes and Noble, 1981), 155–83. See also John
    Marshall, "Pansies, Perverts and Macho Men: Changing Conceptions of Male
    Homosexuality," also in *The Making of the Modern Homosexual*, 150–51; Jeffrey
    Escoffier, "Sexual Revolution and Politics of Gay Identity," *Socialist Review* 81 (1985),
    129–92, and *Socialist Review* 82 (1985), 133–42. Don Mager, "Gay Theories of Gender
    Role Deviance," *Sub-Stance* 46 (1985), 32–36; and Sue-Ellen Case, "Toward a Butch-
    Femme Aesthetic," in *Making a Spectacle: Feminist Essays on Contemporary Women's
    Theatre*, ed. Lynda Hart (Ann Arbor: University of Michigan Press, 1989), 284–86.
4. Sigmund Freud, *Three Essays on the Theory of Sexuality*, trans. James Strachey (1905;
    reprt. New York: Basic Books, 1975), 11 (footnote added 1910); emphasis in the
    original.
5. Judith Butler, *Gender Trouble: Feminism and the Subversion of Identity* (New York:
    Routledge, 1990), 54–55, 60–61.
6. Freud, *Three Essays*, 10.
7. Martin Humphries, "Gay Machismo," in *The Sexuality of Men*, ed. Andy Metcalf and
    Martin Humphries (London and Sydney: Pluto Press, 1985), 84. See also Gregg
    Blachford, who argues that gay macho "may be an attempt to show that masculine or
    'ordinary' men can be homosexual too. . . . " Blachford, "Male Dominance and the
    Gay World," *The Sexuality of Men*, 200.
8. Richard Dyer, "Don't Look Now," *Screen* 23:3–4 (1982), 61–73; Sandy Flitterman-
    Lewis, "Thighs and Whiskers: The Fascination of 'Magnum, P.I.,'" *Screen* 26:2
    (1985), 42–58; Steve Neale, "Masculinity as Spectacle: Reflections on Men and
    Mainstream Cinema," *Screen* 24:6 (1983), 2–16.
9. Marshall, "Pansies," 153–54.
10. Craig Owens, "Outlaws: Gay Men in Feminism," in *Men in Feminism*, ed. Alice
    Jardine and Paul Smith (New York: Methuen, 1987), 220; 219.

11. Sigmund Freud, *Leonardo Da Vinci*, trans. A. A. Brill (1916; reprt. New York: Vintage, 1944), 88.

12. John Rechy, *City of Night* (New York: Grove Press, 1963); Hubert Selby, Jr., *Last Exit to Brooklyn* (1957; reprt. New York: Grove Press, 1986).

13. Sometimes, the interviewees in *Men in Frocks* are defensive about their masculinity, (see Boy George, 112, and Frank Egan, 128); sometimes, they are defensive about their femininity and discuss the denigration of queens in the gay community—see, for example, Terri Frances, 110, and *Rebel Rebel*, 120.

14. Lee Bersani, "Is the Rectum a Grave?" *October* 43 (winter 1987), 208.

15. The transvestic slang, "RG" 43 (1987) is useful for suggesting that even the "real thing" needs to be written in quotation marks, since she is only a product of certain gender codes that privilege the body as essential ground of gender identity—the transvestite contests these codes but also uses them if the impersonation is fetishistic, involving an apparent identification with femininity that is, in fact, a disidentification, through the appeal to the body beneath the clothes as sign of the truth of gender. I discuss this double strategy later in the essay. See Judith Butler, *Gender Trouble*, for a deconstructive critique of the ontology of the body.

16. Bersani, "Is the Rectum a Grave?" 218; emphasis in the original.

17. Ibid., 220.

18. Ibid., 222.

19. Kaja Silverman, "White Skin, Brown Masks: The Double Mimesis, or With Lawrence in Arabia," *Male Subjectivity at the Margins* (New York: Routledge, 1992), 298–338.

20. This book links "Phallicizing" of the ego to fetishism, transvestic fetishism in particular.

21. Marilyn Frye, *The Politics of Reality: Essays in Feminist Theory* (Trumansburg, NY: The Crossing Press, 1983), 137.

22. Judith Williamson, *Consuming Passions: The Dynamics of Popular Culture* (London: Marion Boyars, 1986), 47–54; Erika Munk, "Drag: 1. Men," *Village Voice*, February 5, 1985, 89; Alison Lurie, *The Language of Clothes* (New York: Random House, 1983), 258.

23. The classic psychoanalytic essay on transvestism is Otto Fenichel, "The Psychology of Transvestism" (1930); reprt. in *Psychoanalysis and Male Sexuality*, ed. Hendrik M. Ruitenbeek (New Haven: College and University Press, 1966), 203–10. Fetishism is discussed in Sigmund Freud, "Fetishism," in *Sexuality and the Psychology of Love*, ed. Phillip Reiff (1927; reprt. New York, Collier, 1963) 214–19, and in Jacques Lacan and Wladimir Granoff, "Fetishism: The Symbolic, the Imaginary and the Real," in *Perversions Psychodynamics and Therapy*, ed. Sandor Lorand (New York: Gramercy, 1956), 265–76. See also Kaja Silverman, *The Acoustic Mirror: The Female Voice in Psychoanalysis and Cinema* (Bloomington: Indiana University Press, 1988), 1–42.

24. Ross, *No Respect*, 159.

25. Freud, "Fetishism," 219; 214.

26. Annette Kuhn suggests that films with cross-dressers offer the promise of a multiplicity of gender relations but tend to renege on it ultimately by exposing the body beneath the clothes as the "truth" of gender; see *The Power of the Image: Essays on Representation and Sexuality* (New York: Routledge and Kegan Paul, 1985), 56–57.

27. Neale, "Masculinity as Spectacle," 8–10.

28. Mark Finch, "Sex and Address in 'Dynasty,'" *Screen* 27:6 (1986), 24–42.

29. *Drag Queens* 4:3 (1986), 2.

30. Ibid., 40.

31. Ibid., 7.

32. Ibid., 7.

33. Ibid., 7; 23; 11.

34. Ibid., 32.

35. Frye, *The Politics of Reality*, 128–51.

36. D. N. Rodowick, "The Difficulty of Difference," *Wide Angle* 5 (1982), 7–9. The text Rodowick critiques is the influential essay by Laura Mulvey, "Visual Pleasure and Narrative Cinema," *Feminism and Film Theory* ed. Constance Penley (New York: Routledge, 1988), 57–68.

37. Ibid., 8, where he discusses active and passive desires for a male figure.

38. Griselda Pollock, *Vision and Difference: Femininity, Feminism, and the Histories of Art* (London: Routledge, 1988), 153.

39. Berkeley Kaite, "Transgression is the Law," in *Body Invaders: Panic Sex in America*, ed. Arthur and Marilouise Kroker (New York: St. Martin's Press, 1987), 158. I have used the term *phallic (m)other* because the place of phallic omnipotence and omniscience can be filled by the fantasy of the phallic mother or the primitive father, since neither is imagined to be subject to castration. I will suggest later in the essay that the phallic other may appear to have the phallus by virtue of class or racial difference as well as because of gender, since such differences signify lack or having with respect to the power and privileges that accrue to the phallic subject. Women are not the only ones who do not exist except as a phallic fantasy in the symbolic.

40. Kaja Silverman, "Masochism and Male Subjectivity," *Camera Obscura* 17 (1988), 36; a slightly different version of it appears in *Male Subjectivity at the Margins*. See especially this essay for the subversiveness of masochism, but see also her "White Skin, Brown Masks," and "Masochism and Subjectivity," *Framework* 12 (1981), 2–9.

41. Silverman, "Masochism and Male Subjectivity," 58.

42. For discussions of the literature on Sade, see Jane Gallop, *Intersections: A Reading of Sade with Bataille, Blanchot and Klossowski* (Lincoln: University of Nebraska Press, 1980), and Angela Carter, *The Sadeian Woman and the Ideology of Pornography* (New York: Harper Colophon, 1988).

43. Sigmund Freud, "From the History of an Infantile Neurosis," in *Three Case Histories*, trans. James Strachey, ed. Philip Rieff (1918; reprt. New York, Collier, 1963), 256, 278; and "The Taboo of Virginity," in *Sexuality and the Psychology of Love*, 76–78.

44. Quoted in Gallop, *Intersections*, 57.

45. Two excellent, representative volumes are Mary Ann Doane, *The Desire to Desire: The Woman's Film of the 1940s* (Bloomington: Indiana University Press, 1987), 123–54, and Jane Gallop, *The Daughter's Seduction* (Ithaca, NY: Cornell University Press, 1982), 113–30.

46. Robert Stoller, *Presentations of Gender* (New Haven: Yale University Press, 1985).

47. Kaite, "Transgression is the Law," 164.

48. Jacques Lacan, *Ecrits: A Selection*, trans. Alan Sheridan (1949; reprt. New York: W. W. Norton, 1977), 4–5. Julia Kristeva writes about abjection in *The Powers of Horror: An Essay on Abjection*, trans. Leon Roudiez (New York: Columbia University Press, 1982).

49. Silverman, "Masochism and Male Subjectivity," 62.

50. Jacques Lacan, *The Four Fundamental Concepts of Psychoanalysis*, trans. Alan Sheridan, ed. Jacques-Alain Miller (New York: Norton, 1978), 104.

51. Jacques Lacan, "The Meaning of the Phallus," in *Feminine Sexuality*, trans. Jacqueline Rose, ed. Jacqueline Rose and Juliet Mitchell (New York: Norton, 1982), 83–85.

52. Moustapha Safouan, "Contribution à la psychanalyse du transsexualisme," *Scilicet* 4 (1983), 150–52.

53. Fenichel, "The Psychology of Transvestism," 214–15.

54. Sigmund Freud, *New Introductory Lectures on Psychoanalysis*, trans. James Strachey (1933; reprt. New York: W. W. Norton, 1965), 113.

55. Luce Irigaray, *Speculum: Of the Other: Woman*, trans. Gillian Gill (Ithaca: Cornell University Press, 1985), 73–80.

56. Luce Irigaray, *This Sex Which Is Not One*, trans. Catherine Porter (Ithaca: Cornell University Press, 1985), 76.

57. Butler, *Gender Trouble*, 146–47.

58. Sue-Ellen Case, "Toward a Butch-Femme Aesthetic," 287, 291–92; Jack Babuscio, "Camp and the Gay Sensibility," in *Gays and Film*, ed. Richard Dyer (New York: New York Zoetrope, 1984), 41, 44, 47–49; Richard Dyer, "Getting Over the Rainbow: Identity and pleasure in Gay Cultural Politics," *Silver Linings: Some Strategies for the Eighties*, ed. George Bridges and Rosalind Brunt (London: Lawrence and Wishart, 1981), 60–61; Jeffrey Escoffier, "Sexual Revolution," 140–41; Andrew Ross, *No Respect*, 162; Vito Russo, "Camp," in *Gay Men: The Sociology of Male Homosexuality*, ed. Martin Levine (New York: Harper and Row, 1979), 205.

59. Irigaray, *This Sex*, 76.

60. Nancy Miller, "Emphasis Added: Plots and Plausibilities in Women's Fiction," *PMLA* 96 (1981), 38; Mary Ann Doane, "Film and the Masquerade—Theorising the Female Spectator," *Screen* 23:3–4 (1982), 82; Mary Russo, "Female Grotesques: Carnival and Theory," in *Feminist Studies/Critical Studies*, ed. Teresa de Lauretis (Bloomington: Indiana University Press, 1986), 217, 224; Linda Kauffman, *Discourses of Desire: Gender, Genre, and Epistolary Fictions* (Ithaca: Cornell University Press, 1986), 294–95, 298.

61. Lacan, "The Meaning of the Phallus," 84.

62. Babuscio, "Camp and the Gay Sensibility," 41 (and throughout); Russo, "Camp," 208.

63. Andrew Britton, "For Interpretation: Notes against Camp," *Gay Left* 7 (1978–1979), 12.

64. Gayatri Chakravorty Spivak, "Can the Subaltern Speak?" in *Marxism and the Interpretation of Culture*, ed. Cary Nelson and Lawrence Greenberg (Urbana: University of Illinois Press, 1988), 273–76.

65. Once again, I want to stress that is a problem for theory, and not necessarily for real people.

66. Butler, *Gender Trouble*, 123; Babuscio, "Camp and the Gay Sensibility," 41; Oscar Montero, "Lipstick Vogue: The Politics of Drag," *Radical America* 22:1 (1988), 40–41; Andrew Ross, *No Respect*, 162.

67. Butler, *Gender Trouble*, 123.

68. Case, "Toward a Butch-Femme Aesthetic," 294; see 291 for the assertion that playing the gender roles between women recontextualizes them and "foregrounds" them as myths.

69. Lisa Duggan, "The Anguished Cry of an 80s Fem: 'I Want to Be a Drag Queen,'" *Out/Look* 1:1 (1988), 64.

70. See "A Touch of Class in the Hourglass," *Reflections* 9:1 (1986), 21–29, which features Annie Sprinkle (and other women) in corsets (Sprinkle first appears solo on 22).

71. Teresa de Lauretis, "Sexual Indifference and Lesbian Representation," *Theatre Journal* 40:2 (1988), 177.

72. Jane Gallop, "Beyond the *Jouissance* Principle," *Representations* 7 (1984), 114.
73. See especially chapter 2.
74. Both Case and Ross note that class differences may be a factor in camp, but neither elaborates on the observation or makes it as central to camp as I am suggesting it is. See Case, "Toward a Butch-Femme Aesthetic," 286, and Ross, *No Respect*, 146.
75. Harold Beaver, "Homosexual Signs (In Memory of Roland Barthes)," *Critical Inquiry*, autumn 1981, 113–14; Owens, "Outlaws," 228; see also my discussion above about the implication for egalitarianism of a subjectivity free from castration anxiety, as Owens (and, Owens maintains, Derrida) assume homosexuality to be (Owens, "Outlaws," 219). With regard to the question of the radicality of camp, Bersani, "Is the Rectum a Grave?" points out that a distinction must be made between its effects on the gay couple, who may not have subversive intentions, and its effects on heterosexuals (207). While I believe any politics of consciousness is suspect—as I hope to demonstrate here, the effects, not the intentions, of camp are what count—Bersani's statement does at least suggest the importance of context. Andrew Britton also notes the importance of context in "For Interpretation" when he says that subversion is not intrinsic to a phenomenon but to its context, its reception (12).
76. Sigmund Freud, "Psycho-Analytic Notes on an Autobiographical Account of a Case of Paranoia," in *Three Case Histories*, 1–82.
77. Eve Kosofsky Sedgwick, "Across Gender, Across Sexuality: Willa Cather and Others,": *The South Atlantic Quarterly* 88: 1 (1989), 54–55.
78. Sunil Gupta, "Black, *Brown*, and White," *Coming on Strong: Gay Politics and Culture*, ed. Simon Sherpherd and Mick Wallis (London: Unwin Hyman, 1989), 163–79; Kobena Mercer and Isaac Julien, "True Confessions," *Ten.8* 22 (n.d.), 4–9; Thomas Yingling, "How the Eye is Caste: Robert Mapplethorpe and the Limits of Controversy," *Discourse* 12:2 (1990), 3–28; Jane Gallop, "Annie Leclerc Writing a Letter with Vermeer," in *The Poetics of Gender*, ed. Nancy Miller (New York: Columbia University Press, 1986), 137–56. I discuss Gallop's essay in the second chapter.
79. Homi K. Bhabha, "The Other Question: Difference, Discrimination, and the Discourse of Colonialism" *Literature, Politics, and Theory: Papers from the Essex Conference, 1976–1984*, ed. Francis Barker et al. (New York: Methuen, 1986), 148–72.
80. Frantz Fanon, *Black Skin, White Masks* (New York: Grove Press, 1967), 157. The child's fear of the black man is described on 112.
81. Freud, "Infantile Neurosis," 213, 216.
82. Ibid., 221, 228.
83. Ibid., 210, 278–79.
84. Ibid., 279.
85. Peter Stallybrass and Allon White, *The Politics and Poetics of Transgression* (Ithaca: Cornell University Press, 1986), 156.
86. Bhabha, "The Other Question," 159.
87. Jeffrey Weeks, "Inverts, Perverts, and Mary-Annes: Male Prostitution and the Regulation of Homosexuality in England in the Nineteenth and Early Twentieth Centuries," *Journal of Homosexuality* 6:1–2 (1980–1981), 121–22.
88. Riviere, "Womanliness as a Masquerade," 212.
89. Silverman, "Masochism and Male Subjectivity," 55, 60, 61.
90. For example, see "A Touch of Class," cited in note 70.

91. Zora Neale Hurston, *Their Eyes Were Watching God* (1937; reprt. New York: Harper and Row, 1990), 183; Gayatri Chakravorty Spivak, *In Other Worlds: Essays in Cultural Poetics* (New York: Methuen, 1987), 254.
92. Rechy, *City of Night*, 254.

CHAPTER FIVE

THE SUPREME SACRIFICE?

TRANSSEXUAL IMPERSONATION

It's amazing. I sort of wanted to get rid of it and [then] spend the rest of my life trying to get my hands on one. . . .
—TULA, A BRITISH MALE-TO-FEMALE TRANSSEXUAL MODEL

ostmodernity is fascinated with the failure of sexual difference. From television talk shows to poststructuralist theory, the apparently increasing "in-difference" of the sexes is a central issue. As more women hold jobs formerly reserved for men and more men take an interest in such "feminine" things as clothes, cosmetics, and children—a trend advertisements in particular imply—the sexes seem less and less distinct.[1] But whether this in-difference is viewed as a sign of contemporary culture's health or sickness, it is most often seen from a masculine perspective, which must come as no surprise to feminists critical of the masculinist assumptions of patriarchal society. For the androgynous society, like the androgyne him/herself, as a number of writers on androgyny have pointed out, is usually discussed in terms of feminized masculinity.[2] It is female impersonation that is the subject of countless talk shows and a considerable number of poststructuralist essays. Untill very recently, male impersonation —aside from the brief interest sparked by the Billie Tipton story—has not

figured centrally for postmodernity.[3] Though there is substantial disagreement about the significance of female impersonation in the various discourses circulating about it, they all represent it as transgressive. Because the
female impersonator appears to be an impersonator rather than a "real
woman," his gender act reveals gender to be an act and not a nature, putting
in question commonsense assumptions about biology and sexual identity.
Furthermore, in patriarchal culture, femininity is devalued. As a number of
feminists have demonstrated, in it woman is constructed as man's other, a
negative alter ego he needs in order to feel complete. The feminine, therefore, is associated with lack, what man must repress in order to be whole and
fully masculine. Its uncanny return in impersonation is a fearful reminder
that no man is fully masculine and whole, while the lure of the alternative set
of values it represents—values linked to another way of relating to the self, to
others, to speech, and to desire, according to feminist theorists like Luce
Irigaray—threatens to undermine not only masculinity but also the patriarchal society it sustains.

Because "becoming woman" appears to promise an antiphallic identity and
epistemology, many male poststructuralist theorists have advocated it.
Feminist theorists, however, have been suspicious of this trend, wondering if
it might not be the latest strategy for mastering the loss of mastery associated
with the feminine.[4] Could masculine narcissism be supported rather than subverted by female impersonation? This is the question feminists leave open for
investigation when they refuse to assume that because a man seems feminine,
he is feminine. Like psychoanalysts, they do not take the phenomenon at its
face value but attempt to uncover the hidden desires it may express in disguised or distorted form. For if femininity is a signifier, as Lacanian psychoanalysts have suggested, it is not the direct expression of any essence or
essential identity. It could be assumed by anyone for any number of reasons,
conscious and unconscious. Furthermore, to be feminine is not necessarily to
be feminist, as feminists as different as Mary Ann Doane and Susan
Brownmiller have emphasized.[5] Female impersonation, therefore, may not be
the sign of a particularly femininst change in the social ordering of gender.

TV "TV" AND THE REPRODUCTION OF GENDER

Television has focused extensively on the issue of sexual in-difference and so
has provided the popular framework or "problematic" within which it is
thought about. TV often represents it as the outcome of a battle of the sexes
in which man, as loser, is feminized. Numerous talk shows have featured special segments on feminism, for instance, in which guests take sides on the
issue of whether feminists have unsexed themselves, or men, or both. Has

man capitulated to the demands of woman? This question, the refrain of such shows, is perhaps most urgently asked when it seems a certain pound of flesh has literally been exacted, when man has apparently submitted to a conquering womanliness, signaling his surrender by donning a dress. TV "TV" —televisual transvestism—has proven a particularly titillating scene of battle, a fearsome but fascinating spectacle of man's war with the woman within and the unsexing—or disturbingly double sexing—it heralds. Virtually every issues-oriented talk show—from *Jerry Springer,* to *Oprah,* to *Ricki Lake*—has featured transvestites, gay drag artists, and transsexuals, reviving and allaying anxieties about "normal" gender identity and object choice, and underlining, in the process, the equation of the normal with the masculine. Masculinity is a problem for women only because women are a problem for men: femininity is what must be repudiated, kept in its place. This is the message of talk shows about crises in gender identities.

Crises, of course, must be managed. Talk show hosts and cross-dressers themselves attempt to do just that by linking cross-dressing to "normality." Each type of cross-dresser stakes a claim to it not only by appearing with and appealing to his supportive and loving family (whether spouse or parents) but also by differentiating himself from the others. Typically, transvestites point out that they are strictly heterosexual, gay drag artists that they only wear women's clothes to further their acting careers, and transsexuals that they require *sexual reassignment surgery* (not *sex change operations*) because they were born with the wrong genitals.[6] All types of cross-dressers recognize that a proper gender identity means having a love-object choice and an appearance that are aligned with the genitals, so that the body is installed in heterosexual masculinity and femininity, the cultural norms. They know that femininity is a problem for men. Thus, the transvestite insists he has not made a feminine object choice, while the gay drag artist insists he has not made a feminine identification. Only the transsexual compromises his masculinity with respect to both object choice and identification, apparently wholly embracing femininity and the lack it symbolizes in our culture.[7]

On the one hand, then, transsexuals are closer to normality than other cross-dressers; their genitals, the primary signifiers of gender in our culture, accord with (have been made to accord with) the secondary signifiers of gender: appearance and object choice. On the other hand, transsexuals are at the furthest remove from normality because they have retained nothing of their original biological masculinity; they have given up every claim to it by giving up all its signifiers, especially the primary or master signifier, whose loss cannot be recognized by our culture, which insists on seeing its shadowy presence by imagining there is a scar where, in fact, there are only different genitals. If the double sexing of the transvestite and the female impersonator is singularly disturbing, the unsexing of the transsexual is doubly so: he reveals all too clearly that femininity is the result of a castration, that there is a very real violence done to woman's difference by the patriarchal symbolic. As the hole to man's whole in our culture, woman lacks what man has so he can have it. Normality is on the side of masculinity because our symbolic legislates it. Femininity is its other side, its dark side, signified by what cannot be seen (the scar) or known (the enigma). Fascinating and fearful, femininity returns to haunt man, threatening to unman him.

Because transsexualism literalizes the loss patriarchy tropes as woman, it is especially enigmatic, epitomizing the "social problem" the failure of gender identity poses in patriarchy. How could a man become a woman? Why would a man wish to become a woman? What are the consequences of such "sexual deviance"? Questions likes these comprise the sort of issue television thrives on; it is, therefore, not surprising that transsexualism and other forms of sexual "deviance" have been a topic for talk shows and made-for-television movies. Theorists have argued that television movies exploit the fascination with alternative social forms while normalizing them or containing their fearful potential disruptiveness.[8] Clearly television talk shows participate in the same problematic, though their format does not permit the normalizing resolution which a narrative genre can generate. Rather, talk shows engage in what Roland Barthes calls neither/norism, a "liberal" balancing of oppositions the shows themselves (re)produce as oppositions in order to be able to reject them.[9] "We" (the unified America that talk shows presume to speak to and for) want neither patriarchal men nor feminist women.[10] Like feminists, we want men who can express their "feminine sides," but like patriarchs, we do not want them to do so by dressing in women's clothes or choosing other men as lovers: men should not mistake themselves for women. *Vive la différence!* This is the meaning of talk shows about cross-dressing and gender issues.

But the oscillations of the neither-norism characteristic of these shows maintain the subject on the edge, on the edge of a sexual difference that is neither fully acknowledged nor refused; they cannot position the subject squarely within a proper (properly gendered) identity. Because narrative forms repeat the Oedipal life story, according to Barthes and Kristeva, they would seem better suited to solving the problem of sexual identity, a problem faced by all children before they enter the symbolic.[11] Narrative can resolve the shifting identifications and object choices with which cross-dressing confronts both the subject and object of its spectacle of the play of difference. A "good story" (like the good mother of psychoanalytic object-relations theory) tries to fix up a mixed-up subject by fixing an identity in flux firmly on one side or the other of the gender divide. Of course, the inevitable failure of every such attempt is measured by the repetition of the oedipal scenario and its pleasures across a plethora of discourses. The etymology of "entertainment," "holding in place," is significant in this regard: anxieties about difference (and its failures) are replayed in the mass media as variations on a theme, interpellating the subject into difference by offering a reward, pleasure.

By narrativizing social problems the talk shows (in conjunction with other media) produce, television movies can mobilize different strategies of containment. Indeed, with respect to cross-dressing and sexual difference, the TV movie's normalizing strategies are more effective, since talk shows tend to endlessly reproduce the oscillations they would resolve, while the story about discovering identity (as Foucault has argued, for modern man always in large part about uncovering the secret of sexual identity[12]) has a definite ending, usually in the renewal of heterosexuality through marriage. TV movies, like films, reproduce the gender hierarchy through the story they tell. And like films, they also reproduce it through the way they tell it, which Laura Mulvey and other feminists have demonstrated is from a masculine, heterosexual point of view.[13] According to Mulvey, cinema positions the spectator as masculine through its activation of scopophilia, pleasure in looking. She argues that cinema aligns the gazes of the spectator, the camera, and the male protagonist, constructing the subject of the gaze active and masculine and the object of his look as passive, feminine, and different—a difference that is made to symbolize lack or castration and is therefore frightening.

Cinema is able to allay the castration anxiety produced by the image of the woman through a regression to three masculine "perversions": sadism, voyeurism, and fetishism. Mulvey associates the first two with film narrative. If the woman is castrated, the threat she poses is contained by sadism; the male protagonist (as voyeur) sees that she deserved to be punished for her guilty desires, which he uncovers during the course of the story. Fetishism, on the other hand, does not require a narrative, to which it may even be antithetical, since it involves a moment of contemplation of the film image (of woman) and, therefore, an arresting of narrative progression. The fetishist disavows the woman's lack by overvaluing her physical attributes or articles of her clothing and, by extension, her whole body, which he reads as beautiful and desirable, lacking nothing. Because the viewer shares the male character's controlling, knowing gaze (his sadistic voyeurism) or his willful ignorance of difference (his fetishism), he is constituted as masculine. Mulvey argues that women in the audience participate in this masculine perversity vicariously, by virtue of their never fully resolved bisexuality, which allows them to regress to an earlier, masculine (and hysterical) identification.[14] Their only other option is to be the object, rather than the subject, of desire, effected through a feminine and masochistic identification with the heroine as victim of a sadistic story, punished for her difference.

Cinema thus reproduces patriarchal subject positions by representing the meaning of woman as sexual difference, a sexual difference both acknowledged and denied through voyeurism and fetishism, which require feminine masochism and exhibitionism. If the masculine look constitutes its subject against a feminine object that it sees as different, the feminine look constitutes its subject, paradoxically, as an object; it demands a becoming. Hence woman's alleged narcissistic involvement with her image, her inabilility to have any distance on it and so to know anything about it. But as feminists have been concerned to point out, because images of women address masculine rather than feminine desires they arise from masculine narcissism. Man feels whole at woman's expense. Woman's real difference is not represented in the patriarchal symbolic, in which it is misrecognized as lack. The symbolic, therefore, is acutally a masculine imaginary, in which man's refusal to accept his own castration or lack is facilitated by the regressive perversity promoted by a range of cultural practices. Man's misrecognition of himself and his other, woman, is sanctioned—indeed, solicited—by patriarchy.

Feminists have sought to intervene in the masculine imaginary by calling attention to it as such, emphasizing the defenses that shore up man's illusion of wholeness by protecting him from his own "feminine" lack. Accordingly, they have shared postmodernity's fascination with the failure of sexual difference, in particular of heterosexual masculinity, interrogating film and other cultural practices for moments of slippage, when man's anxieties about his "natural" masculinity are foregrounded, revealing the latter to be a construct precariously maintained by regressive voyeurism and fetishism. At such moments, masculinity is undermined and man's masquerade of wholeness is unveiled as such, uncovering the fact that he is castrated or lacking rather than whole. Fetishism is a particularly vulnerable defense strategy not only because it disrupts the flow of the film narrative and its sadistic drive toward containment of the threat woman poses, as Mulvey points out, but also because it involves a double attitude: at once a refusal and a recognition of sexual difference. It keeps the threat of castration alive even as it attempts to allay the anxiety that threat generates and so is a position of knowledge as well as ignorance. Man fetishizes woman in order to fetishize himself.[15] Mulvey argues that an excess of fetishism, which she suggests occurs in Josef von Sternberg's films, subverts its defensive function, provoking the unpleasurable awareness of woman's difference and the self-difference and wound to man's narcissism that she symbolizes.[16] Film (and television movies), therefore, could shake up rather than shore up masculine identity.

Cross-dresssing would seem to involve just such a threatening excess of fetishism, since in it the voyeuristic element that enables the masculine subject to maintain a distance from the feminine fetish object is absent, and the subject quite literally fetishizes himself. The female impersonator, psychoanalysts say, is usually a fetishist whose "perversion" takes the form of transvestism; fetishizing himself, he displays himself in an exhibitionism that is the reversal of voyeurism into its opposite.[17] He confuses what are supposed to be polar extremes: voyeur/exhibitionist, fetishist/fetish, self/other (or subject/object); he is not able to sustain the distance and difference between them assumed to be necessary for identity. The transvestite desires, and desires to be, the "better woman," the phallic woman who promises that there is no sexual difference, whose prototype is the mother of the Lacanian imaginary that precedes the symbolic and the systems of difference (including sexual difference) it institutes. The transvestite's femininity, therefore, is only a disguise. In fact, he feminizes himself in order to "masculinize" (phallicize) himself; masquerading as the phallic woman, he is able to have (the illusion of having) the phallus, resolving in the imaginary his castration anxiety and securing (or at least attempting to better secure) a masculine, phallic, and "whole" identity. Mixing object love and identification, the transvestite is narcissistic; he loves only (his fantasy of) himself.

Eugenie Lemoine-Luccioni suggests that transsexualism is an excessive transvestism: while the transvestite just wants to pass as a woman, the transsexual wants to be the real thing.[18] She notes, however, that the border between the two is fragile.[19] In fact, for many transvestites the sexual excitement initially associated with cross-dressing disappears, although the desire to cross-dress remains as strong as ever.[20] Evidently the fantasy of being feminized takes the place of sexual satisfaction (at least partially), as it does for transsexuals, according to Harry Benjamin, the doctor who coined the term *transsexualism*.[21] Transsexuals, like transvestites—and in psychoanalytic theory, women—invest their libido narcissistically, even to the point of frigidity, concentrating on their image. Their desire is to be desirable, and they express a fetishistic concern with getting right all the details of the woman's "look"—a concern shared by their surgeons, who think they know just how much hair a "real" woman should have, as well as the proper size for her nose, breasts, and vagina, the voice quality that is suitable, and the clothes and makeup that are appropriate, as any description of transsexual surgery reveals.[22] It is this desire to create the "perfect" woman—perhaps more perfect than the "real thing"—to which critics of transsexualism like Janice Raymond object.[23]

In the Lacanian paradigm, this desire would be characterized as the desire to be the phallus, which is associated with femininity. Woman masquerades as the phallus (it is, of course, impossible to be the phallus) so that man can parade his phallus, the woman he needs to feel complete. Lacan states that with regard to the phallus, the child moves from being it to having or not having it, the masculine and feminine positions. Femininity is a masquerade due to "the intervention of an 'appearing' which gets substituted for the 'having' so as to protect it on one side and to mask its lack on the other. . . ."[24] Because the system of sexual difference is organized around an appearing with respect to one term, *the phallus*, femininity is of necessity an appearing to have. Woman can only appear to be the phallus for man by appearing to have the phallus or what signifies having the phallus, its metaphoric and metonymic attributes, in particular, "her" fetishes. Being and having are confused in the phallicizing (virilizing) effect of fetishistic masquerade. The same is true for male-to-female transsexuals, who—like women—sustain only an oblique relation to symbolic castration, remaining (at least partially) in the imaginary, beyond or before castration, caught up in the masquerade of being the phallus, according to Catherine Millot.[25]

As Millot points out, a narcissistic image of self-perfection (the Lacanian mirror other as ego ideal) is one equivalent of the imaginary phallus.[26] However, that image is necessarily fetishistic, since appearing to be the phallus means appearing to have it. The transsexual, like the transvestite, wishes to be a "she-male," the phallic woman who lacks nothing. While the transvestite finds both "feminine" fetishes and the penis indispensable for phallic imposture, the transsexual can only lose lack by giving up the penis. Paradoxically, a real castration is demanded as the (imaginary) solution to castration anxiety. Becoming woman, the transsexual would refuse rather than accept lack and symbolic castration; as long as s/he has a penis, s/he is subject to sexual difference and the lack linked to being only one sex, rather than being beyond or before sexual difference itself. Millot concludes that the transsexual seeks to be an androgyne, a third, angelic sex outside the lack legislated by the symbolic and its complementary and therefore incomplete genders.[27]

She argues that transsexual androgyny results from a foreclosure of the name of the father, a default of that law that founds both society and the subject, the incest prohibition and its legislation of difference between mother and child, self and other, man and woman. Castration, like incest, goes beyond the law, since it is a refusal of a limit to the desire to be the phallus for the (m)other and an attempt to maintain the subject in the pre-oedipal indifference of the imaginary, on the edge of the symbolic and, therefore, of subjectivity itself.[28] Yet the transsexual is not psychotic, despite the apparent foreclosure of the name of the father. Rather, s/he knows a "real" woman cannot have a penis, but insists s/he really is a woman just the same. Like the transvestite and the fetishist, then, the transsexual is at once aware but ignorant of sexual difference, disavowing it by perversely acting out the fantasy of a double sexual identity that is a nonidentity. In order to better enact this fantasy, s/he demands surgery, but the ultimate effect of the latter, according to

Millot, is that of a symbolic cut that allows the subject to assume her castration through a real castration.[29] Or, as Moustafa Safouan describes it, transsexuals sacrifice the penis to save desire and subjectivity, thereby becoming the only real women.[30]

But to write in this way of real women and real castration is to mistake the penis for the phallus, a constitutive error in patriarchy. With respect to the phallus, man—like woman—is situated in the mode of appearing. Appearing masks a lack both for and of the woman: man fetishizes her (masks her lack) in order to fetishize himself (masking his own lack). In addition, he fetishizes himself by fetishizing the organ on which his identity hangs, misrecognizing the phallus as the penis. It is a misrecognition of which woman, too, is a dupe because it is engineered by the patriarchal symbolic (and repeated by Lacanian psychoanalysts). Man, like woman, is both fetishist and fetishized, voyeur and exhibitionist, subject and object of the knowing and desiring gaze. However, he disavows his phallic imposture as imposture by legislating the credulity that supports it, culturally validating the misrecognition of the penis as the phallus so that his phallic imposture does not appear as such. Nevertheless, the fact that he attaches himself to an endless chain of substitutes—women, cars, clothes, and so on—for the real organ (the penis) that substitutes for the imaginary organ (the phallus) reveals the degree to which he remains anxiously incredulous.

Fetishism always involves incredulity, an oscillation between belief and disbelief in the (m)other's phallus and the possibility of achieving wholeness in her. Confusing identification and object choice, it is characteristic of the imaginary, but it is also characteristic of the symbolic, which is really a phallic imaginary organized around certain privileged fetishistic misrecognitions and phallic impostures, including mistaking the penis for the phallus. According to Jane Gallop, to repeat the imaginary as imaginary is to enter the symbolic and so to be cured of narcissistic defenses like fetishism.[31] In order to break with the imaginary, the masculine subject must recognize his misrecognitions as misrecognitions, understand his imposture as imposture. He must see what has been invisible: the "feminine" fetishism and exhibitionism sustaining the simulation of a masculine identity that parades itself as a nature, as the reverse of the masquerade of femininity that it imagines it has repudiated. Millot and Safouan assert that becoming woman has this effect on the transsexual, who accepts lack in assuming femininity.

But if transsexualism is not so much a psychosis as a perversion like transvestism, then the achievement of a cure must be in doubt, since perversions are notoriously difficult to eliminate—especially when they are promoted by the symbolic itself, as phallic imposture is. Becoming woman may not cure the transsexual; indeed, two of the foremost authorities on transsexualism note that surgery very often provides only a brief satisfaction before the transsexual renews the demand for a more perfect feminization.[32] It is a demand women themselves express. Because femininity is nothing but a masquerade, like masculinity it implicates the subject in phallic imposture and, therefore, is a site of ignorance rather than of knowledge about itself. Only once the significant differences between women (in particular, differences of class and race) are taken into account, can feminine phallic imposture be interrogated. In a symbolic that is not just patriarchal but also bourgeois and racist, some women do have what other women lack: signs of a "proper" class and racial identity. They appear to have the phallus because they have what is associated with it and can dissociate themselves from the class and racial other onto whom lack is projected. Disidentifying from the "other" woman, the female fetishist is a "better" (phallic) woman. Becoming woman, the transsexual, too, would be distinct from the unbecoming women who signify lack; s/he exchanges one fetishism for another, employing feminine masquerade as the "cure" for anxiety about masculine phallic imposture.

THE RENÉE RICHARDS STORY

Perhaps the best known case of transsexualism in America is that of Renée Richards, tennis star, doctor, and naval officer. Her autobiography, *Second Serve*, tells the story of how "a perfectly normal American boy," who seemed solidly middle class and male, was sexually transformed "from a successful Adam into a triumphant Eve."[33] How could a man married to a model, the father of a son, a well-respected opthamologist, and former captain of the Yale University tennis team be tempted to undergo emasculating surgery? The made-for-television movie based on the autobiography aired on CBS (May 13, 1986), and set out to answer this question.[34] Dr. Richard Radley (played by Vanessa Redgrave) is clearly uncomfortable with what the book terms "masquerades"[35]—not only his cross-dressing as Renée but also the cross-dressing as Dick, since Dick/Renée always seems to be miming the masculine or the feminine, rather than simply *being* masculine or feminine. S/he is torn between two gender identities and feels keenly the need to choose one identity or the other—and the genitals to match, because in our culture they are the definitive signifier of gender. The movie narrates Dick's battles with a femininity in himself that he is not able to overcome, ultimately fixing him as her in a sexual difference that is the happy ending: Dick makes the supreme sacrifice on the operating table, and Renée wins the war of the sexes within.

But the movie is unable to fully contain the disturbance created by Dick's unnatural attitude to something that should be natural—gender. In fact, his unnatural attitude reveals gender to be an attitude, socially constructed, rather than a nature. Just as Renée's femininity inhabits his masculinity, so does Dick's masculinity inhabit her femininity. Dick/Renée is masculine and feminine, active and passive, subject and object, including subject and object of the knowing and desiring gaze, both before and after s/he has settled on one sex. Miming the feminine and miming the masculine serve as defenses against a femininity that threatens to engulf him/her, annihilating subjectivity altogether: the difficulty of sexual difference is inextricable from the difficulty of difference itself. Paradoxically, Dick loses lack and gains a "whole" self when he becomes Renée: he gives up the penis in order to have the phallus—a happy ending indeed.

Dick's miming the feminine is signaled in the show by his dressing in what is marked as unnatural feminine attire. It is unnatural primarily because as a masculine character in a realist drama, Dick is not supposed to change sex. His masculinity is indicated in a number of ways. He is a doctor. He is athletic: he plays competitive tennis. He drives a flashy sports car. He wears "respectable"—not flashy—men's clothing (the dandy risks femininity). Most significantly, he has a girlfriend; since the movie assumes heterosexuality is natural, this is the strongest piece of evidence for his masculinity. In the final scene, when Renée asks her young son, Andy, if he has understood what happened, he tells her, "It seemed pretty clear to me. You and mom got divorced because two women can't stay married." This is not only apparently a naive statement about what transsexualism signifies, since the movie itself endorses it; in fact, it is endorsed by many doctors involved in transsexual counseling, who cannot conceive of a lesbian transsexual and may forbid the surgery if lesbianism seems the likely outcome.[36] The heterosexuality of both Dick and Renée is never openly questioned in the movie but is represented as if it were simply a consequence of genitalia. The shift in the gender of Dick's object choice (after surgery) seems to be more effortless than the shift in Dick's gender (the surgery is apparently quite painful).

If the viewer doubts these are necessarily the signifiers of masculinity, Dick's analyst does not, and continually reassures himself (and Dick) that Dick must be a man because all the signs are right. For instance, after Dick has gone to a bar that features a female impersonator, Dr. Beck tells him that he did not really enjoy the show, listing the reasons why he could not have in the form of an unself-conscious tautology—and tautology, like neither/norism, is characteristic of the operation of bourgeois ideology, according to Barthes.[37] "You're a masculine character. You're athletic, you like fast cars, and with Gwen [Dick's girlfriend] the sex is fine," he says. Though he does not mention appearance, later he recommends that Dick grow a beard to "put off" Renée both literally and figuratively. And it works. The shot following the scene of this advice is of Dick scrubbing for surgery. His bearded face is framed in close-up in the mirror over the sink, and as he stares intently at it, Renée's voice-over informs us that whenever he looked in the mirror all thoughts of Renée disappeared. The art of the beard here recalls Sigmund Freud's comments on woman's one art, that of weaving, modeled on the "beard" nature has given her to veil her shame.[38] The beard is a fetish; like all clothing—as Freud's allusion to weaving suggests—it is a phallic covering, meant to signify that Dick has the phallus.

In *Second Serve* the fetishism of the beard, as well as of the car, sports, girl-friend, and—of course—the penis itself are pointed out to the spectator as defenses against a threatening femininity, as constructed rather than natural, not only by the way the camera looks at Dick but also by the way the other characters look at him and by what they say. Paradoxically, Dick's apparently natural masculinity is marked as unnatural, as a collection of fetish signifiers that can only maintain itself by exhibiting itself over and over again. As Jacques Lacan has noted, "Virile display in the human being itself appears as feminine."[39] Masculine "parade" becomes a kind of feminine "masquerade" when man's investment in showing off his phallus comes under scrutiny; his phallic imposture is revealed as such, and the game is up. *Second Serve* seems to situate the spectator as scrutinizer, catching man in the act: the gender act as an act. It constructs a voyeuristic and fetishistic gaze at man, making him an object of knowledge (if not of desire) in the way that films ordinarily do woman. This gaze uncovers the foundation of subjectivity in phallic impos-ture, fetishism and exhibitionism of/for the other, rather than in the expres-sion of an essence, whether biological (the genes) or philosophical (the *cogito*). Steve Neale suggests that when films turn man into a spectacle, they disavow homosexuality, mediating the gaze through the male characters's looks, as in the classic Hollywood text, but marking those looks as aggressive rather than desiring by situating the characters in scenes of ritual combat, such as sporting events.[40] In *Second Serve*, however, a confusion of aggression and desire, identification and object choice, occurs throughout—between Dick and Renée, Dick/Renée and his/her others, and Dick/Renée and the spectator. This confusion repeats that of the imaginary but repeats it with a difference, a critical difference: it puts masculinity in question, whereas the classical Hollywood text puts femininity in question. By making man, the (supposed) universal, human subject, into a spectacle of phallic imposture, *Second Serve* unveils his inescapable "femininity," revealing the uncertainty of all sexual identity in the splitting of the subject, who can never be whole.

The fetishistic spectacle of masculinity is perhaps most obviously feminine and feminized in the narcissism of the look in the mirror, as in the scene in *Second Serve* of the camera's contemplation of Dick's contemplation of his beard. The camera turns him into a woman, an object of the fetishistic gaze, even as Dick believes he has returned to being a man. Yet the distance that Mulvey and other film critics have associated with fetishism collapses into closeness at this moment of identification with the image. The narcissistic impulse of fetishism is unveiled in transvestism as the subject both fetishizes himself and displays himself, confounding voyeurism and exhibitionism, and confusing the difference between the subject and object of the gaze. However, Dick's transvestistic identification is not with the phallic woman, which is how psychoanalysis classically diagnoses transvestism, but with the phallic man; this scene at once represents, solicits, and undermines phallic imposture.

In Dick's relations with other men, he is also the object of the gaze—in particular, the sadistic gaze Neale characterizes as a defense against homosexuality. This is very evident with Dr. Beck, who aggressively asserts he knows what Dick wants and intends to make sure he gets it. In one scene, when Dick attempts to resist, Dr. Beck responds with shouts, with prescriptions for tranquilizers, and with something close to physical violence; he is apparently ready to talk, drug, or beat Dick into submission to masculinity. The aggressivity of this episode brings into the open the sadomasochistic basis of Dick's relationship with him and, indeed, with most of the other male characters, which is often disguised as "competitiveness" (the demonstration of both athletic and heterosexual romantic prowess). Dick's desire is acted out in displacements of the beating fantasy, which according to Freud is regressive in its masculine enunciation, associated with the little boy's negative oedipal or homosexual desire for his father, expressed masochistically, in a "feminine" fashion.[41] That is, because the boy's desire for the father is incestuous it must be repressed. It can only be expressed regressively: in the fantasy love is camouflaged as punishment as the boy regresses from the genital to the anal-sadistic stage of sexual development and takes his pleasure with his beating. Furthermore, the homosexual nature of the wish is hidden because the father is disguised as the mother who, therefore, is a phallic mother. This fantasied relation to the father is feminine, Freud says, because femininity, passivity, and masochism are linked.

In fact, Dick literally feminizes himself in one very dramatic "coming out" scene with his friend Josh, who quickly becomes sadistic. When Dick appears at Josh's apartment in his "femme" attire for the first time, Josh is cruel. He invites the neighbors over and makes fun of Dick in front of them. After he tells Dick he will get the same treatment every time he visits crossdressed, Dick insists Josh will never "humiliate" him out of it. Indeed, humiliation would seem to be part of Dick's pleasure in it, the only way he can satisfy a homosexual desire; the autobiography tells us he went back to

Josh's repeatedly, although the movie only shows the first visit, perhaps because the homosexual overtones are more obvious when Dick is "dressed" (the autobiography also reveals Dick has had a number of homosexual encounters, which the movie represses entirely). Femininity is a socially sanctioned way to have relationships with men—as long as it is "real" femininity. This is brought home by a presurgery scene in which Dick goes to a bar in Spain dressed as Renée. When he begins to flirt and then dance with another man, some soldiers in the crowd become hostile, accusing him of homosexuality; eventually they brutally assault him.

In *Second Serve*, the homosexual fantasy of being loved and humiliated by the father often seems to take the form of a feminine Oedipal enunciation: it is a girl rather than a boy the father loves and beats. The fantasizing subject denies his homosexuality by changing his own gender rather than that of his object. It is a curious metamorphosis, evidently not one Freud encountered, since he does not discuss it in his essay. The transformation proper to the male subject, which Freud does discuss, is the masculine oedipal enunciation: the father is disguised as the mother in the conscious form of the fantasy. During Dick's childhood, his mother, Dr. Muriel Bishop (a psychiatrist), and his sister insisted on dressing him in drag for a party against his will, as a flashback in Dr. Beck's office indicates. Though Dick and his father struggle with the women in the family over this, they do not prevail, and the movie suggests that their capitulation sanctions a repetition of the scene of cross-dressing with the sister, to which the mother gave tacit consent, as another flashback implies. In it, Dick and his sister, both dressed in her clothes, stand in front of a mirror staring at their reflections. "I like you when you're pretty," she says, echoing the words of the first incident. Then his mother appears in the doorway and smiles; Dick's voice-over states that Dr. Bishop wanted to be a good mother but did not have the feeling for it.

The movie here offers the explanation of transsexualism adhered to by the well-known expert on the subject, Dr. Robert Stoller, who says that too much mother and too little father make for a feminine boy. The phallic mother refuses to let boys be boys, maintaining the child in a feminine dependence on her, so that he does not successfully separate himself from her. Such a blame-the-mother approach is characteristic of object-relations theorists like Stoller, who fail to recognize that the phallic mother is the child's fantasy because they share this fantasy and participate in the paranoia in which it results. As Monique Plaza points out, in general, psychoanalysts are all too ready to displace the "madness" of children onto mothers without any consideration of the contradictory injunctions to which the mother is subject in capitalist patriarchy.[42] According to psychoanalytic theory, when the little boy is unable to accede to sexual difference, he is also unable to accede to difference itself and separate from the mother. Object-relations theorists assume masculinity and femininity are there from the start (perhaps as biological essences), rather than produced through the resolution of the castration complex and the separation from the mother that it legislates. Like Stoller, they indict the mother for impeding the boy's assumption of a masculinity to which he was always already destined, just as the movie implies that initially there was no woman trapped inside Dick's body but only women on the outside who forced femininity upon him.

The boy cannot accede to difference because he is haunted by a femininity that overwhelms him in a pre-oedipal paranoia in which subject and object, self and other, boy and mother are terrifyingly indistinct. This has been theorized as peculiar to women (precisely because the symbolic expects them to identify with the mother rather than to break with her) and is frequently a theme in women's genres like the gothic, as several feminists have pointed out.[43] But *Second Serve* suggests Dick suffers from it, the first scene of his cross-dressing particularly emphasizing it. The camera's gaze is clearly voyeuristic as it moves in through the window of the Warwick Hotel and watches Dick watching Renée's face emerge in the bathroom mirror as he shaves. Then there are a number of highly fetishistic shots that focus on parts of Renée's body as she dresses: her hairy chest, her stockinged legs, her arms in long gloves. Finally we see the whole of her as she emerges from the lobby and are able to scrutinize her intently in the next shot as she sits at a counter sipping a milk shake, framed not only by the camera but by the soda shop window. Throughout this, Renée never speaks; she functions as pure spectacle—spooky spectacle, the music on the sound track suggests, lest we take any pleasure in it. (The spilling over of emotion into music is characteristic of melodrama, and as such is another motif of the Gothic.) We have witnessed the uncanny unmanning of Dr. Richard Radley, and it is not supposed to be a pretty sight. Indeed, the aggressivity of the fetishism is not so much reassuring as threatening because it implies a body in pieces and, therefore, the annihilation of the subject in the loss of the ego (disintegration is as characteristic of the imaginary and imaginary processes like fetishism as is the fictive integration of the self through an identification with a phallic image of wholeness). When voyeurism can no longer maintain a distance from its object, when the subject both wants and wants to be what s/he sees, the relay of gazes common to classical film is troubled, threatened with a homosexuality it cannot contain—a passive, feminine desire for the mother, the phallic (m)other for whom the castrating father figure is a screen—exactly the opposite of what Freud says about the beating fantasy. The look is then transvestistic: the subject fetishizes himself and displays himself, displacing the opposition between voyeurism and exhibitionism and deconstructing the gender binarism by deconstructing the binarisms on which it is grounded.

This transvestistic oscillation has been discussed by Mulvey as characteristic of the feminine look and femininity,[44] but in *Second Serve* it is associated with the masculine look and a masculinity that mimes itself in a desperate attempt to extricate itself from femininity and the homosexuality with which it is linked. When Dick looks, he sees Renée, a monstrous figure of femininity with whom he is quite literally identified: he both looks at and looks like Renée, a confusion the proliferation of mirror shots underlines. Whether Dick mimes the masculine or the feminine, he is threatened with—and threatens the spectator with—homosexuality and femininity. Dick must become "the real thing" for that threat to be domesticated, and for him that means miming not "the" feminine but a particular kind of femininity, one that will pass for being (rather than impersonating) woman. By the end of the movie Renée has learned to represent femininity so convincingly that she seems to be a natural at it, disappearing into her role. The apparent surrender to the mother proves to be a victory over her, securing Renée's subjectivity and her sense of narcissistic wholeness.

Before the surgery, Renée's femininity is marked as unnatural because she does not quite get it right—her style is tacky, and her taste is bad. Good taste is always that of the middle class, practical but elegant, as Brownmiller makes clear in her 1984 book on femininity. The story she tells there of "progress" in male fashion (she does not seem to believe there has been any in women's wear) privileges the values associated with bourgeois masculinity: she praises "functional utility," and "dynamic action combined with serious responsibility."[45] Brownmiller's hero is clearly the business man in his sack suit, whom she urges feminists to emulate. The feminine facsimile is the working woman (not to be confused with the working-class woman) in the skirted suit, which John Molloy advises career girls to wear in *The Woman's Dress for Success Book*, and which is perennially recommended in magazines aimed at a bourgeois female audience. The idea behind dressing for success is to look authoritative like a man without looking like a man—Molloy says that the imitation man look is too cute and sexy for an image of corporate responsibility.[46] Good taste is the sign of quiet authority; clothes that are loud call attention to the fetish signs as fetish signs and suggest the authority is an imposter. Dick's clothes are tasteful, not flashy, but Renée's clothes, flashy and tasteless, expose the truth about the Dick beneath the skirts: before her surgery, Renée looks like a transvestite instead of a "real" woman.

In "overdone" or overly dowdy clothes and wearing too much makeup, Renée reveals her lack of mastery of the artifices of femininity and thereby calls attention to the artificiality of her femininity. According to Luce

Irigaray, when femininity draws attention to itself as artificial rather than natural, as female impersonation rather than the real thing, it disrupts the masculine imaginary and the scopic regime of voyeurism and fetishism that subtends it.[47] Admittedly, Irigaray has in mind a female female impersonation, what she calls mimicry, but as Mary Russo and Karen Newman have suggested, mimicry may be more effective when practiced by men, the implication being that otherwise it looks too much like the real thing and, therefore, risks reinscribing woman in the same old story.[48] According to Irigaray, to mime the feminine is to "assume the feminine role deliberately . . . so as to make 'visible,' by an effect of playful repetition, what was supposed to remain invisible: the cover-up of a possible operation of the feminine in language."[49] The mimic denaturalizes ideology by calling attention to the conventions that encode her as woman; she repeats the masquerade of femininity with a playful difference that is a critical difference, producing the knowledge that it is not a nature but an alienating identity constructed "for" women on behalf of men.

Irigaray and other femininist critics suggest that woman must enter into mimicry and cease the masquerade in order to break with her image and thereby shatter the mirror she has become for man. Disidentifying from her image, woman could know something about it, and so, apparently, could man. Irigaray speaks of the mimic's difference as a "visible" difference; other theorists who have discussed it associate it with hyperbolization, italicization, and exaggeration—all postmodern, parodic strategies.[50] In fact, likening mimicry to female impersonation because it burlesques the real thing is revealing, since feminists have often associated transvestism with a malicious travesty of femininity on the grounds of its bad taste. For instance, in her book on fashion, Alison Lurie writes "that the transsexual "usually prefers the sort of clothes a woman of his own age and social position would choose."[51] This critique has affinities with radical lesbian analyses of homosexuality and drag, which are accused of what Marilyn Frye terms "fetishistic phallophilia."[52] Because drag is excessive, theatrical, it is said to make a mockery of women. The transvestite, fetishistic in his outlook, is charged with failing to sympathize deeply enough with his role to be able to realistically represent it. The class anxiety is transparent here. A real woman is a real lady; otherwise, she is a female impersonator. What has passed for "passing for" rather than being womanly—the mimicry or parody of femininity— covers up certain unexamined notions of femininity that are class-biased and ethnocentric.

Second Serve demonstrates this logic. It must convince us that a woman (actress Vanessa Redgrave) is a man (Dick) pretending to be a woman (Renée). This is made especially difficult because the movie opens with a sequence of Redgrave as Renée in the operating theater and then on the streets of New York, so that there is no chance we might mistake her for a real man in the next sequence, in which she plays Dick. This beginning serves to anchor her voice-over; no doubt it is also necessary because of the anxiety over what is a story of a "real" as well as symbolic castration. The movie, therefore, mirrors the logic of transsexuals themselves, who insist that they are women trapped in men's bodies. If Dick is Redgrave, then he really has been a woman all along, and so he has nothing to lose by surgery; femininity is more than second nature for Renée. This poses a problem, however, for Redgrave's impersonation of Dick's impersonation of Renée, which must be seen as unnatural. *Second Serve* solves the problem by representing Redgrave as having good, middle-class taste when she is masquerading as a genuine woman (as Renée), and as having bad or gaudy taste when she is miming or impersonating a woman (as Dick as Renée).

It is this bad taste that transvestites are themselves concerned with educating into middle-class sensibility so that they can "pass" more effectively. For instance, in 1987 on the *Donahue* show, JoAnn Roberts, a transvestite guest, touted the good-grooming guide s/he had written, revealingly entitled *Art and Illusion*, noting that cross-dressers too often dress like tramps or hookers.[53] Predictably, the beauty tips in it are not much different from those some former Miss Americas gave on a Donahue show: look natural.[54] To construct femininity so that it looks natural rather than constructed, whether one is a male or a female impersonator, means to construct it with reference to middle-class codes of behavior and fashion. Dick learns to do this by the time he becomes Renée: he tones down his eyeshadow and wears the skirted suits advocated by Molloy. The movie represents Renée as a real woman when she is classy, at a controlling distance from what signifies "no class" or mimicry as female impersonation.

However, Renée is still engaged in mimicry, though not what Irigaray describes as mimicry. Instead, hers resembles the mimicry discussed by Homi Bhabha as a tactic of imperialism. "Colonial mimicry is the desire for a reformed, recognizable Other, as a subject of a difference that is almost the same, but not quite," he writes.[55] The (colonized) other's difference is produced and disavowed by the (imperialist) self, which requires the other to mime the self and to fail in that mimicry, to fail to "pass." As Molloy makes clear, the middle-class woman mimics the masculine, not the feminine, but with a feminine difference that makes it female impersonation just the same. Thus Renée still practices medicine, plays a mean game of tennis, and drives fast cars—but in skirts—tasteful, not flashy, skirts. Dick's problem, which was also Renée's problem, mimicry, has been resolved—by more mimicry. To be a subject is to engage in phallic imposture. Yet Renée's phallic imposture does not appear as such because lack has been displaced from the middle-class woman onto the "other" woman, whose femininity is repudiated. Renée is a "real" woman because the other is not—what Lacan calls "not-all"; lack.[56] When Dick parts with (being) this fascinating and fearful phallic (m)other, who is, after all, not the real mother (Dr. Bishop) but a fantasy woman, he seems to secure his gender identity and his object choice. He gives up the penis in order to have the phallus, signified by middle-class power and privilege.

Second Serve strives to contain the anxieties raised by the "camp" attitude toward gender, which makes it mimicry. Mimicry reveals not only the subject's gender identity but also his/her class (and ethnic) identity to be unfixed, unstable; it is a defense against the loss of (phallic) wholeness such instability threatens.[57] But because mimicry is fetishistic, it is a defense that creates anxieties even as it attempts to resolve them. As disavowal, it involves a double attitude: (in)credulity about phallic imposture. Thus, though the movie appears to secure Renée's middle-class and heterosexual feminine identity, settling the unsettling question of Dick's gender that generated its narrative, because it must rely on mimicry in order to counter mimicry, its strategies of containment inhabit and are inhabited by what they would oppose. Fetishism, including fetishistic phallic imposture, maintains the subject on the edge, on the edge of sexual, class, and racial differences that are neither fully refused nor recognized. The disavowal of uncertainty can only result in uncertainty, oscillation.

The cover of the book (as a kind of commentary on its contents) conveys this through a curious appeal to a biology whose significance it undermines. It is dominated by photos of Dick and Renée cleverly framed in tennis racquets. Dick's handle is up and crossed at the top by the letters of the title so that it looks like the biological sign for masculinity. Renée's handle, much truncated, is down and crossed at the bottom by her name so that it looks like the biological sign for femininity. Her portrait is higher than Dick's, suggesting the feminine is in the ascendant. But within the photo Renée is active (usually correlated with masculinity), both writing a note and talking on the phone, obviously in the middle of conducting her medical practice, while in his photo, Dick is just standing around, already the object of our gaze, feminized. Biology cannot guarantee who has the phallus, whose imposture is more convincing (for the subject and for the symbolic), since the penis is not the phallus, despite a certain similarity between the two that we are encouraged to (mis)recognize. If the spectator can never quite be sure who appears in Dick's/Renée's mirror or what might be found under his/her skirt, s/he is assured of the importance of good taste—not surprisingly, exactly the theme of many commercials. Because class fractures the simple binarisms of psychoanalytic and feminist discourses focused too exclusively on sexual difference, it can also suture the wound inflicted on the feminine other by the masculine self, grafting on a phallus. Dick's/Renée's gender act is a class act, and that makes all the difference s/he desires.

THE SUPREME SACRIFICE?

Poststructuralist theorists like Jacques Derrida have suggested that becoming woman could deconstruct phallocentrism.[58] However, a consideration of the Renée Richards story and of male transsexualism in general reveals female impersonation to be consistent with, rather than in contradiction to, an imaginary regression to fetishism. In fact, because subjectivity itself is based in phallic imposture or mimicry, "real" women, too, are female impersonators, fetishizing themselves by fetishizing "other" women whose difference (especially of class and race) can signify phallic lack or presence. But as Millot and Safouan indicate, "being" the phallus can as easily take the form of male impersonation; female transsexualism, like its masculine counterpart, can be explained as a transvestic defense against castration anxiety.[59] Indeed, masculinity itself is such a defense, though it has not appeared as such because the misrecognition of the penis as the phallus has been naturalized in patriarchy so that both men and women are duped by it.

Man, like woman, only comes into being when "photo-graphed," as Lacan terms it, when fixed or framed by the look of the (phallic) (m)other, who returns to him an image of wholeness with which he jubilantly identifies.[60] Yet since he has to exhibit himself in order to exist at all, he is caught in a fetishism that must expose his imposture. Paradoxically, virilization is feminizing: man must display his virility, but the signifier cannot stand up to that demand. Fetishism generates anxiety, and the solution to such anxiety is more fetishism; there is no real movement into the symbolic through an acceptance of castration. Instead, man passes for a desiring subject, engaging in phallic imposture by surrounding himself with the signs of what he has to lose so he can signify he has something to lose and, therefore, something to desire. Because the symbolic is actually an imaginary—a white and bourgeois as well as masculine imaginary—it is produced by and productive of fetishistic subjects anxious about "in-difference" and castration; therefore, it solicits fetishism in both men and women as it promotes the narcissistic desire to be (seen as) whole.

Once "proper" (masculine, white, and bourgeois) identities are called into question, however, as is currently occuring, the phallic signifiers fail in their function, and fetishism intensifies (with respect to a white, Anglo, middle-class norm)—though the very "excess" of fetishism reveals the subject's masquerade of wholeness to be an imposture. As Anne Hollander points out, the new masculine ideal of androgyny invites men to exhibit their virility in a "feminine" way, through surface adornment.[61] Like Catherine Millot and Francette Pacteau, she associates the androgyne with the erotic angel who is beyond sexual difference. The androgyne does not fix the look and thereby gender the subject; rather, s/he invites identification with—instead of desire for—an exciting image of wholeness that is neither one sex nor the other and so is not lacking anything.[62] Androgyny promotes a decentered subjectivity and a disseminated sexuality that have been associated with femininity; Hollander makes this connection when she suggests that the disturbing sensuality of angels is read as feminized.[63] The angel is the phallic or fetishized woman.

But any touch of "otherness" can generate the phallic effect, including racial or class otherness: rock star Michael Jackson excites such strong feelings because he crosses not only gender but racial categories. There is an "androgyny" of race and class that like androgyny "proper," generate and have been generated by fetishism and the (imaginary) confusion of self and other, subject and object, fetishist and fetish, which fetishism promotes. Furthermore, such fetishistic "androgyny" is complicit with commodity consumption; in fact, they are inseparable. As Judith Williamson has noted, advertising represents to us the object of desire—but that object is ourselves, ourselves as whole, a wholeness the commodities advertisements claim they can produce.[64] The commodity, like the fetish (and the fetishized other), is what we need to be seen as complete; buying it, like buying transsexual surgery, is an act of faith in the possibility of becoming the phallic (m)other. In the postmodern age, the narcissistic attempt to secure identity through fetishism therefore contributes to an increasing commodification of the self and others and supports the form of late capitalism.

Television, rather than film, has been discussed as characteristic of postmodernity. It is said to be more fragmentary than cinema because its "flow" is diverse: different types of programming, perhaps most importantly commercials, succeed one another, and there is a variety of camera "looks," including filmed versus "live" footage, whereas movies consist entirely of single-camera-style filmed footage. Furthermore, the viewing experience is not one of concentrated attention, as in the cinema; instead, the spectator watches TV with the lights on, surrounded by chattering family members. Television theorists suggest that these differences make for a dispersed look or "glance" and, therefore, a decentered spectator, who is interpellated as an only ambiguously gendered or perhaps feminine consumer rather than the masculine subject that films produce.[65] Nevertheless, such a spectator is still fetishistic, making an imaginary investment in the self as whole. Television has not broken down fetishism but intensified it, naturalizing even as it exposes the phallic signifiers of "proper" gender, class, and racial identities and reproducing the anxiety which sustains fetishistic commodity consumption. When fetishistic "excess" is the norm, when subjectivity is not so much "photo-graphed" as "tele-vised," it must be asked whether TV "TV" really represents the supreme sacrifice and acceptance of lack or castration that advocates of female impersonation suggest it does.

NOTES

1. In particular, see Elisabeth Badinter, *L'Un est l'autre: des relations entre hommes et femmes* (Paris: Odiles Jacob, 1986), for the argument that contemporary culture is invested in androgyny.
2. See Anne Hollander, "Dressed to Thrill: The Cool and Casual Style of the New Androgyny." *New Republic* 28 (January 1985), 28–33; and Cynthia Secor, "Androgyny: An Early Reappraisal." *Women's Studies* 2:2 (1974), 161–69.
3. Billie Tipton was a female jazz pianist who masqueraded as a man for many years in both her professional and her private life; see *People* (February 20, 1989), 95ff for a brief account of her unmasking at her death. Recently, several books on female masculinity and male-to-female transexualism have appeared.
4. See the collection of essays in *Men in Feminism*, ed. Alice Jardine and Paul Smith (New York: Methuen, 1987), in which the role of men in feminism is debated by a number of important literary cirtics; the women who contributed are, in general, rather suspicious of men's motives for wanting to be "in" feminism. See also Alice Jardine, *Gynesis: Configurations of Woman and Modernity* (Ithaca: Cornell University Press, 1985), and Jane Gallop, *Thinking Through the Body* (New York: Columbia University Press, 1988), 91–118; both consider the meaning of male theorists' "becoming woman."
5. Mary Ann Doane, "Masquerade Reconsidered: Further Thoughts on the Female Spectator," *Discourse* 11:1 (1988–89), 42–54; and Susan Brownmiller, *Femininity* (New York: Fawcett, 1984).
6. The implication is that they are women trapped in the wrong body, so that they suffer from a kind of "birth defect" which requires "corrective" surgery rather than a surgical "change"; see Suzanne Kessler and Wendy McKenna, *Gender: An Ethnomethodological Approach* (Chicago: University of Chicago Press, 1978), 122; they discuss the transsexual birth defect theory on 117.
7. Transsexuals have been, not are—indeed, required—to be heterosexual; see note 36.
8. See Laurie Schulze, "Getting Physical: Text/Context/Reading and the Made-for-Television Movie," in *Cinema Journal* 25:2 (1986), 35–50; and Elayne Rapping, "Made for TV Movies: The Domestication of Social Issues," in *Cineaste* 14:2 (1985), 30–32.
9. Roland Barthes, *Mythologies*, trans. Annette Lavers (New York: Hill and Wang, 1972) 153.
10. Jane Feuer demonstrates that the mode of address in *Good Morning, America* "is embedded in a mutually reinforcing ideological problematic of national and family unity" (18). While the problematic is the same for talk shows, they are structured differently, since the host does not mediate between interviewees in different parts of the

country, nor does he seem to invite us into a living room. Rather, these shows achieve what could be called the pluralist effect not only through a "neither-norism" of content but also through the setup, in which the host mediates between guests with opposing opinions and between guests and the audience, including live callers, in a physical analogue to neither-norism. Pluralism, of course, pays lip service to diversity while eradicating any real difference, since it assumes we are all the same beneath what is only a superficial otherness.

11. See Roland Barthes, *The Pleasure of the Text*, trans. Richard Miller (New York: Hill and Wang, 1975); and Julia Kristeva, *Desire in Language: A Semiotic Approach to Literature and Art*, trans. Leon Roudiez et al. (New York: Columbia University Press, 1980). Both talk about the irruption into the Oedipal text of *jouissance*, a non-oedipal or pre-oedipal pleasure that undoes the subject rather than reconfirming his ego's fictive unity.

12. Michel Foucault, *The History of Sexuality*, vol. 1, of *The Hisotry of Sexuality*, trans. Robert Hurley (New York: Vintage, 1980).

13. Laura Mulvey, "Visual Pleasure and Narrative Cinema," in *Feminism and Film Theory*, ed. Constance Penley (New York: Routledge, 1988), 57–68. Though TV movies and cinema films are very similar formally (in fact, some TV movies were first shown in cinemas), there is at least one significant difference between them: TV movies are interrupted by commercials, which limits the sustained and fascinated gaze of the cinema. Nevertheless, because other TV genres are far more fragmentary than TV movies and because the latter do attempt to produce something like the cinema experience and require a more concentrated attention than most television programming, their similarities rather than their differences are emphasized here. In fact, the confusion of looks discussed in the TV version of *Second Serve* (below) is due primarily to the nature of the topic being narrativized rather than to the medium's difficulty with the filmic system. However, the difference TV makes in spectatorship is important and is addressed in the conclusion of the essay, in which the transvestistic content of the Renée Richards story is linked to television's construction of a transvestistic spectator.

14. Laura Mulvey, "Afterthoughts on 'Visual Pleasure and Narrative Cinema' Inspired by *Duel in the Sun*," in Penley, ed., *Feminism and Film Theory*, 69–79.

15. Kaja Silverman brings this out very clearly in her reading of Freud's discussion of fetishism in *The Acoustic Mirror: The Female Voice in Psychoanalysis and Cinema* (Bloomington: Indiana University Press, 1988), 13–22.

16. Mulvey, "Visual Pleasure," 68.

17. See Otto Fenichel, "The Psychology of Transvestism," (1930); reprt. in *Psychoanalysis and Male Sexuality*, ed. Hendrik M. Ruitenbeek (New Haven: College and University Press, 1966), 203–20; and George Zavitzianos, "The Object in Fetishism, Homeovestism and Transvestism," *International Journal of Psycho-Analysis* 58 (1977), 487–95.

18. Eugenie Lemoine-Luccioni, *La Robe: essai psychoanalytique sur le vêtement* (Paris: Seuil, 1983), 121.

19. Ibid., 126.

20. Peter Ackroyd, *Dressing Up: Transvestism and Drag: The History of an Obsession* (New York: Simon and Schuster, 1979), 14.

21. Harry Benjamin, "Transsexualism and Transvestism as Psycho-Somatic and Somato-Psychic Syndromes," *American Journal of Psychotherapy* 8 (1954), 224.

22. See, for example, Dr. Erwin Koranyi's book on transsexualism, *Transsexuality in the Male: The Spectrum of Gender Dysphoria* (Springfield, MA: Thomas, 1980.) He advises electrolysis not only for the chest and face but also the forearms, describes rhinoplasty as a "feminizing operation," states that breast augmentation "greatly increases the subjective feelings of femininity," discusses the exact diameter and length a constructed vagina should be, and suggests that "a suitably soft and feminine voice" can be self-taught, obviating a transsexual's need for surgical "feminization" of the larynx, which too often leads only to hoarseness. Nicole Kress-Rosen, in "Le Transsexualisme de Stoller" *Ornicar* 22–23 (1981), 188, notes that well-known and well-respected transsexual expert Dr. Robert Stoller works with a stereotypical definition of femininity, so that he judged as unfeminine the mothers of some of the transsexuals he saw because they wore suits! Transsexuals are aware that a doctor's sexist and conservative notion of femininity is a problem; one of those interviewed by Anne Bolin in *In Search of Eve: Transsexual Rites of Passage* (South Hadley, MA: Bergin, 1988) explicitly expressed her anger at having to conform to a doctor's idea of a woman in order to be approved for surgery (51).

23. Janice Raymond, *The Transsexual Empire: The Making of a She-Male* (Boston: Beacon Press, 1979.)

24. Jacques Lacan, "The Meaning of the Phallus," in *Feminine Sexuality*, trans. Jacqueline Rose, ed. Jacqueline Rose and Juliet Mitchell (New York: Norton, 1982), 84.

25. Catherine Millot, *Horsexe: essai sur le transsexualisme* (Paris: Point Hors Ligne, 1983), 33.

26. Ibid., 34.

27. Ibid., 62–64, 124–27.

28. The peculiar orothography of "(m)other" is a reminder that the place of phallic omnipotence can be filled by the fantasy of the phallic mother or the primitive father, since neither is imagined to be subject to castration. The phallic other may exercise her fascination through class or racial difference as well as through gender difference, since such differences, like sexual difference, signify phallic lack or having. Women are not the only ones who do not exist except as a phallic fantasy in Western culture, as becomes clear in the overlooked class dynamic of transvestism.

29. Millot, *Horsexe*, 134. For some, however, surgery precipitates psychosis.

30. Moustafa Safouan, "Contribution à la psychoanalyse du transsexualisme," *Scilicet* 4 (1983), 150–52.

31. Jane Gallop, *Reading Lacan* (Ithaca: Cornell University Press, 1985), 60.

32. In *Presentations of Gender* (New Haven: Yale University Press, 1985), Dr. Robert Stoller only briefly mentions transsexuals' despairing recognition that a true sex change is not possible (163), though he discusses at length why he does not believe surgery is the answer to the sexual discomfort transsexuals feel (see especially 165–67). Kress-Rosen, "Transsexualism," 187, points out that in an earlier volume devoted to transsexualism Stoller suggests the euphoria succeeding the surgery is short-lived because the organs acquired are so imperfect (187). Benjamin, "Transsexualism," 228, asserts unequivocally that transsexuals are dissatisfied with the femininity achieved by surgery and renew their demand for feminization.

33. Renée Richards (with John Ames), *Second Serve* (New York: Stein, 1984), cover notes.

34. For legal reasons, Richard Raskind is called Richard Radley in the television movie. Other names appearing in the autobiography have also been changed.

35. Richards, *Second Serve*, 135–50.

36. In the *Guidelines for Transsexuals*, the literature from the Erikson Educational

Foundation, a psychiatrist is quoted to the effect that he helped a patient realize he was not a transsexual by pointing out to him the "contradiction" between wanting the surgery and still relating sexually to women; Stoller, *Gender*, 18. Similarly, Bolin writes that in the literature, "a long-term and deeply abiding attraction to genetic males is viewed as intrinsic to true transsexualism" (62). This has resulted in the need for transsexuals to lie about their sexual orientation in order to be able to qualify for surgery, though the situation improved considerably in the 1990's.

37. Barthes, *Mythologies*, 152–53.

38. Sigmund Freud, "Femininity," (1933), in *New Introductory Lectures on Psychoanalysis*, trans. and ed. James Strachey (New York: W. W. Norton, 1965), 117.

39. Lacan, "The Meaning of the Phallus," 85.

40. Steve Neale, "Masculinity as Spectacle: Reflections on Men and Mainstream Cinema," *Screen* 24:6 (1983), 2–16.

41. Sigmund Freud, "A Child is Being Beaten" (1919), in *Sexuality and the Psychology of Love*, trans. James Strachey, ed. Phillip Reiff (New York: Collier, 1963), 107–32.

42. Monique Plaza, "The Mother/the Same: Hatred of the Mother in Psychoanalysis," *Feminist Issues* 2:1 (1982), 75–99.

43. See Mary Ann Doane, *The Desire to Desire: The Woman's Film of the 1940s* (Bloomington: Indiana University Press, 1987); and Claire Kahane, "Gothic Mirrors and Feminine Identity," *Centennial Review* 24:1 (1980), 43–64.

44. Mulvey, "Afterthoughts."

45. Brownmiller, *Femininity*, 86.

46. John Molloy, *The Woman's Dress for Success Book* (New York: Warner, 1977), 28.

47. Luce Irigaray, *This Sex Which Is Not One*, trans. Catherine Porter (Ithaca: Cornell University Press, 1985), 76.

48. See Mary Russo, "Female Grotesques: Carnival and Theory," in *Feminist Studies/Critical Studies*, ed. Teresa de Lauretis (Bloomington: Indiana University Press, 1986), 216; and Karen Newman, "Renaissance Family Politics and Shakespeare's *The Taming of the Shrew*," *English Literary Renaissance* 26 (1986), 98–100.

49. Irigaray, *This Sex*, 76.

50. Mary Ann Doane refers to "hyperbolisation" in "Film and the Masquerade—Theorising the Female Spectator," *Screen* 23:3–4 (1982), 82; and Nancy Miller discusses "italicization" in "Emphasis Added: Plots and Plausibilities in Women's Fictions," *PMLA* 96 (1981), 38. Irigaray's references to mimicry as a "playful" repetition of the masquerade (76) also suggest some sort of parodic or ironic distance on femininity.

51. Lurie, 259.

52. Marilyn Frye, *The Politics of Reality: Essays in Feminist Theory* (Trumansburg, NY: Crossing, 1983), 137–39.

53. JoAnn Roberts (pseudonym), *Art and Illusion: A Guide to Crossdressing* (King of Prussia, PA: Creative Design Services, 1986); and see "Crossdressers," *Donahue* (Metromedia transcript #2234, August 19, 1987).

54. "Beauty Pageant Makeovers," *Donahue* (Metromedia transcript #2392, March 31, 1988).

55. Homi Bhabha, "Of Mimicry and Man: The Ambivalence of Colonial Discourse," *October* 28 (1984), 126.

56. Jacques Lacan, "God and the *Jouissance* of The Woman," in Rose and Mitchell, eds., *Feminine Sexuality*, 144–45.

57. This argument has been enabled by the work of Peter Stallybrass and Allon White. In their book on the Bakhtinian carnivalesque they discuss desire and subjectivity in terms of class as well as gender, addressing differences ordinarily not significant for psycoanalytic theory; see *The Politics and Poetics of Transgression* (Ithaca: Cornell University Press, 1986). Bhabha has engaged in a similar effort to broaden the explanatory base of psychoanalysis, using it to account for the constitution of raced subjectivity. See Homi K. Bhabha, "The Other Question: Difference, Discrimination, and the Discourse of Colonialism," in *Literature, Politics, and Theory: Papers from the Essex Conference, 1976–84*, ed. Francis Barker et al. (New York: Methuen, 1985), 149–70.

58. Jacques Derrida, *Spurs: Nietzsche's Styles*, trans. Barbara Harlow (Chicago: Chicago University Press, 1979).

59. Millot, *Horsexe*, 121; Safouan, "Contribution," 158.

60. Jacques Lacan, *The Four Fundamental Concepts of Psychoanalysis*, trans. Alan Sheridan, ed. Jacques-Alain Miller (New York: W. W. Norton, 1978), 106.

61. Hollander, "Dressed to Thrill," 28.

62. Francette Pacteau, "The Impossible Referent: Representations of the Androgyne," in *Formations of Fantasy*, ed. Victor Burgin et al. (New York: Methuen, 1986), 77.

63. Hollander, "Dressed to Thrill," 32.

64. Judith Williamson, *Decoding Advertisements: Ideology and Meaning in Advertising* (New York: Boyars, 1978); see especially 60–70.

65. For a more thorough introduction to the question of film versus television spectatorship, see John Fiske, *Television Culture* (New York: Methuen, 1987); Sandy Flitterman-Lewis, "Psychoanalysis, Film, and Television" in *Channels of Discourse: Television and Contemporary Criticism*, ed. Robert Allen (Chapel Hill: University of North Carolina Press, 1987), 172–210; and E. Ann Kaplan, "Feminist Criticism and Television," in Allen, ed., *Channels of Discourse*, 211–53; Tania Modleski's discussion of the feminization of mass culture is also relevant; see "Femininity as Mas(s)querade: A Feminist Approach to Mass Culture," in *High Theory/Low Culture: Analysing Popular Television and Film*, ed. Colin MacCabe (New York: St. Martin's, 1986), 137–52. In a recent book, taking issue wth the theoretical hegemony of the televisual "glance," John Thornton Caldwell argues even network television has, since 1980, invited a more sustained gaze through a "stylistic exhibitionism" adopted to combat loss of viewers to cable and satellite television; see *Televisuality: Style, Crisis, and Authority in American Television* (New Brunswick: Rutgers University Press, 1995).

THEORETICAL IMPERSONATION

MEN AND FEMINISM

> *Our interpretations will not be readings of a hermeneutic or exegetic*
> *sort, but rather political interventions in the political rewriting of the*
> *text and its destination. This is the way it has always been. . . .*
> —JACQUES DERRIDA, *THE EAR OF THE OTHER*

I
t seems indisputable that feminism has secured a place in the U.S. academy, given the numbers of books, essays, conference papers, and course offerings in the field. The virulent antifeminism of some of the diatribes in the press against multiculturalism and "political correctness" in our culture is a testimony to the importance of feminism in the cultural imagination of those outside the academy as well. The relative success of feminism (indicated even by fears of its success) implies a change in the contemporary scene, perhaps particularly the academic "beehive," as Jacques Derrida has troped it, and, therefore, a change in the subjects of that scene, for whom a new set of attributes is supposed to have become desirable.[1] Jane Gallop's assertion, "Not to be a feminist in this age is to be lacking, inadequate," is a measure of that change.[2] It seems the desire of the "other" may now be "feminist," and since it is the other in whom man finds his desire, according to Jacques Lacan, men's penetration of feminism—or feminism's penetration of men—has become an issue. There are currently enough books and essays

about this to constitute it as a subfield—although it is evidently one unlikely to gratify those in it; for all too often the "beehive" is stirred up by the man who calls himself a feminist, proving it to be a hornet's nest. Yet it is women who claim to feel the sting, as many argue that "male feminism" is nothing but a "sting" or con—a rebuke male feminists in turn experience as stinging.

Many of the essays in the several anthologies now in print that engage the issue testify to man's discomfort with woman's discomfort with his attempt to join the feminist hive.[3] Evidently the "femmaninist" (to employ a neologism coined by Peggy Kamuf) is the bee in the feminist bonnet, and he does not like that role.[4] When he looks at the feminist looking at him, he is unhappy with what she sees: the "man" hidden within the femmaninist, the phallus he thought was eliminated by his feminist togs. The feminist gaze discomfits him, unsetting his gratifying symbolic identification. But he does not so much reflect upon this as reflect it back in a kind of double sting—or con. Feeling a phallic thrust to the critique, he insists it is the female feminist who is the real femmaninist, a phallic woman who demonstrates her complicity with the law of the phallus by checking sexual identity cards, in Derrida's memorable phrase, merely inverting rather than displacing phallic identities.[5] Such a woman is a queen bee, an impersonator whose belief in sovereign identity makes a burlesque of genuine feminism.

Whose feminism is the real thing and whose a theoretical impersonation? What is the place of experience and identity in feminist politics? Who can speak as a feminist, and what does it mean to do so? Does postmodern man's new valorization of the feminine, of "becoming woman," make for an unbecoming feminist? Just what sort of feminism—and feminist—do we desire? The answers to these questions that different theorists of feminism have offered must be read not for their truth value but for their political efficacy, as my epigraph by Derrida suggests.[6] We must attend to the letter of these texts, but in order to rewrite and reroute them, a political intervention that is *necessary* in both senses of the word, as a responsibility and an inevitability. Because an author's intentions are never entirely legible in a text—not even to the author—interpretation is imperative. The reader bears an ethic-political responsibility to the letter whose "truth" she forces and delivers, the violence of writing that reading entails.[7]

Representation is inevitably violent because of the responsibility to difference that writing and reading never can fully discharge. "Responsibility annuls the call to which it seeks to respond," Gayatri Chakravorty Spivak flatly asserts at the opening of an essay on the topic.[8] The responsible subject cannot live up to her responsibility because she reduces self and other to knowable objects, subjects whose needs and desires can be calculated. The second half of Spivak's essay is devoted to a discussion of just such a failure to be responsible by representatives of two Western organizations who would not hear what subaltern peasant fishermen and farmers had to say about the mid-1990s World Bank-coordinated *Flood Action Plan for Bangladesh*; their responsibility to subaltern difference was thus abrogated. Spivak closes with a reading of one passage of a Western essay about the *Plan* that is a reminder of her often repeated dictum, "People are different from the object of emancipatory benevolence."[9] Commenting on the explanations of the "good Europeans" for the reluctance of the poor of Bangladesh to leave the land except as unwilling refugees—that the subaltern fear they will lose common lands to agribusiness or are unable to find waged work in rural areas—Spivak writes, "There is, according to the view I am discussing here, no gauge of intention but rational expectations, logical self-interest, reason written by something confusedly called European common sense. The subaltern mental theater is no bigger than this, just as for population control the subaltern female is nothing but a crotch."[10] That final analogy underlines the violence of the objectification through Western subjectivation with its brutal metonymic reduction of the woman to her genitals, even as Spivak has insisted, in an earlier essay concerning clitoridectomy, that anti-sexist work may require just such a reduction.[11]

The other as "subject" is always, according to Derrida, "a principle of calculability—for the political . . . in the question of legal and human rights . . . and in morality"; therefore, he suggests, "Something of this call of the other must remain nonreappropriable, nonsubjectivable, and in a certain way nonidentifiable, a sheer supposition, so as to remain *other*, a *singular* call to response or to responsibility. . . . This obligation to protect the other's otherness is not merely a theoretical imperative."[12] However, Derrida insists that the responsibility to the other requires action, rather than indecision in the face of the undecidability of what is called for, though the result is the ineluctable assimilation of other to self. Elaborating on identification and the narcissistic assimilation of difference as a kind of cannibalism whose literal examplars might be Jeffrey Dahmer or Hannibal Lecter in *Silence of the Lambs*, as Diana Fuss has suggested, Derrida writes, "The moral question is thus not, nor has it ever been: should one eat or not eat . . . but since *one must* eat in any case and since it tastes good to eat, and since there's no other definition of the good *(du bien)*, *how* for goodness sake should one *eat well (bien manger)*?"[13] Or as Spivak puts it, "[A]n ethical relationship with the other entails universalizing the singular," a gesture that is appropriative and narcissistic as absolute alterity is named and incorporated by and as the subject like the subject of the West.[14] For that reason "all sustained 'activists' know that victories are warnings . . . often silencing that knowledge in the interest of the decision," Spivak notes. "Derrida attempts to deconstruct that gap. It is not that we must not take sides. We must continue to know, and to make known, 'which is the least grave of these forms of complicity' [with Western metaphysics]," she concludes, quoting Derrida's *Of Spirit*.[15] If there just is narcissism—"without a movement of narcissistic reappropriation the relation to the other would be absolutely destroyed," Derrida says—there nevertheless can be no just narcissism, as the life drive or eros and the death drive and its aggressivity will never achieve a fair balance in the cathexes of self and other.[16]

How, then, to write and read feminism in a movement of that narcissism more "generous, open, extended" for which Derrida calls, one more "hospitable" to the other's difference, to sexual difference, including the sexual difference of the subaltern woman absolutely different from the First World white woman?[17] Ethico-politics condenses aporias of social contact and contract, coercion and consent, calculation and what resists it that (con)found feminist subjects and collectivities no less than any others. Writing and reading feminism involves an interrupted address like that to "the nation" as outlined by Homi Bhabha in "DissemiNation," in which the "the people" are at once subject and object, speaking and spoken, "constructed in the performance of narrative" and "*a priori* historical presence," performative and constative iteration.[18] Bhabha thus recalls that the members of the imagined community of the nation are desiring subjects, split by the language of the Other, who is also a split and desiring subject. Never quite coinciding with their uttered *I*, nor certain about the *you* into which they are interpellated in discursive and other exchanges, the members of a community, including those hailing and hailed by feminists, confront the paradoxes of responsibility to difference, their own as well as the differences of others, of which desire is an expression. How is the subject named and naming, and what desires are thereby "assumed"—assigned or identified with even if only through negation and denial? Psychoanalysis, like deconstruction, emphasizes the inadequacy of every answer given to these questions, which are ultimately undecidable because of the absolute alterity of the other. It insists that desire insists and cannot be satisfied: both subject and other always want something more and other than what they have demanded in the Other's signifiers, something that it is impossible to put into words or know and that is beyond the pleasure or reality principles of any utilitarian scheme.

Who can responsibly presume to know what is in another's best interests? Can men in feminism determine what women "should" desire if they know what is good or them? The issue of enunciation is key for feminists, but makes men anxious because it is linked to the place of identity politics and essentialism in feminism, which could leave men with no place in it at all, exposing them as theoretical impersonators. Yet identity politics should also make women uneasy, since its forgetting of the split between enunciation and utterance, self and other, can lead to the construction of a universal "woman" whose desires and oppressions all women are assumed to know as "sisters." When differences among women are disavowed, "other" women can only participate in feminism as theoretical impersonators. What Spivak has termed "strategic essentialism" has now supplanted "equal rights" as a rallying cry for feminists and others working in fields that address the subcultures of subalterns, the cultural productions of such diverse groups as diasporic and postcolonial subjects, ethnic and racial minorities, lesbians, gays, transgenders, and other queers, and the working class.[19] Once upon a time we hoped all men would become feminists, but as early as 1983 feminist philosopher Moira Gatens was citing "the number of men who have built their academic reputations on feminism and 'teach' feminism" as clear proof that feminism had already been co-opted.[20] Can a politics founded on identity do justice to difference, including the self-difference of a group and its members? What assumptions about identity and community, especially political identity and community, should feminists bring to their praxis?

Are feminists more afraid of the differences between men and women than of the differences among women? Are men in feminism out to take over the hive and eliminate women altogether, as is suggested by the provocative title of Tania Modleski's *Feminism without Women?*[21]

KILLER BE(E):
FEMINIST THEORY AND SEXUAL ONTOLOGY

Men in Feminism (1987), the first of several volumes on the topic of its title, is filled with anxiety about "political correctness."[22] To lack the right politics is to lack the phallus, or in this case, to have the phallus, which becomes the mark of lack in what is, at least for the men who contributed to the anthology, an inverted economy of sexual difference. Their essays are literally "cases," since the female feminists function as the men's analysts, frustrating their desire to see themselves whole in the mirror of feminism.[23] That male feminism may be caught up in an imaginary specular economy (whatever other functions it may have) is evident from the very first essay of the book, in which Stephen Heath writes, "the most any man can do today [is] to learn and so to try to write or talk or act in response to feminism, and so to try not in any way to be anti-feminist, supportive of the old oppressive structures. Any more, any notion of writing a feminist book or being a feminist, is a myth, a male imaginary with the reality of appropriation and domination right behind. But who am I to say this?"[24]

Heath recognizes the risk of appropriation and therefore interrogates his own enunciation. His question foregrounds the fact that the "I" of the utterance, which might indeed be offering savvy feminist advice, is radically split from the "I" of the enunciation, which might offer that advice in order to be situated in the place of knowledge, beyond lack and desire. As Toril Moi notes in her critique of Joseph Boone's critique of the book, "good faith" guarantees nothing.[25] The male feminist necessarily engages in double-talk.

But female feminists, too, practice double-talk. In a duplicity that seems to smack of bad faith, women have deconstructed masculine identity even while they have affirmed feminine identity through both continued support for affirmative action and other, less obviously "strategic" essentialisms. This has arisen from the wish to address the oppression arising from the devaluation of the feminine as signifier of something lacking and of those who bear its marks, principally women. But if the phallus is not the penis, as feminist psychoanalytic theory insists then lack need not be represented only by women. Even "the male body can signify castration and lack, can hence function as the object of voyeuristic looking, insofar as it is marked as such . . . disfigured in some way, or . . . racially or culturally other," as Steve Neale notes.[26] When the men of *Men in Feminism* search out the holes in the logic of feminists, whether female or male, they mark an other against whom they measure themselves so as not to come up short, feminizing that other as lacking what they have. Furthermore, by representing feminists that way, men profit from their critical speculations, filling the hive with their happy hum, having once again asserted their right to be the masterful subjects of discourse.

A feminist point of view must be concerned with the ethico-politics of the representation of the feminine other, which, as Spivak has discussed at length in "Can the Subaltern Speak," embraces not only *depiction* (what Marx terms *darstellen*, speaking about) but also *delegation* (what Marx terms *vertreten*, speaking for and instead of).[27] From such a perspective, the male contributors to *Men in Feminism* remain caught up in the very problems they discover. Their contributions seek to determine—to describe and prescribe—what a woman/feminist wants and then to demonstrate that the man in question has the right stuff, while his rivals for her affections are seriously lacking. But this conception of what it means to be a male feminist is not much different from what it means to be a heterosexual man in our culture, which is one of the problems that feminism addresses. It seems to be the same old story of masculine narcissism and competition, with a new cast of feminist characters. Once again, men have arrogated to themselves the power to know and fulfill a woman's wishes, and in doing so, they remain caught in a masculine imaginary, a specular speculation, capitalizing on differences reduced to the same.

In her contribution to the volume, Elaine Showalter uncovers a common sadistic fantasy of male feminism, in which men "discipline" women about feminism by "showing the girls how to do it," counseling women how best to practice feminism.[28] It is a scenario that recurs throughout the book, for example, when Robert Scholes advises feminists to stay away from deconstruction in the name of an essentialist feminism, and when Andrew Ross insists that feminists deconstruct identities in the name of an antiessentialist feminism.[29] This move to put women in their place (of lack) may be accompanied by or effected through what Nancy Miller, reviewing Denis Donoghue's review of several feminist publications, describes as "playing women off each other," and what Elizabeth Weed, in her discussion of one of Ross's essays, characterizes as "indirectly implicating the victim."[30] A particularly telling instance of this occurs in the final essay in the book, a conversation between Alice Jardine and Paul Smith, the editors. Jardine attempts to draw a parallel between the situation of male feminists and feminism and white feminists and black feminism. When she suggests "there is very little place [in black feminism] . . . [for] a white feminist to play with the rhetorical field," her sexualized metaphor emphasizes the analogy with men in feminism even as it also curiously portrays white feminists as libertines.[31] But Smith does not hear what was intended, a charge he has earlier leveled against the female feminists in the book who did not perceive the irony in his troping of men in feminism as a "penetration."[32] He asks Jardine why women are willing to invite black feminists to join "the movement," while men are told they must present their credentials, an allusion to Derrida on checking identity cards. Though Jardine has suggested that men, like white feminists, should not imagine it is their right to speak in the name of a movement that is responding to an oppression for which they must take some responsibility, Smith inverts the binarisms, making men equivalent to black femininsts, just two groups of similarly marginalized "others" buzzing about the hive, importuning the white queen to let them in. As the rest of his dialogue makes clear, however, these phallic women could not be phallic without the addition of the male feminists who will make them whole. Ever chivalrous, the male feminist is eager to come to the aid of the woman in need—a need for which he is on the lookout.

This sort of chivalry reaches new heights in Smith's solo essay, where, as Weed points out, he presents himself and his fellow male feminists as the saviors of a feminism on the brink of conformity and homogenization, as a crucial "difference within" that only he and other men are able to supply, despite the analogy with black feminists in the joint essay.[33] Men in feminism, he asserts, can "help to subvert, unsettle and undermine the (seemingly rather fast to settle) laws of the discourse. . . . This they might do purely by virtue of existing in it as a difference."[34] As Tania Modleski notes, it is a remark seemingly calculated to bring about the abuse that is heaped upon him subsequent to making it, suggesting that he is perhaps not so much a sadist as a masochist, a particularly crafty "bottom" who knows how to get a woman on top so he can take correction—like a man?—even as he also offers correction (purely and virtuously) to those women really in need of it.[35] The others, the "real" feminists, he simply admires—as Heath has suggested he should.[36] Many of the male contributors to the volume seem to alternate between just such sadistic gazing and worshipful, masochistic contemplation of female feminists in an ambivalence characteristic of the fetishist, who both worships and castrates the fetish object, according to Sigmund Freud.[37] The male feminist's knowledge of feminism is therefore self-interested and self-pleasuring, however hard he may try to efface the desiring body behind the neuter mask of "truth."

The fetishism of such male feminist desires is phallic, even if heavily veiled in feminism, making him something of a female impersonator, as Showalter asserts and Scholes implies. Like Joan Riviere's feminine masquerader, the male feminist disavows castration, hiding the fact he believes he has the phallus by donning the mask of lack itself, a feminism never entirely disjunct from the feminine with which it is metonymically linked—and for which it metaphorically substitutes in all the essays and in the title of the book itself. That fetishism assures him he is indeed lacking nothing, not even feminism.[38] Reasoning similarly, a number of feminists have questioned the motives and effects of postmodernist transvestism. Ruth Savaggio suggests that "in a game where the object is to subvert mastery, everyone wants to be the woman.[39] Jardine asserts such impersonation might allow men to master their loss of mastery through and by feminine alterity itself.[40] Gallop argues that when postmodernism insists on dephallicization, being antiphallic becomes the new phallus, with women lacking once again. "Postmodernist thinkers are defending against the downfall of patriarchy by trying not to be male," she writes. "In drag, they are aping the feminine rather than thinking their place as men in an obsolescent patriarchy." This, she adds, is "the father's last ruse to seduce the daughter and retain her respect," and she wonders what the place of the woman who identifies with the man who identifies with the woman can be.[41] However, Freud has already discussed just such a transvestic identification in "A Child Is Being Beaten."[42] The woman is in the feminine masochistic position once again, but by way of a homosexual cross-identification, incestuously desiring her father as a little boy, repressing that desire, and disguising it not only by regressing to an anal-sadistic phase, in which beating is loving, but also by absenting herself from the scene, looking on as her stand-in, the little boy, enjoys all the painful pleasure of being the object of the father's desire.

Gallop's allusion is to a feminism—and even a femininity—without women, which Modleski also anticipates and deplores in her 1991 book.

Such a feminism threatens to become a token in a phallic game played by the fathers, in which a man determines what feminists should want and then demonstrates he has it by unveiling the (w)holes in the arguments of others, whether men or women. These (w)holes waver in their signification: sometimes they are signs of phallic lack and sometimes of phallic presence, although such presence, paradoxically, may signify lack in the logic of a postmodernist fetishism, which masculinizes in order to emasculate. But this fetishism can have another man as its object, rather than a woman, and its subject can oscillate between sadistic voyeurism, masochistic fetishism, and a fetishistic transvestism that is also exhibitionistic. This is especially clear in those moments when the male feminist employs the rhetorical device of paralipsis, doing what he says he will not, burying his Caesar in order to praise himself by ventriloquizing the other's phallic desires and deploring them. Critiquing Smith's use of the metaphor of the "penetration" of feminism, Cary Nelson "knows" and rejects what Smith wanted to accomplish by it. "In highlighting the tendency to see all male feminist discourse exclusively in terms of sexual difference he [Smith] hoped, perhaps, to persuade women to read men's feminist writing more diversely . . . ," Nelson writes. "I fully sympathize with him here, but, again, I do not think this is yet the time for men to make that request of feminism. I have made that request myself often enough in the past, but I do not make it anymore."[43] Nelson allows Smith to voice his wish for him, putting it under the sign of negation so as to disavow it ("I know I should not ask this, but just the same—"). He adopts Smith's "I" in order to disidentify from it, wishing his wish upon Smith so he will not have wished it himself, a defense Smith himself uses during his conversation about Heath with Jardine.[44]

"I am tired of men arguing amongst themselves as to who is the most feminist," Claire Pajaczowska complains, "frustrated by an object feminism becoming the stakes in a displaced rivalry between men because of a refusal by men to examine the structure of the relations between themselves."[45] Both Eve Kosofsky Sedgwick and Luce Irigaray have articulated compelling critiques of the sexist and homophobic oedipal politics of such exchanges of women between men.[46] In *Men in Feminism*, that rivalrous exchange often goes beyond the personal, involving critical (af)filiations and the powerful disciples of the theoretical "schools" of deconstruction and psychoanalysis, which could subsume feminism. When Jonathan Culler claims "reading as a woman" as an example of a deconstructionist approach, he represents deconstruction as the master discipline and himself as a proper disciple, naming himself (and his critical practice) through the mediation of the figure of femininity.[47] While—in his critique of Culler—Scholes problematizes deconstruction's relation to feminism, he maintains the same hierarchy. His essay is addressed to Derrida across the body of one particular type of feminist criticism (though he writes as if essentialist feminism were in effect the essence of feminism, as Fuss has noted) despite its attempt to deconstruct "for" feminism the kind of "dire mastery" a theoretical apprenticeship can involve.[48] The narcissism of the masculine imaginary clearly need not be disrupted by a fascination with feminism, even when men exchange (comments about) male feminists, rather than women, or fetishize the female feminists with whom they identify as whole, rather than lacking.

Or even when the male feminists are gay identifed. In his essay in *Men in Feminism*, Craig Owens, the only self-identified gay contributor to the volume, suggests that gay men are "outlaws," outsiders in a society based on the prohibition of incest and homosocial rivalry through the exchange of women.[49] A homophobic homosociality should not be confused with homosexuality, he argues, and criticizes Irigaray for conflating just these two concepts. According to Owens, such a confusion is itself homophobic; in addition, it is reductive and, therefore, complicit with race and class oppression because it exempts women from any responsibility for such oppression by reading the symbolic order as organized entirely around the exchange of women by men who unconsciously desire men. Undoubtedly, Owens is right to insist that Irigaray's reading is reductive, and not just strategically so—she does not often address racism and classism, especially in her early work, and is therefore insufficiently attentive to the impact of differences between women on both feminist theory and practice, as well as on women's lives. However, Irigaray cannot be so readily accused of homophobia. While she does not maintain the consistent distinction between homosexuality and homosociality that structures Sedgwick's work, Ingaray does say that if the penis becomes a means to pleasure it cannot symbolize the phallus.[50] This suggests that gay men, like feminists, may oppose a homosocial patriarchy, and is not congruent with the kind of radical feminism represented by feminists like lesbian philosopher Marilyn Frye, who argues that all gay men are "phallophilic" and so no less sexist than straight men.[51] Irigaray's assertion might even be read as implying that gay men cannot be misogynist, which is what Owens declares. Such a claim can only be based on an inversion of the confusion Owens attributes to Irigaray. To confound the homosexual and the homosocial, Irigaray must reduce the latter to misogyny, ignoring homophobia; to confound the homosexual and the feminist, Owens must reduce the homosocial to the homophobic, ignoring misogyny or assuming it is somehow the same—but only for men, since women, like Irigaray, can be homophobic. Whereas for Frye gay men must be antifeminist because they do not find women desirable, for Owens gay men must be feminist because they do not find women desirable—positions that are equally problematic. Gay men are as capable of misogyny as women are of homophobia as a response to the symbolic castration that has made them subjects; this means that women can be misogynist, and homosexuals homophobic—a charge leveled by some against Brandon Teena/Teena Brandon, who saw "her" as a victim of "lesbophobia," including her own.[52] Nor am I as certain as Irigaray that the penis ceases to be confused with the phallus when it becomes a means to pleasure; such a confusion can be the very source of pleasure, especially in a culture in which the most common fetish may be the penis itself.

It is therefore not surprising to find gay-identified men participating in the kind of rivalry informing many of the essays in *Men in Feminism*. In his critique of the book, Boone suggests that he can disrupt what he quite rightly recognizes as the "two-dimensional oppositionality" of its format, which reproduces gender difference as a binary opposition, by exposing the differences between men.[53] One of the most important of these is sexuality, Boone notes, and "many of the men in the academy who are feminism's most supportive 'allies' *are* gay."[54] Boone's deconstruction of the binarism through the revelation of the differences within one of the two opposed terms involves emphasizing the *me* in *men*, which he writes as "me(n)" to indicate that his *me* differs from *men* in general, as a supposed unity, and particularly from the men in *Men in Feminism*. Boone characterizes those men—or, rather, allows Jardine to characterize those men for him—as "straight, white academics" and, therefore, as having clear "limitations" as male feminists. They are, "more likely than not," Boone writes, to be "'in(to)' feminism in the most troublesome sense of the word."[55] Boone utilizes Smith's controversial sexual metaphor to subtly exculpate gay men: since they are not "into" women, they cannot be "into" feminism in a penetrating way, which is "a strictly heterosexual gesture of appropriation."[56]

Although Boone's identification with gay men is implicit throughout the essay, he never explicitly identifies himself as anything other than a "male feminist," despite his call for men to "forge self-definitions of themselves *as men* that make room for the acknowledgment of a difference and a sexuality that is truly heterogeneous."[57] In fact, his identification with a younger generation of academic men supposedly educated in feminism is more marked than his identification with gay scholars; this broad group is the first of those "marginalized male voices" to which Boone calls attention in his list of areas from which a male feminism might emerge.[58] For Boone the main character flaw of the male contributors to *Men in Feminism* is not their sexual or racial identities but their fame, which seems to guarantee they can never be more than appropriators of feminism. First on Boone's list of "directives for literary feminists" is the command to "stop looking to prominent figures like Derrida for the final word on men's potential to theorize their relation to feminist theory and practice."[59] This order, and the assumption that such men lack anything interesting to contribute to the discussion, is another enactment of academic rivalry, as Moi has pointed out.[60] Boone demands that feminists recognize the little me the big men have obscured or rendered invisible so that male feminism will no longer appear to be "a struggle for power among superpowers." Superpowers, of course, have big guns; Boone's metaphor is therefore symptomatic of rather than subversive of the phallic rivalry of oedipal anxiety, a "palace revolution of the young Turks," as Moi phrases it.[61]

In the inverted economies of difference currently operating in an academic and popular imaginary structured by liberal guilt and its rejection, even the difference of oppression can be disavowed. With so many men already claiming to be in the position of the victim, suffering the effects of "reverse discrimination," it cannot be surprising to hear voiced an overt desire to be in that place by some who identify with feminism. Told by one male friend that her position as marginal was ideal, Rosi Braidotti asks, indignantly, "In whose imaginary?"[62] Clearly, when to have is to lack, to masculinize, to emasculate, men would be different, "becoming woman" (as Derrida would have it)—but the "better" woman, the "proper" feminist, the "femmaninist," and so the same. The theoretical impersonator would be more feminist than the female feminist, and more feminine than the woman: according to Smith male feminists "conflict with the law in a way possibly more pointedly than women"; they suffer more than women for their feminism.[63] However, as Kaja Silverman has demonstrated in a reading of Lawrence of Arabia, such masochism may support rather than subvert a phallic identity; just as the white European proves he is better at suffering Arab identity than Arabs themselves, so the male feminist proves he is better at suffering feminism than women.[64]

It is no wonder that so many women have been critical of men's penetration of feminism: they fear that the feminist hive will be taken over by men acting like killer bees since the latter all too often disregard the risk of appropriation and their responsibility to feminine alterity. Whereas male feminists would check their identities like coats at the door, many women would check them like sentries on guard duty. "Qui vive?" is increasingly the demand to the person who would speak as a feminist, a demand for a fixed identity as answer to the question of ontology and preface to any remark, a magic password—or confession invalidating whatever follows. Hence the suspicion with which deconstruction in particular has been viewed by many feminists: because it is rigorously antiessentialist, it is at odds with "strategic" (or other) essentialisms and identity politics (which might explain why it has been deployed by so many male feminists). The "woman" that deconstruction valorizes is not so much a "real" woman as a means of dismantling "the subject" —before women have been able to speak as such, according to many feminists, among them Modlesk, Braidotti, Nancy Miller, Teresa de Lauretis, and Margaret Whitford.[65] "Identity may be illusory, but men are still speaking, and speaking *for and in the place of women*," Whitford notes.[66] Derrida's "becoming woman" therefore may be the most egregious theoretical impersonation of all. He has even said himself that "deconstruction is not feminist . . . if there is one thing it must not come to it's feminism."[67] According to Derrida, however, the effacer of difference is the sexual ontology many feminists assume or advocate, identity predication associated with the "deathly patronymic" that poses no challenge to phallocentric metaphysics, the "Killer *be*."[68] Does Derrida's becoming woman make for a most unbecoming feminist? Is deconstruction a co-optation of feminism by an antifeminist man in drag, or does it disturb feminism in a productive fashion?

QUEEN BEE? DERRIDA'S *SPUR*-IOUS TRANSVESTISM

Derrida's impact on literary and cultural studies has been tremendous, as the number of his disciples (and critics) indicates. Derrida would not see himself as a founding father of a critical "school"; he has said often enough that deconstruction is not a theology or even a methodology with certain unvarying rules or strategies to be applied to whatever text is to be deconstructed. For Derrida (if not for all of his followers) a text is never merely an example of deconstruction, with undecidability its theme; to treat a text as such is to fail in one's responsibility to read it. Nonetheless, as a number of critics have pointed out, in his interviews Derrida has identified certain "protocols" of a deconstructive reading.[69] In raising the question of proper identities and the violence of naming, deconstruction problematizes not only the object(s) of knowledge but also the knowing subject, usually described as "Western man." Deconstruction can be a powerful political practice when it addresses the aporias of subjectivity as well as objectivity, including that of the would-be deconstructive reader who disguises his agency through personification, resituating himself as a transcendental subject of knowledge by pretending to allow the tropes to "speak for themselves." When man as reading/writing/knowing subject is called into question through an analysis of his troping of the world, so is phallogocentrism, the system in which he is reproduced as transcendent identity. The best Derridean analyses accomplish this "soliciting" or shaking of the phallogocentrism of the symbolic.

It is phallogocentrism that feminists, too, would undermine. Given deconstruction's potential utility for and interest in critiquing the patriarchal symbolic, it is not surprising that feminists have employed it in their critical

practice. In fact, though he has been critical of feminism, Derrida has at times
suggested that the link between deconstruction and feminism is strong.[70]
Deconstruction challenges hierarchical and oppositional logic, revealing all
identities to be fictions of the discourse in which they have been constituted.
As Spivak says, "The useful part of deconstruction is the suggestion that the
subject is always centered.[71] Deconstruction is committed to antiessentialism
as a way of disclosing and disturbing that centering. Given that one binary
pair that it can be used to trouble is masculinity/femininity its appeal for feminists is obvious. Proper identities are associated with the name of the father,
the patronymic. Woman, having no name or signifier of her own, is that difference between father and son that does not signify and yet disrupts the perfect—deathly—repetition of the same. Through woman, man sees himself as
a (phallic) whole, and seeing through her, he cannot see her difference;
instead, she is perceived as his negative alter ego or complement. Yet man's
alienation from the image she mirrors back to him is threatening. He does not
perfectly coincide with his (better) self but is different, a difference the feminine other is made to represent. She is difference so that he may be the same,
an impossible and therefore anxiety-provoking equation, since it is through
her that he would be "himself." Because woman poses a threat to the western
notion of identity, she also poses a threat to the epistemology it grounds (and
which in turn grounds it): patriarchal rationality. Deconstructive readings
demonstrate man's self-difference so as to trouble his illusory self-identity and
the phallogocentric symbolic it sustains, including his foundational truths and
ways of knowing. It can be no surprise that one of the names Derrida gives to
such troubling self-difference is *woman.*

However, it is only one term in a series of Derridean signifiers for self-
difference, perhaps the best known of which is *différance.* Derrida coined that
neologism to suggest both the idea of differing (a spatial relation between
signifiers and their paradigmatic sets) and deferring (a temporal, syntagmatic
relation between signifiers).[72] Différance deconstructs the structuralist opposition between synchrony (structure and meaning as static) and diachrony
(structure and meaning as changing through time). It ensures that the signifier "plays" in a potentially endless "game" of substitution or displacement,
one signifier for another, each bearing the *trace* of the others, without mind-
ing its "proper" business and fixing a final signified: a meaning, truth, name,
or identity. The spacing/timing of différance undoes the difference of binary
oppositions, revealing them to be in process. Différance, Derrida writes,
"could be said to designate the productive and primordial constituting
causality, the process of scission and division whose differings and differences
would be the constituted products or effects" ("Differance," 137). Sexual
identities, like all identities for Derrida, are characterized by différance and

undecidability, with woman in particular linked to that instability. Woman represents difference; man, therefore, experiences his self-difference through femininity.

Derrida makes this point through readings of Freud and Lacan (among others), since in their work woman functions as a symptom of man. For Freud, femininity signifies the difficulty of sexual difference because it is the site of its own hysteric failure. He believes woman is more bisexual than man, as a number of his feminist commentators have pointed out.[73] Both sexes have difficulty with castration, assigned to woman, and with passivity, "presented for them [women] constitutionally and imposed upon them socially," according to Freud.[74] The Freudian libido is in effect masculine because it resists expression in passive rather than active aims; as Freud explains, "More constraint has been applied . . . when it is pressed into the service of the feminine function."[75] For Lacan, too, woman signifies castration. Although he insists both sexes are symbolically castrated, he does not completely distinguish the penis from the phallus, imaginary from symbolic castration. Woman is only a phallic fantasy of castration or its opposite; there is no signifier of her difference. However, in the seminar *Encore*, Lacan says woman also exceeds the alterity arising from her relation to the phallic function (as neither having nor being the phallus).[76] She is "not all" in the phallic: she signifies phallic lack, but she also has access to a non–phallic, supplementary *jouissance* outside the symbolic and representation. Derrida does not address this more radical alterity theorized by Lacan, concentrating instead on the role of woman's castration for psychoanalysis in the production of sexual identity.

Woman figures self-difference for Derrida not because of the psychic rejection of woman's castration and passivity but because of a lack of essence that he argues is expressed in fetishism. "And what I try to say particularly in *Spurs* is that woman has no essence of her very own, and that that's the phallocentric gesture. It's the gesture of considering that there is 'la femme' and that she has her very own essence, " he explains in an interview.[77] Woman does not—and should not—assume her "proper" place in a gendered world; rather, she engages in a very improper dissimulation of femininity in which she should continue, miming the feminine without being feminine, putting it on (and putting man on) in order to suggest she could take it off, as several feminist theorists of mimicry have also sought to demonstrate, among them Luce Irigaray, Mary Ann Doane, Mary Russo, and Judith Butler.[78] Behind the fetishistic accoutrements of femininity (woman's "veils") there is nothing: if the mask does not express woman's "truth" or essence, it does not conceal it either, as such feminists as Susan Brownmiller have argued.[79] Style is the woman herself. The Derridean fetishist, unlike the fetishist of classic psychoanalysis, is not male but female—or rather, neither, since s/he seems to oscillate between the poles of sexual difference. S/he appears to play with difference, refusing to accept—or refuse—the lack or castration the symbolic would assign. All that s/he lacks for certain is an essence or identity.

In *Spurs*, Derrida elaborates on woman's fetishistic style as distance from "her" identity, a distance into which man is seduced. "The seduction of woman operates from a distance, distance is the element of its/her power," he writes. "But from this song, this charm, one must keep a distance, one must keep a distance from distance, not only, as one might believe, in order to protect oneself against this fascination, but also in order to feel it/test it."[80] This is the sort of advice men give to one another, he adds, situating as potentially masculine the enunciation of what may be only a fantasy of woman. That fantasy is fetishistic. It expresses a double attitude toward woman and the feminine which is characteristic of fetishistic disavowal, and its playing with distance and nearness, disidentification and identification, as man is seduced by and into the feminine, is typical of transvestic fetishism as defined in classical psychoanalytic theory. As analyst Otto Fenichel notes of the transvestite, "To him the fetish becomes a fetish only when brought in to relation with the person of the patient, not . . . as an object in itself."[81] According to Derrida, to know/test women's charms man must be at a distance from them, yet this distance fails: "Distance is necessary . . . it is necessary to keep one's distance . . . which we lack, what we fail to do. . . ."[82] The transvestistic fetishist cannot maintain the desirable distance, the distance necessary for masculine identity and desire. As the "feminine operation" becomes his own, man, too, "sacrifices" what he does not lack, the phallic signifier as fetish or "spur" to his difference from—and mastery of—woman's otherness. The woman's nonidentity seduces him into the loss of his own: he oscillates between fetishistic disidentification and transvestistic identification.

Woman's adornments, particularly her veils, are crucial for this effect, though if Derrida doesn't detail these as leather, rubber, or the sexual paraphernalia—as others, such as Anne McClintock or Lorraine Gamman and Merja Makinen do in their discussions of female fetishism—it is because he is addressing fetishism as a psychic structure associated with phallogocentric man and not as a set of relatively fixed symptoms or signs.[83] They mask the lack of the truth of femininity or femininity as the truth of castration, signifying that the "fact" of castration is neither true nor false but undecidable. "The feminine distance abstracts truth from itself in a suspension of the relation with castration," Derrida asserts.[84] Woman does not believe in "her" castration, the truth her veils seem to hide from man. But if woman is not lack, neither is she not lacking, since that "is the masculine concern, the concern of the male who is never sufficiently skeptical or dissimulating," according to Derrida.[85] Woman does not believe in castration or its opposite, anticastration. Derrida insists that a reversal "would only deprive her of her powers of simulation . . . [and] would, return her, in truth, to the same. . . ."[86] Inversion of the binary opposition masculine/feminine, having or lacking the phallus, reinscribes woman in the regime of truth, which is phallogocentric. Because she knows this, Derrida says, woman plays with "her" castration, miming its effect, her identity. For, as Derrida notes, woman has been the allegory of truth, though she does not believe it herself. "And she is woman precisely because she herself does not believe in truth itself, because she does not believe in what she is, in what she is believed to be, in what she thus is not, " he writes.[87]

Truth is a fetish in that it enables the disavowal of the absence of the real in the signifier. Truth is not "Truth." The literal is always already figurative because language cannot transparently reflect reality and has no metonymic or existential link to it; rather, language substitutes for it as a metaphor does for its tenor, thereby constituting and not simply reflecting reality. Truth is a surface, the play of signification rather than the referent it would re-present for us, just as style is the woman herself. The fetishistic play of veils and adornments is the truth of woman because the naked truth about her cannot be unveiled by stripping away man's "rhetoric," as the feminist hermeneutist believes. Paradoxically, Derrida "unveils" for us the fetishism of our attitude toward representation by fetishizing the woman and her veils. Signs, like women, are fetishes. The way they work might be expressed in the kernel sentence of the fetishistic fantasy as Octave Mannoni has described it: "Je sais bien, mais quand même"; we know our representations are not "the real thing," but just the same. . . .[88] We disavow the lack of the real in them, as Christian Metz has demonstrated in cinematic spectatorship, but only when they "work" for us, seducing us into a belief in (their) realism.[89] If we "see through" them, they do not function as fetishes at all.

For Derrida, fetishism is the nexus of discourses of gender and representation, discourses of identity in the broad sense. He would use man's fetishism to undo representation's fetishism and, therefore, its effects, including man himself. Derrida plays on and exacerbates the confusion of fetish and fetishist in several passages about woman's displacement of the distance/nearness binarism in order to deconstruct man's identity. Both man and woman participate in the fetishistic feminine operation, according to Derrida. Nevertheless, he tropes that operation as feminine. If man differs from himself it is because woman differs from herself and figures for him the knowledge of his own otherness. He knows his self-difference through what he represents as her self-difference, her seductive and self-distancing dissimulation of an identity. Because it is "her" self-difference, however, woman's femininity might also guarantee man's masculinity. Fetishistic disavowal is double, both knowledge and ignorance. Man is of two minds about the truth of her castration and, therefore, his.

Man is also of two minds about the truth of Truth, which Derrida has represented not as the traditional allegorical figure of a naked virgin (truth as unveiling, *aletheia*) but as a female impersonator swathed in veils with which she fetishistically plays.[90] Derrida's woman is both the subject and object of fetishism, seducing man into the sexual undecidability she signifies. His deconstruction of the gender binarism is effected through hers. Woman's style is a writing of the body said to dispossess both genders of self-possession, of style as authorial *property*, the expression of an essence or identity, whether biological or psychic. She disrupts the functioning of the phallus for man and for herself as she (dis)places them beyond an economy of truth and/as castration and into sexual *différance*. Derrida writes his desire for such a decentered, polysexual (non) identity through the figure of a woman who is fetishized as fetishistic: his style becomes hers before it can be reappropriated as his again. In an interview with Verena Andermatt Conley in which he discusses writing polysexual desire, Derrida says, "The style does not come back to me, it makes me come to myself from the other. Let us say that this is my sexual difference."[91]

Man expropriates his "proper" style by appropriating woman's improper style, which deconstructs the proper, property, and propriation, the transcendental grounds of a patriarchal symbolic. Man cannot "have" woman, fix her as his property, make her reflect his identity back to him. For, as Spivak points out in a review article on *Spurs*, woman can fake an orgasm. "Women," she writes, "'acting out' their pleasure in the orgasmic moment, can cite themselves in their very self-presence. It as if the woman is quotation marks and vice versa. If men think they have or possess women in sexual mastery, they should be reminded that, by this logic, women can destroy the proper roles of master and slave. Men cannot know when they are properly in possession of them as masters (knowing them carnally in their pleasure) and when in their possession as slaves (duped by their self-citation in a fake orgasm). Woman makes propriation . . . undecidable."[92] Rather than giving herself, woman "gives herself for" and fakes it. Through her citational strategy, she suspends "truth," "identity," and "property."[93] Her mimicry undoes the possessor/possessed binary opposition, even as she circulates in the gift exchanges of patriarchal society; for woman and truth are not property, but gifts, according to Derrida, and as gifts they have no inherent meaning, essence, or identity from which those who give or get them could profit. The gift is "aneconomic" in that "it opens the circle so as to defy reciprocity or symmetry, the common measure, and so as to turn aside the return in view of the no-return," Derrida explains.[94] Paradoxically, if the gift is recognized as a gift, if there are benefactors and beneficiaries, then there is not the gift but economy as profitable speculation, which is why the gift is a figure of the impossible. In *Spurs*, Friedrich Nietzsche's womanly style is one such undecidable gift, as would be that of *Spurs* itself. Both play with meaning, rather than fixing some "truth," and so "remain indefinitely open, cryptic and parodying."[95] Derrida says that the determination of meaning is a political act, rather than a simple unveiling of truth. "It is we who have been entrusted with the responsibility of the signature of the other's text which we have inherited, " he writes, adding "the signature is not only a word or a proper name at the end of a text, but the operation as a whole, the text as a whole, the whole of the active interpretation. . . . It is in this respect that we have a political responsibility."[96] Because the "stylate practice" of the feminine is the gift that can undermine a phallogocentric epistemology and phallogocentric identities, Derrida would give his readers woman, rather than the present-absent phallus as woman's castration in what Derrida regards as the specular economy of psychoanalysis.[97]

Spurs continues the critique of the phallogocentrism of psychoanalytic theory articulated in a number of essays, the best known of which may be "Le Facteur de la Vérité," published just three years earlier, a reading of Lacan's seminar on Poe's "The Purloined Letter." In that seminar, Derrida asserts, woman becomes "the figure of castration *and* of truth. Of castration as truth. Which above all does not mean, as one might tend to believe, to truth as essential dislocation and irreducible fragmentation. Castration-truth, on the contrary, is that which contracts itself . . . in order to bring the phallus, the signifier, the letter, or the fetish back into their *oikos* [home], their familiar dwelling, their proper place."[98] Not a gift that disseminates, the phallus instead inseminates with its truth of a lack that exacts restitution most properly from woman. In psychoanalytic theory, man accrues a certain phallic surplus value from his exchanges of or with women, whereas "dissemination figures that which *cannot be* the Father's," Derrida asserts in an interview that predates "Le Facteur de la Vérité" but anticipates many of its arguments. "To write—dissemination: is this not to take into account castration . . . by once more putting at stake its position as a signified or transcendental signifier (for there can also be a transcendental signifier, for example the phallus as the correlate of a primary signified, castration, and the mother's desire), the ultimate recourse of all textuality, the central truth, or truth in the last analysis . . . ?" Derrida asks rhetorically (it calls for an affirmative answer).[99] As Derrida sees it, in the end, that is what Lacan is saying. Derrida thus finds exemplary the literary misquotation literally at the end of Lacan's seminar, in which Lacan slips up and writes "destination" *(destin)* instead of "plan" *(dessein)*. For Derrida this demonstrates Lacan's commitment to closure à la lettre: the letter or signifier always arrives at its destination, a final meaning or signified truth, an identity that negates and sublates what Derrida sometimes calls *destinerrance*—the divisions, diversions, divergences, and *différance* though which the signifier plays without end or transcendent telos.

In a brilliant reading of Derrida's reading of Lacan's reading of Poe, however, Barbara Johnson demonstrates that reading and writing are as endless for Lacan as for Derrida. "When Derrida says that a letter can miss its destination and be disseminated, he reads 'destination' as a place that preexists the letter's movement. But if, as Lacan shows, the letter's destination is not its literal addressee, nor even whoever possesses it, but whoever is possessed by it, then the very disagreement over the meaning of 'reaching the destination' is an *illustration* of the nonobjective nature of that 'destination,'" she concludes.[100] She even wonders if they might not be saying the same thing— which would seem to follow from the evidence she discovers of a repetition compulsion, with Derrida doing what he accuses Lacan of doing, which is also what the characters in Poe's story do. Each tries to right a wrong, Johnson suggests, only to repeat it, albeit not exactly, since it "becomes the new injustice" (Lacan's to Poe's textuality and to woman, Derrida's to Lacan's textuality and to psychoanalytic theory, but also, as I will argue, to woman).[101] They engage in what she terms "blank-filling," which conjures at once fixing the truth or meaning of the text by arresting the play of the signifier in a final signified, and making restitution to woman by returning her purloined letter (whether the Lacanian lack of the phallic signifier or the Derridean fetish style of the disseminating letter that veils that lack).[102] Johnson shows that Lacan's prose is not as decidable as Derrida argues, and that Derrida, the would-be champion of undecidability, tries repeatedly to close down the play of the Lacanian signifier. Ironically, as she points out, though time and again Derrida has insisted truth is nothing but its veils, style, and simulations, rather than some higher-order Idea that can be unveiled in an *aletheia*, he complains in this essay that Lacan's language is dissimulating and can be stripped of its deceptive style to reveal its truth: "Lacan's 'style,' moreover, was such that for a long time it would hinder and delay all access to a *unique* content or a single unequivocal meaning determinable beyond the writing itself."[103] Thus Johnson concludes, "If at first it seemed possible to say that Derrida was opposing the unsystematizable to the systematized, 'chance' to psychoanalytical 'determinism,' or the 'undecidable' to the 'destination,' the positions of these oppositions now seem reversed." She adds, "Lacan's apparently unequivocal ending says only its own dissemination, while 'dissemination' has erected itself into a kind of 'last word'. . . . 'Undecidability' can no more be used as a last word than 'destination.'"[104]

As Spivak reminds us, responsibility annuls the call to which it seeks to respond. Nevertheless, she insists we must calculate which is the least grave of these failures.[105] Johnson finds more than the injustice in the name of justice which is the effect of encountering the impossibility of responsibility; she discovers the repetition of another, perhaps more unjust and violent doubling: the rivalry and aggression of the imaginary relation that can be linked to what Spivak describes as the "ethical alibi" for the desire to punish outlined by Nietzsche in *The Genealogy of Morals*.[106] The men in Poe's story, Lacan, and Derrida engage in what Johnson terms "one-upmanship" motivated by the wish for revenge for a wrong done them (whether real or imagined), and not simply for a wrong done another, woman. "Correction must thus posit a previous pretextual, pre-textual crime that will justify its excesses . . . ," Johnson notes, pointing out that Derrida has complained of Lacan's aggression in a long footnote in the interview which antedates but anticipates "Le Facteur de la Vérité"—and he airs this complaint again in a more recent essay uncannily like that footnote in structure and substance.[107]

One result of this, as in *Men in Feminism*, is that woman becomes an object of exchange between male rivals anxious about "lack," though at issue here, ostensibly at least, is the woman's potential "lack," rather than the men's. Irigaray makes a similar point in her discussion in "Belief Itself" of Derrida's reading in *The Post Card* of Freud on the death drive, while marking her own repetition compulsion with respect to Derrida in the title of her essay, which recalls Derrida's theories of belief, faith, and speculation. "The son merely listens to the father's game . . . takes the measure of the father's game, intends to take him by surprise," Irigaray asserts. "He is not encountering *her* but the father who encounters her. . . . By this retroaction the son gives himself or gives himself back, with or without her, a *face* that can be present, rediscovered, behind the father's back."[108] As Johnson explains, "The reader is comprehended by the letter: there is no place from which he can stand back and observe it. . . . The opposition between the 'phallus' and 'dissemination' is not between two theoretical objects but between two interested positions."[109] Men (and women) meet in language; there is no metalanguage purged of the violence of the letter, the drive to mastery, and the transferential interests of exchange. Yet they are subverted in an instant by an effect of lack, a catachresis as paradoxical as *différance*, woman, the gift, or responsibility. Lack makes both separation and joining traumatic because we cannot get things right with the Other; something always goes awry despite our calculations. Responsibility annuls the call to which it seeks to respond; nevertheless, there is the gift; we might even call it the gift of lack. Placeless, lack displaces; possessed by it, one is dispossessed of having, mastery, and self-interest. Thus framed, Johnson's Derridean quotation, "lack has no place of its own in dissemination," becomes its uncanny double, with a Lacanian meaning

Derrida cannot have intended (and yet, he has proclaimed it a "a formula to be read however one wishes"): lack can turn up anywhere in dissemination because it is nothing other than the letter and its violent effects on those who arrest its errancy, whether righting its wrongs or repeating them.[110]

Can we be surprised, then, to find Lacanian theorist Slavoj Žižek complaining about poststructuralism, whose exemplar for him is Derrida, in almost the same terms in which Derrida griped about Lacan more than a decade and a half earlier? Critiquing the critique of the theory of the phallic signifier as the signifier of lack, Žižek asks in an interlude between one of his many apparent digressions into jokes or summaries of short stories or films, "How can one not recognize, in the passionate zeal with which the post-structuralist insists that every text, his own included, is caught in a fundamental ambiguity and flooded with the 'dissemination' of the inter-texual process, the signs of an obstinate *denial* . . . a barely hidden acknowledgement of the fact that one is speaking from a safe position, a position not menaced by the decentered textual process?" Answering what was evidently a rhetorical question, he asserts, "The whole effort to write 'poetically,' to make us feel how our own text is already caught in a decentered network of plural processes and how this textual process always subverts what we 'intended to say' . . . masks the annoying fact that at the root of what post-structuralists are saying there is a clearly defined theoretical position which can be articulated without difficulty in a pure and simple metalanguage."[111] Once again, blanks are filled; a wrong is righted as another wrong; rivalry, mastery, and interest intervene in the response to the call—or "poetry"—of the Other. The purloined letter returns to dispossess critical self-possession and profitable speculation, out-distancing the subject's distance from his object, as Derrida might put it, expropriating the appropriator and preserving something of the Other's difference as what exceeds our calculations, refuses our demands, and leaves unsatisfied our desires.

The Derridean fetishist is like Nietzsche; a man identifying with woman and taking her as his object choice, he affirms the other in himself through the dissimulating woman, who "affirms herself, in herself *and in man.*"[112] The female fetishist as a figure of man's self-difference is a masculine fetish, yet Derrida endows her with a Nietzschean will of her own: she *affirms herself, in herself,* as well as in man. His sexual difference must be hers, too. Derrida makes his fetish woman complicit with his desire, even the source of it, since he claims he identifies with her desire. But a fetish is fundamentally inanimate, a construction with no life or desires of its own, as the etymology of the word suggests: it is adapted from the Portuguese *feitiço,* meaning "charm or sorcery," a substitute use of the adjective *feitiço,* "made by art, artificially, skillfully contrived," for African amulets (the adjective itself derives from the Latin *factitius*, "made by art," from *facere*, "to make, do").[113] Even the fetish's seductive qualities are not "proper" to it, as is clear from the example with which Freud opens his essay on fetishism. The "shine on the nose" that Freud's patient "exalted" in certain women was subjective, the effect of his desires rather than theirs. According to Freud, it is quite literally a discursive construct, an effect of the agency of the letter in the unconscious of the young man, who had been brought up in an English nursery before he moved to Germany and "almost completely" forgot his mother tongue: "The fetish," he writes, "which derived from his earliest childhood, had to be deciphered into English, not German; the *Glanz auf der Nase* [shine on the nose] was really "a glance at the nose;" the nose was thus the fetish, which, by the way, he endowed when he wished with the necessary special brilliance, which other people could not perceive."[114]

Derrida's fetish woman, brilliantly disavowing castration, is endowed with his own disavowal of castration, animated by it like Olympia, the "automatic doll" with which the hero is obsessed in "The Sand-Man," the E. T. A. Hoffman tale Freud discusses in "The 'Uncanny.'"[115] Nathaniel's love for her is blind because her eyes are really his, stolen by the castrating Sand-Man when he was just a child. Like Nathaniel, Derrida is fascinated by his vision of and in woman, seduced by his double, who seems to satisfy his desire for her desire to disavow castration. She is the imaginary feminine other in whom man would see himself as whole because her desire complements his, substituting fetishistic disavowal for hysteria (although desiring the other's desire is a symptom of hysteric identification, suggesting that the Derridean fetishist is also a hysteric—a hysteric who desires a fetishistic desire).[116] As such, she has little to do with "real" women, which is why she can be a gift even for Derrida's women (feminist) readers.

The disjunction between this woman and those who circulate in the world as women has led many feminists to view deconstruction with suspicion; as Culler has noted, they "are rightly disturbed that in this deconstructive paleonomy 'woman' may no longer refer to actual human beings. . . ."[117] For Derrida, femininity signifies self-difference; it is really an "arche-femininity," like the "arche-writing" he discusses in *Of Grammatology*.[118] The feminine (and what is metonymically linked to it—woman, the hymen, invagination) is to be located in a series of concepts like writing and *différance* that deconstruct the logic of identities. They "no longer simply designate figures for the feminine body," just as writing no longer means the same thing when it is used to displace the opposition between speech and writing.[119] In deconstruction old terms are retained, yet changed. As Derrida explains in *Positions*, that double gesture includes first a reversal, so that the hierarchy of terms in a crucial binary opposition is overturned, and then a displacement of the difference between those terms by means of that reversal. He emphasizes that both stages are indispensable, writing, "To overlook this phase of overturning is to forget the conflictual and subordinating structure of opposition. Therefore one might proceed too quickly to a neutralization that in practice would leave the previous field untouched, leaving one no hold on the previous opposition, thereby preventing any means of intervening in the field effectively. We know what always have been the practical (particularly political) effects of immediately jumping beyond oppositions, and of protests in the simple form of neither this nor that."[120] On the other hand, privileging reversal without displacement is "simply residing within the closed field of these oppositions," thus confirming the phallogocentrism which they sustain.[121] By demonstrating that what has been devalued always already inhabits what has been overvalued, deconstruction seeks to undermine the truth and identity effects of a discourse.

Woman, writing, simulacrum are not, strictly speaking, equivalent to the devalued terms of a hierarchical opposition; rather, each is also the difference between that and the dominant term, the undifferentiated matrix or *différance* out of which differences arise through a suppression of the doubling and division of that origin. Such concepts figure what "can no longer be included within philosophical (binary) opposition, but which, however, inhabit philosophical opposition, resisting and disorganizing it, without ever constituting a third term," a Hegelian synthesis or sublation of difference into a higher unity.[122] Their deconstructive force comes from their proximity to the devalued term, from which they can never finally be distinct, so that their deployment has the power of a reversal even as they are resignified in order to effect a displacement, rather than a mere inversion, of a binary opposition. "There is one meaning to the word 'woman' which is caught in the opposition, in the couple, and to this extent you can use the force of woman to reverse, to undermine this first stage of opposition," Derrida writes. "Once you have succeeded, the word 'woman' does not have the same meaning. Perhaps we could not even speak of 'woman' anymore."[123]

Like undecidability, woman is only a space holder—a fetish—for what would be completely other and, therefore, unrepresentable in dialectical logic, what Derrida calls "polysexuality," a sexuality not "immured in the figure two" that "arrest[s] desire at the wall of opposition."[124] However, as long as there is no outside to the system, as long as its outside is inside it as its necessary other (as woman is man's self-difference), it must be deconstructed from within. The system makes terms available that can be appropriated, revalorized, and resignified in order to subvert the structure of binary oppositions in which they appear; they make the difference that can unsettle difference. Thus "woman" (self-difference) displaces woman (difference), which displaces women, "the real, historical beings and social subjects who are defined by the technology of gender and actually engendered in social relations," according to Teresa de Lauretis.[125] This is the path traced by man on his self-resistant way to polysexuality, a Derridean "trace" without a trace of real women, as many feminists have complained.[126] For Derrida's "woman" is more "arche-feminine" than feminine, more "feminine" than a real woman, and spoken of and by a fetishistic transvestite, a "woman"—identified man who desires to escape sexual difference in undecidability and polysexuality.

"How does the feminine as the 'dark side' of Western theoretical discourse relate to the speech, the intelligence, and the discursivity of real-life women?" Rosi Braidotti wonders. "And if it does not relate to it at all, what is its value for feminism?"[127] The recall of the "real" as the excluded or appropriated in Derridean woman is a rejoinder to a responsibility that annuls the call to which it seeks to respond. Each encounter with alterity is less than satisfying; the connection with the other impossible, unjust; the trauma of lack and insufficiency in object relations repeats as the subject confronts the enigmatic signifiers of the other's desire in the call. What does she want? Inevitably, there is violence in the writing of self and other that constitutes an answer, as Johnson shows in Derrida's representation of Lacan and woman, and as Irigaray shows in his representation of Freud and woman. That violence structures Derrida's writing and reading of Nietzsche, Heidegger, and woman in *Spurs*. "Even the strongest personal good will on Derrida's part cannot turn him quite free of the massive enclosure of the male appropriation of woman's voice," Spivak asserts, having argued that "female personhood" cannot be entirely excluded from Derrida's "female element" as he "might insist."[128] In *Spurs* and elsewhere Derrida claims that he can occupy a feminine position by writing himself into one, as when, in response to a question from Peggy Kamuf about writing from the feminine, he says, "[I]f we consider for example what is called a writing man—for example me, to the extent that I'm supposed to be a man—then writing on woman should be less writing on woman than writing from or on the basis of . . . what comes to me from a feminine place."[129] Derrida signals his interest in the enunciation and not just the utterance of the feminine, speaking as, not just about, woman. Spivak notes that of all the names he has given to undecidability, woman is unique because "she can occupy both positions in the subject-object oscillation."[130] By arguing that writing style produces gender style, displacing the opposition between metaphorical and real bodies, however, Derrida demonstrates he believes what Spivak says is impossible: that he can become a woman at the stroke of a word.[131]

In *Spurs*, that word is *hermaphroditic;* as a modifier for *phallus* or *spur* (the phallic signifier) it seems to perform what some feminists see as risk-free transsexual surgery. The tail of Derrida's text is the fetish example of the umbrella, a signifier for the undecidability of the Nietzschean text as woman which is in both a metaphoric and a metonymic relation to the Derridean writing about it. According to Derrida, examples produce a signature effect; they reflect something of the subject who chose them.[132] The umbrella signifies textual/sexual indeterminacy because it is double, at once folded and unfolded, phallic and femininely veiled. The umbrella is a phallic symbol, Derrida says, like "the hermaphroditic spur of a phallus modestly enfolded in its veils, an organ at once aggressive and apotropaic, menacing and menaced."[133] An umbrella can be turned inside out; Derrida insists the phallus, too, can be invaginated, a claim he repeats in his reading of the fetish example of the shoes in a Van Gogh painting discussed by Heidegger and Meyer Schapiro. "Like a glove turned inside out," he writes, each shoe sometimes has "the convex 'form' of the foot (penis) and sometimes the concave form enveloping the foot (vagina)."[134]

This is aggressively antiessentialist: it would not seem the phallus could make its possessor feminine and undecidable, yet Derrida turns that signifier of having into a signifier of lack. Just as such feminists as Irigaray and Hélène Cixous reclaim the signs of feminine lack as signs of a feminine specificity in order to be able to speak as feminine subjects, Derrida reclaims the sign of masculine power and privilege as a sign of lack so he too can speak as woman. His deconstructive reconstruction of the feminine has an uncanny resemblance to theirs, even as his deconstructive reconstruction of the masculine does not. Irigaray and Cixous speak from the either/or of sexual difference but fill feminine lack with meanings incompatible with the function of mirroring or complementing man, resistant to appropriation for his self project as imaginary ego-fortress. Derrida speaks from a sexual difference signified by the neither/nor of sexual différance that is also a both/and and therefore a neuter totality all too like the phallocentric masculine he would critique. In determining the least grave complicity with the metaphysical, Derrida has done what he warned might reinscribe a binary hierarchy: rushing too quickly to the displacement of sexual difference that must succeed the reversal of its oppositional terms. If Irigaray and Cixous risk essentialism and the reinscription of women in the same old place of lack without a difference, Derrida "risks" an antiessentialism that may resituate him in the same old place of having (the phallus and the power and privilege it can bring) without a difference.[135] Derrida's transsexual surgery is reversible, its effects as undecidable as the phallus/sheath opposition. A certain vatic authority accrues to the subject with such sexual property. He can speak as both man and woman, lacking nothing—not even lack. The phallic sheath is therefore a condom, providing protection from contact with the feminine as a position within sexual difference, rather than beyond or before it in sexual différance.

Sarah Kofman points out that Derrida's bicolumnar, double writing in *Glas* and elsewhere may be a strategy of mastery rather than a reflection of division and difference in a discourse unable to unify self and other.[136] Double-voiced hermaphroditic writing also may be a strategy of mastery. Traditionally, the disembodied voice has been the voice of authority in documentaries; it is represented by the speech of a white, middle-class man with a "neutral" non-accent.[137] Even when that voice is embodied in a visible commentator, it still pretends to be a universal point of view speaking the impartial truth, rather than a particular perspective arising out of limited interests and desires. In newscasts, it has been quite literally a talking head, the body hidden behind a desk and within the sack suit of the businessman. Avant-garde documentary filmmakers have suggested that embodying the voice of "truth" could crack its neuter and neutral persona, revealing its limitations, including its pretense to absolute knowledge.[138] Feminists, too, have insisted on embodying the truth, not only revealing the desiring masculinity behind patriarchal representations that have masqueraded as the truth about women and the world, but also revealing the body behind their own words, locating them in the specific experiences and desires of the woman who enunciates them. This is to dephallicize the operations of phallic power, according to Jane Gallop, revealing phallic imposture to be an imposture.[139]

Derrida's hermaphroditic body, and the strongly cathected metaphor for it which is the fetish umbrella unveiling the invaginating phallus, does away with limitations altogether. His "transsexual" subject recalls the fetishistic worship of the hermaphrodite as a god possessing special powers.[140] Derrida reifies the upright speech of undecidability his fantasmatic part object enables. He risks no metonymic contamination with limitation, partiality and specificity, as he might have done had he claimed the anal "hymen" as the masculine marker of lack/femininity, a privileging of which could signify homosexuality, as Alice Jardine has noted, or had he elaborated circumcision as a figure of castration, as he has done elsewhere.[141] Instead, he arrogates to himself the phallic privilege of marking the other as lacking, in need of advice. He knows what is best for women, he claims, and it is not feminism because "feminism is nothing but the operation of a woman who aspires to be like a man."[142] Derrida, like Nietzsche, identifies with the better woman, the one with style, who does not believe in woman's essence, whether it is conceived to be the same as man's or different (anti-castration or castration). He becomes the affirmative woman who does not stop at the second stage of deconstruction but displaces the gender binarism after reversing it rendering it undecidable infemale fetishism.

As a fetishistic transvestite, however, he disavows sexual difference, elimi-
nating the risk of an ethical decision when confronting alterity through a program of "perversion" calculated to secure the jouissance of the Other, with
whom he identifies as phallic woman. He is "horsexe," *outsidesex*, as Lacanian
analyst Catherine Millot says of those transsexuals who would be both sexes
or neither by incarnating the phallus.[143] They thereby seek to escape the limitation, difference, and division of having a sex and the envy, jealousy, and
other lacking and desiring emotions that sexed subjects feel—and in so doing
would give up their access to what Lacan terms *masquerade*, the element of
deception in gender performances arising from the distance sexed subjects
take toward them. Millot contrasts such transsexuals with those who are inside
the sexed symbolic and therefore desiring men and women with a symbolic,
discursive identity at odds with their psychic sexual identity. While the latter
can benefit from surgery and hormone therapy as potentially traumatic alter-
ations of the body, the former might experience a psychotic break as a result.
She argues that their particular transgender psychic structure is sometimes
stable only as long as the medical establishment does not collaborate with
their desire to be an exception to the law of sexual difference, *The Woman* or
the Primal Father, (of Freud's *Totem and Taboo*), who experience a nonphallic
jouissance prohibited by the law.[144]

Some lesbian, gay, and feminist theorists share with psychoanalytic critics
a suspicion of a queer or transgender position defined as beyond sexual difference and expressed through conscious gender alternations or other "play."
They are critical of both the voluntarism such theories presume and the
implication that there is an "I" before gender acts, unmarked by sexual difference and therefore whole, rather than divided, and neuter; such a subject
is inevitably masculine in patriarchal culture. Bernice Hausman, for example,
points out that transsexual performance artist, theorist, and activist Kate
Bornstein's promotion of consensual gender play assumes complete self
determination and mastery.[145] Pat Califia argues that gender is more than a
prison and that Bornstein would not call for the elimination of race as the
solution to racism.[146] She worries that transgender advocacy of the dissolution of gender will precipitate new "sex wars" like those which in the past
have divided the feminist community over butch-femme and other sexual
role playing.[147] Biddy Martin is critical of what she sees as queer theory's
desire to transcend gender as an identity it constructs only as confinement
rather than creative possibility. She finds that femininity in particular is
demonized as the narrow alternative to queer sexual liberation. While Lee
Edelman praises queer theory for being "utopic in its negativity," describing
it as "a force of derealization, of dissolution into the fluxions of a subjectless
desire," Martin critiques just that, asserting, "In some queer work, the very

fact of attachment has been cast as only punitive and constraining because already socially constructed, so that indifference to objects, or the assumption of a position beyond objects—the position for instance of death— becomes the putative achievement or goal of queer theory."[148]

As Kaja Silverman reminds us, desire at the level of the unconscious primary processes of unbinding and metonymic sliding is in Lacan's words, "acephalic," without a self or ego, "the desire for nothing," a pure death drive.[149] "At the deepest recesses of its psyche the subject has neither identity nor nameable desire," she writes, but qualifies that, adding that at the level of the lived expression of desire in the fantasy structuring object relations, "the fantasmatic and the *moi* [ego] together work to articulate a determining vision of each, a placement of the subject."[150] The death drive is always fused with the binding and appropriating force of eros, according to Freud; in Lacanian terms, the ego cathects love objects modeled after itself, in which it sees itself idealized, even as the death drive dissolves and renews those relationships.[151] "The object relation must always submit to the narcissistic framework and be inscribed in it," Lacan says.[152] Or as Derrida writes, "I believe that without a movement of narcissistic reappropriation, the relation to the other would be absolutely destroyed, it would be destroyed in advance."[153] The subject is always centered, and at the expense of the other. (Were it otherwise, there could be no subject responsible to the other's call she will have annulled; responsibility and the subject are exactly this double bind.) Nevertheless, as Stuart Hall points out, Derrida often privileges dissemination over "the cut of identity" as a positioning within and through meaning, thereby sacrificing specificity.[154] In *Spurs*, his fetishistic transvestistic mimicry of the feminine "says" différance but performs identity. Through his style, Derrida becomes the phallic woman, not the father but the phallic mother of a critical practice under which feminism would be subsumed, as he wields phallic power over the women and men he *feminist-izes*.

A "maverick" feminist like Emma Goldman, with whom he identifies in "Choreographies," Derrida would save woman from falling into phallogocentrism. Derrida has said that if you know what you want to give and to whom you want to give it, it is no longer a gift but an object of profitable exchange.[155] Clearly, Derrida wants to give the "gift" of deconstruction to feminists, who he imagines are badly in need of it. However, Derrida's gift of a cure for feminism could be poison from a feminist point of view of concern for women's voices and consciousnesses, as Frances Bartkowski has pointed out.[156] In deconstruction, woman is under erasure, silenced, absent, as man speaks of, for, and instead of her, even *as* her, once he has done away with the difference between woman as trope or signifier of excluded otherness and women as others deprived of certain rights and privileges in patriarchy. Ventriloquizing woman, polysexual man questions women's demands for those and other rights, including the right to represent themselves. Such women have failed in their feminine duty to difference, which is inextricable from serving as the instrument of male self-deconstruction. As Spivak notes, Derrida appropriates woman's voice (and other body parts, such as the hymen).[157]

For the male deconstructor as transvestic fetishist, woman is both there and not there. It seems that if feminists do not claim a specificity and speak from its place men will continue to represent women on their own behalf, as Derrida does. Feminists have urged men to think their place as men and investigate masculine subjectivity; that is frequently a strength of Derridean analysis. But Derrida's place in *Spurs* and some of the other work in which he takes up the feminine is never really put in question. He grafts on signs of difference which prove to be defenses against it, rather than an encounter with it. Paradoxically, Derrida's emasculation is a masculinization, a *Spurious* transvestism, as his representation of woman allows him to master his relation to the other, to whose call he fails to respond. The patriarch as theoretical impersonator, he substantiates Lacan's claim that the phallus plays its role best when veiled, even when swathed in tropes of femininity.

[R]ENUNCIATION: IMPERSONATION AND FEMININE SPECIFICITY

It is all too easy to demonstrate that both male feminists and antifeminists (including those whose antifeminism purports to be the best kind of feminism, like Derrida) oscillate between a sadistic and fetishistic voyeurism, in which they direct a theoretical gaze at what male and female feminists lack in order to satisfy themselves that they have it, and a fetishistic and transvestic exhibitionism, in which they solicit the gaze of the phallic other (critical father or mother) in order to lose themselves in it, identifying with the phallic ideal as whole, lacking nothing. It is all too easy and even pleasurable, which might indicate that the fantasy has a feminine as well as a masculine enunciation. If all the bees in this hive are eager to be feminists of the right stripe, they also all have stingers. Female feminists have played the dominatrix with relish, soliciting the tongue lashings gotten and given, rather than functioning as analysts by reflecting men's desires back to them. Responding to men's critical comments by returning them to their "proper" place as masculine and phallogocentric even when they purport to be critiques of phallogocentrism, we have allowed our own desires to remain unanalyzed. Chief among these is the desire to be the subjects of a critique of phallogocentrism without reproducing it, to desire differently, and so to be absolutely and essentially different from "the male subject." Feminists such as Nancy Miller have insisted we read for such differences, beginning with the signature of a text, whose importance poststructuralist theory called into question at the very moment when writing by women was being rediscovered and taken seriously.[158] Hence the confidence with which some women have asserted identities, providing a litany both of their own "subject positions," so as to "situate" or "embody" their feminist/feminine knowledges, and of those authors whose works they read.

However, the best of intentions cannot prevent such "strategic essentialism" from becoming reductive when authors' remarks are made to reflect the identities assigned them. Once feminists have been labeled *male* or *female*, readers conclude that the most significant effect of men in feminism is the reconstitution of the gender hierarchy as men tell women how to be better feminists, reconfirming the mastery of the feminine a feminist other had seemed to threaten. *Qui vive?* As a metonym of the author's anatomy, itself understood as a metaphor of the author's identity, the signature seems to answer that question clearly. Anxious to discover the truth about feminist imposters, women have sought to see through the rhetoric in which men have dressed up their claims and have fixed upon the signature, erecting it between us and the terrible vision of lack—the lack of a fixed identity and final signified as controlling authorial intention or essential expression. That fetish signature cannot quite unveil the organ of the writing body displaced by the body of writing. The violence of writing repeats as women, outdistancing their distance from men, defend themselves from the deconstructive defense of transvestic fetishism with transvestic fetishism, veiling themselves in the apotropaic signifiers of the "real."

What feminist would dare to take issue with a belief in "real-life women"? To do so is apparently to make a sacrifice more costly than that symbolic pound of flesh that women never had anyway. As Modleski argues, "I worry that the complicated belief structure [Denise] Riley and other [antiessentialist] feminists counsel us to adopt as a *female* form of disavowal (which in its Freudian version would be 'I know very well I'm not a woman, but all the same . . .') might be said not so much to counter masculine disavowal as to participate in the same phobic logic. Given that fetishistic disavowal in the male is the means by which the psyche avoids facing the fact of woman's difference, the fact of her *being* woman, the feminist anti-essentialist, with her fears of being decapitated by her 'essentialist' sisters, might be confirming the very horror that is at the root of male castration anxiety and the dread of woman."[159] Even women sympathetic to deconstruction disavow it through the "real." Diane Elam critiques the naïve appeal to experience by showing that it is a discursive construction that cannot ground women as a class, rather than a given or universal and common property.[160] Drawing on Butler's work, she also accepts the more radical argument that bodies too are discursively (and institutionally) constituted—and suggests they are deconstituted and reconstituted, not only by Derrida and Irigaray but also by transsexuals, intersexuals, and "gender blenders." Nevertheless, she is compelled to situate Derrida firmly within sexual difference, rather than différance, insisting, "If Derrida is positioned 'as a woman' in philosophy, he is still *not* a woman."[161] Her qualification of his philosophical femininity, framed by quotation marks that put it in doubt, contrasts sharply with her emphatic negative to the question of Derrida's discursively or institutionally unspecified womanliness as the predication of the sheer assertion of being through that *is*. "Woman" very definitely exists outside the *mise-en-abyme* of representation that disturbs the ontological, yet she is ineluctably "mise-en-abyme," as Elam's book's subtitle declares. Elam is split over this, of two minds about it; she disavows it.

Spivak too cannot make up her mind once and for all whether *woman* should be veiled in quotation marks, as the oscillation in her readings of Derrida's "woman" over the years suggests. If in 1983 she accuses Derrida of appropriating woman by trying to purge the "female element" of "female personhood," ten years later, in a return to *Spurs*, she reverses herself, writing, "My previous position on this essay of Derrida's was polemical. I suggested that it was not right to see woman as sign for indeterminacy. But today, negotiating, I want to give the assent *for the moment* to Derrida's argument."[162] There is something troubling in her encounter with the Derridean feminine, so much so that Spivak finds herself repeating it, torn between her responsibility to women and "woman." Failing to satisfy the claims of this double bind, she is driven to renew her efforts to do so; whatever she says about it can only be "for the moment," rather than her final word. For if the appeal to "woman" displaces the "real-life woman" so as not to foreclose the question of the referent, to retain it as a question, rather than to appropriate its difference in the predication of a (Western) "subject," when dominant feminists act in the name of that referent, they displace "other" women, whose differences and desires they too readily presume to know and satisfy in their ethico-political programs. The differences within "woman," between women, return, like the repressed, to fracture a tidy gender binarism and disrupt women's imaginary identities as the pure victims of oppression rather than oppressors of other women who disturb the familial paradigm of feminist sisterhood.[163] Spivak urges us to divide the name we would appropriate for ourselves and ask "not merely who am I? but who is the other woman? How am I naming her? How does she name me? Is this part of the problematic I discuss?"[164]

Modleski's production of Sojourner Truth as the woman in the name of

THEORETICAL IMPERSONATION

whom we must resist antiessentialism is a "fetish example" illustrative of a feminist imposture about the importance of "differences within" (her name itself seems to anticipate a Derridean problematic of truth as a temorary arrest or "sojourn" in a process of deferral and destinerrance). Commenting on the productive ambivalence of Truth's negative interrogative, "Ain't I a woman?" Modleski suggests the question invites both "yes" and "no" answers: "'yes' in terms of her 'experience,' which in some major respects reduces her to her biology—to being the white man's breeder, and 'no' in terms of an ideology based on a notion of frail white Southern woman-hood."[165] But then Modleski forecloses on the very ambivalence of the disvowals she has just praised, asserting, "It seems to me politically irresponsible for (white) feminism to refuse to grant Sojourner Truth the status of a woman for it would then be in complicity with the racist patriarchal system that [she] . . . was protesting and that has denied, and in important ways continues to deny, this status to the black female."[166] However, as Hortense Spillers has argued, black women have a different history from white women with respect to the notion of maternity—to be a breeder is not to be a mother.[167] And as Sander Gilman has shown, 19th century discourses about female genitalia distinguished those of white, middle class women from those of black women like the "Hottentot Venus," Saartje Baartman.[168] The history of biology is therefore the grounds of a sexual difference, rather than a commonality, between black and white women. Furthermore, as Deborah McDowell has pointed out, Sojourner Truth is the fetish example that white women always produce when demonstrating a concern for race and the materiality of a critique, as if to be absolved from knowing anything else about black women's history, which is also white women's history, since as a race and sex we are implicated in it as oppressors structurally, if not personally.[169] Symptomatically, race drops out of Modleski's analysis throughout much of the rest of *Feminism without Women*, which allows her to make sometimes suspect generalizations about women, such as those about women's rejection of war, to which one can assent only if all women are imagined to be white, middle class and First World.

Another other also frequently drops out of sexual difference in feminist objections to deconstructive "transsexualism"—the "real-life" hermaphrodites and transsexuals equally displaced by Derrida's "woman" with her hermaphroditic spur of an invaginating phallus, as recent intersexual, transsexual, and transgender activism might suggest to us. But again, "real life" can function apotropaically as a defense against what it excludes as it names. Transgenders too are caught up in the double bind of (in)justice from which an appeal to a real identity, the writing of an *I* or *we* with a presumptive referent, is no defense. Representations of the transgendered by the transgendered necessarily fail to meet the responsibility to the call of the other, including those "other" transsexuals or transgenders whose differences cannot be appropriated in a gesture of identification without violence. For that reason, Jacob Hale's "Suggested Rules for Non-Transsexuals Writing about Transsexuals, Transsexuality, Transsexualism, or Trans____" also must apply to transsexuals.[170] Furthermore, no such program of rules can finally enable transgenders, women, or any other collective subject to master the relation to the others in our midst, and more and different rules still will not solve the problem. As psychoanalytic feminist theorist Renata Salecl notes, paraphrasing Marxist theorist Claude Lefort, "[T]he very fact that it is impossible to determine the character of the bearer of human rights is what gives the idea of rights its critical potential," adding as a gloss a direct citation from Lefort: "their formulation contains the demand for their reformulation."[171] Undoubtedly, we are meant to catch the double meaning of "contain" in that phrase.

For Salecl, rights are a catachresis, just as the name is for Spivak. Spivak urges us to preserve the name as paradoxical "misname" by giving it to that disenfranchised other whom we cannot imagine as a reference and appropriate for our self-consolidation. She also warns us to eschew that nominalism she finds even in Derrida when in the face of the undecidable, he decides against the feminist, who he insists cannot be a name for "woman" so he can preserve that one particular name for différance.[172] Spivak reminds us that such names are selected because of their role in a history of violence: they are what displaced the unnameable suppressed in the constitution of a particular hierarchical binary difference in which they are devalorized. We must work to neutralize their deconstructive efficacy. Rights are caught up in a similar history of violence, and like particular names, misname what is desired, never quite living up to the idea of rights as an "empty universality" substituting for something which has been irrevocably lost.[173] Salecl's formulation alludes to symbolic castration, and indeed, she likens rights to the *objet a*, the "object" the subject loses when it gains itself in the separation from the phallic mother. Like the idea of rights, it is empty of particularity in that it has no embodied (imaginary) form, and like the idea of rights when realized as particular rights, its exchange between desiring subjects always leaves them wanting, no matter what particular objects they have been given.[174]

The name—like rights or the *object a*—is also an empty universality, according to Žižek, since it is the retroactive constitution of an identity beyond and before any particular descriptive features, which will change over time. It is assumed upon the passage through symbolic castration, which catalyzes the play of the signifier in the symptoms, fantasies, meanings and masquerades that would make up for it.[175] They are the multiplication arising from division, the addition supplementing the originary subtraction or separation of the (potential) subject from the mother. Lack makes possible having and all the effects of propriation and predication, including expropriation and reappropriation; indeed, it is nothing else but these effects. Given this catachrestical figuration of lack and the identity that is its effect, Rey Chow argues that the name is in effect an anti-essential essence for Žižek, who critiques both essentialism and deconstructive anti-essentialism.[176] She finds it functions as such for Spivak too, who emphasizes that the name is an enabling violation. We cannot do without it, since essentialism is irreducible in any decision about what is undecidable on the basis of which we act, but because the other nevertheless remains undecidable, absolutely different from a given name and program organized around it, naming is always already a misnaming, and benevolence is violence.[177]

Anti-essentialism brings to crisis the essentialism through which we manage our relations to alterity, whether our own or that of others. Distinguishing between "*as* or *is* a woman" in Derrida's or any other's "case," we cannot help but make the wrong decision about which difference to preserve, so we commit an injustice, the violence of the one an alibi for the violence of the other. We disavow difference through names as through fetishes, for the name, like the fetish, is only a veil thrown over a void, a style of avoiding it that nevertheless brings us back to it again. Such style is more than a conscious fashion statement, just as "strategic essentialism" is not a tactic fully within our control. Calculating with the incalculable in our programs or stratagems for avoiding risks in relations to others, we cede desire, which psychoanalysis warns against, and responsibility, which deconstruction warns against. Desire and responsibility are two names for the incalculable, the disturbance to calculation that thereby renews it.

They might even be the same name: perhaps, as Chow suggests, Žižek and Spivak are more or less saying the same thing in advocating "enthusiastic resignation" to lack and antagonism or "affirmative deconstruction" of all that we love.[178] Chow (re)names what repeats in these two formulations "ethics after idealism," a phrase that disavows the differences between Žižek and Spivak, displacing and reconciling their antagonism so that she may embrace them both—and in so doing, displacing and reconciling the antagonism between ethics and idealism also. For her "ethics after idealism" evidently cannot do without a movement of idealizing, reconciling appropriation of differences; ethics "after" idealism *takes after* idealism, mimes it, might even be its double. Chow has not transcended idealism any more than Derrida has when he insists on his difference from Lacan or from feminists. His opposition, as a negation, is caught up in the dialectic, just as is Chow's reconciliation of those two "disciples" of Derrida and Lacan, Spivak and Žižek (and so

too is Barbara Johnson's reconciliation of the masters themselves). We cannot say "no" to idealism without remaining within it; there is no outside to it,
no "after" except that which takes after it. But perhaps Derrida and Chow
represent two styles of this "after idealism," two different ways of avoiding
the void that is ethics as catachresis and impossibility. One is after idealism,
out to get it, to give as good as it gets, tit for tat; outdistancing the distance
from the other it critiques it finds itself repeating what it condemns. The
other too is after idealism, but by miming it, eschewing opposition and speculating on antitheses it reconciles by bringing them so near they are touching
what may be the limit to their difference. We might call these two ethical
styles the optic and the aptic as Derrida does—or perhaps the masculine and
the feminine.[179]

"There is not narcissism and non-narcissism; there are narcissisms that are
more or less comprehensive, generous, open, extended," Derrida asserts.[180]
Narcissism invests both eros and aggression in the ego, rather than the
Other, but never entirely, just as object-cathexes never completely displace
ego-cathexes if there is a subject. "'You' keeps me a little from death,"
Derrida says in an essay on touch (touch also has been a central trope for
Irigaray in her writing of the feminine).[181] Does one of these two styles of
ethical speculation strike a better balance between self and other? How can
we say "no" to one of them if there is to be a relation to the other?
Theoretical speculation about men in feminism or anything else must confront these questions, which in the end return us to ourselves. The call of the
Other to which we seek to respond inevitably does so, inviting critical, even
aggressive, but also loving, self-reflexive analysis, as well as writing and reading those calculating investments in the other that are the limits to calculating with the self. Ultimately, however, our position can only be determined
by triangulation, by the Other who receives our message and countersigns
our letters, responding to our call with the signifiers of her own desire as she
too speculates on identity.

NOTES

1. See Jacques Derrida, "Women in the Beehive," trans. James Adner, in *Men in
    Feminism*, ed. Alice Jardine and Paul Smith (New York: Methuen, 1987), 189–203.
2. Jane Gallop, *Thinking through the Body* (New York: Columbia University Press, 1988),
    106.
3. See Jardine and Smith, eds., *Men in Feminism*, the first of such anthologies; see also
    Engendering Men: The Question of Male Feminist Criticism, ed. Joseph Boone and
    Michael Cadden (New York: Routledge, 1990) and *Between Men and Feminism*, ed.
    David Porter (New York: Routledge, 1992). In addition, *Gender and Theory: Dialogues
    on Feminist Criticism*, ed. Linda Kauffman (New York: Basil Blackwell, Ltd., 1989)
    includes several essays in the "genre."

4. Peggy Kamuf, "Femmeninism," in Jardine and Smith, eds., *Men in Feminism*, 78–84.

5. Jacques Derrida, "Choreographies" (Interview with Christie McDonald), trans. Christie McDonald, *Diacritics* 12:2 (1992), 69.

6. Jacques Derrida, *The Ear of the Other: Otobiography, Transference, Translation*, trans. Peggy Kamuf and Avital Ronell, ed. Christie McDonald (New York: Schocken, 1985), 32; Throughout this book, Derrida is concerned with the politics of a Nietzschean philosophy.

7. In "Force and Signification," in *Writing and Difference*, trans. Alan Bass (Chicago: University of Chicago Press, 1978), Derrida aligns force with writing as the "indefinite referral of signifier to signifier" and "becoming," or progression toward the future. He opposes it to form as the fixity of meaning or structure which presumes a *telos* and simultaneity or fixing/freezing of time. The former is Dionysian, the latter Apollonian. Yet he also insists that this opposition must be deconstructed because "difference" does not belong to one or the other, to diachrony or synchrony (history or structure). Writing, finally, cannot be thoroughly Dionysian. Meaning must be "forced" through the play of the signifier, but force must also submit to meaning, a submission "in which the same can always lose (itself)" in its own self-difference (the self-sameness or identity of both force and meaning, history and structure); the citation is on 29.

8. Gayatri Chakravorty Spivak, "Responsibility." *Boundary 2* 21:3 (1994), 19.

9. Spivak repeats this in a number of places. See, for example, her *The Post-Colonial Critic: Interviews, Strategies, Dialogues*, ed. Sarah Harasym. (New York: Routledge, 1990), 136.

10. Spivak, "Responsibility," 63.

11. Gayatri Chakravorty Spivak, "French Feminism in an International Frame," *In Other Worlds: Essays in Cultural Politics*. (New York: Methuen, 1987).

12. Jacques Derrida, "'Eating Well,' or the Calculation of the Subject: An Interview with Jacques Derrida," trans. Peter Connor and Avital Ronell, in *Who Comes after the Subject?* ed. Eduardo Cadava, Peter Connor, and Jean-Luc Nancy (New York: Routledge, 1991), 108.

13. Derrida, "'Eating Well,'" 115. Fuss discusses Dahmer and Lecter in *Identification Papers* (New York: Routledge, 1995), 83–106.

14. Gayatri Chakravorty Spivak, "French Feminism Revisited," in *Outside in the Teaching Machine* (New York: Routledge, 1993), 154.

15. Spivak, "Responsibility," 25.

16. Jacques Derrida, "There Is No *One* Narcissism (Autobiophotographies)," trans. Peggy Kamuf, in *Points: Interviews, 1974–1994*, ed. Elizabeth Weber (Stanford: Stanford University Press, 1995), 199.

17. Ibid.

18. Homi K. Bhabha, "DissemiNation: Time, Narrative, and the Margins of the Modern Nation," *The Location of Culture* (London: Routledge, 1994), 147.

19. Spivak is generally credited with coining the phrase "strategic essentialism" in an interview with Elizabeth Gross (Grosz) for *Thesis Eleven*, nos. 10–11 (1984–85), which is reprinted as "Criticism, Feminism, and the Institution," in *The Post-Colonial Critic*; 11. Spivak expresses reservations about the concept in a later interview with Ellen Rooney, "In a Word: *Interview*," *differences* 1:2 (1989), 127–28.

20. Moira Gatens, "A Critique of the Sex/Gender Distinction," in *A Reader in Feminist Knowledge*, ed. Sneja Gunew (New York: Routledge, 1991), 143; and 155, note 21.

This essay was originally published in 1983; however, the issues it addresses are still very current, as is its concern about men in feminism, as Modleski's more recent title suggests (see note 21, below).

21. Tania Modleski, *Feminism without Women: Culture and Criticism in a "Postfeminist" Age* (New York: Routledge, 1991).

22. See note 3 above for a partial list of others on men in feminism.

23. I am indebted to John Murchek for the suggestion that the women act as psychoanalysts as much as analysts in the usual sense of the term.

24. Stephen Heath, "Male Feminism," in *Men in Feminism*, 45.

25. Toril Moi, "Men Against Patriarchy," in Kauffman, ed., *Gender and Theory*, 182.

26. Steve Neale, "Sexual Difference in Cinema—Issues of Fantasy, Narrative, and the Look," *Oxford Literary Review* 8:1–2 (1986), 130.

27. Gayatri Chaktavorty Spivak, "Can the Subaltern Speak?" in *Marxism and the Interpretation of Culture*, ed. Cary Nelson and Lawrence Grossberg (Urbana: University of Illinois Press, 1988), especially 274–80.

28. Elaine Showalter, "Critical Cross-Dressing; Male Feminists and the Woman of the Year," in Jardine and Smith, eds., *Men in Feminism*, 119.

29. Robert Scholes, "Reading Like a Man," in Jardine and Smith, eds., *Men in Feminism*, 204–18; Andrew Ross, "Demonstrating Sexual Difference," 47–53, and "No Question of Silence," 85–92; both in Jardine and Smith, eds., *Men in Feminism*.

30. Nancy Miller, "Man on Feminism: A Criticism of His Own," Jardine and Smith, eds., in *Men in Feminism*, 139; Elizabeth Weed, " A Man's Place," in *Men in Feminism*, 72.

31. Alice Jardine and Paul Smith, "A Conversation," in Jardine and Smith, eds., *Men in Feminism*, 256; Hereafter cited parenthetically as "Conversation."

32. Ibid., 254.

33. Weed, "A Man's Place," 73.

34. Paul Smith, "Men in Feminism: Men and Feminist Theory," in Jardine and Smith, eds., *Men in Feminism*, 39. Smith's phrasing suggests that men's work of unsettling things is both passive and pure. This fantasy of men as better feminists, or at least as necessary to feminism, is shared by K. K. Ruthven, as Naomi Schor points out in her review of his *Feminist Literary Studies: An Introduction* see *Paragraph* 8 (1986), 8.

35. Modleski, *Feminism without Women*, 69.

36. The first ending of Heath's "Male Feminism" advises men to admire feminism. The second ending—a postscript—recognizes and comments on the fetishism of the attitude of admiration. I would note as well the exhibitionism of the need to display that admiration, to be seen/heard talking about it.

37. Sigmund Freud, "Fetishism" (1927), trans. Joan Riviere, in *Sexuality and the Psychology of Love*, ed. Philip Rieff (New York: Collier, 1963), 219.

38. Joan Riviere, "Womanliness as Masquerade" (1929); reprt. in *Psychoanalysis and Female Sexuality*, ed. Hendrik M. Ruitenbeek (New Haven: College and University Press, 1966), 209–20.

39. Ruth Salvaggio, "Psychoanalysis and Deconstruction and Woman," *Psychoanalysis and . . .*, ed. Richard Feldstein and Henry Sussman (New York: Routledge, 1990), 157.

40. Alice A. Jardine, *Gynesis: Configurations of Woman and Modernity* (Ithaca: Cornell University Press, 1985).

41. Gallop, *Thinking through the Body*, 100.

42. Sigmund Freud, "A Child Is Being Beaten" (1919), trans. James Strachey, in *Sexuality*

and the Psychology of Love, ed. Philip Rieff (New York: Collier, 1963), 107–32. For two readings of this essay—which arrive at very different conclusions—see Mary Ann Doane, *The Desire to Desire: The Woman's Film of the 1940s* (Bloomington: Indiana University Press, 1987), 17–20, and Kaja Silverman, *Male Subjectivity at the Margins* (New York: Routledge, 1992), 185–213.

43. Cary Nelson, "Men, Feminism: The Materiality of Discourse," in Jardine and Smith, eds., *Men in Feminism*, 168.

44. See Jardine and Smith, "A Conversation," 247, where Smith ventriloquizes a desire for Heath and explicitly identifies with him even while disidentifying from him: "I suspect that feminists are being played to here: you women are right and I (Heath) am going to please you" [Smith's parenthesis]. Elsewhere Smith has described this structure of knowledge as paranoid, based on the mechanism of projection, in which fantasies about the other are assumed to be the truth. See Paul Smith, *Discerning the Subject* (Minneapolis: University of Minnesota Press, 1988), 83–99.

45. Quoted in Heath, "Male Feminism," 2.

46. Eve Kosofsky Sedgwick, *Between Men: English Literature and Male Homosocial Desire* (New York: Columbia University Press, 1985); Luce Irigaray, "Commodities among Themselves," in *This Sex Which Is Not One*, trans. Catherine Porter (Ithaca: Cornell University Press, 1985), 170–91.

47. Jonathan Culler, *On Deconstruction: Theory and Criticism after Structuralism* (Ithaca: Cornell University Press, 1982), 43–64.

48. The allusion is to François Roustang's study of discipleship in psychoanalytic circles, *Dire Mastery: Discipleship from Freud to Lacan*, trans. Ned Lukacher (Baltimore: Johns Hopkins University Press, 1982). Fuss discusses Scholes in "Reading Like a Feminist," *Essentially Speaking: Feminism, Nature, and Difference* (New York: Routledge, 1989), 23–28, especially 25–26.

49. Craig Owens, "Outlaws: Gay Men in Feminism," in Jardine and Smith, eds., *Men in Feminism*, 219–32.

50. See Irigaray, "Commodities among Themselves," 193.

51. See Marilyn Frye, *The Politics of Reality: Essays in Feminist Theory* (Trumansburg, NY: The Crossing Press, 1983), 128–51.

52. It might be argued that feminists could not be misogynist, just as gays could not be homophobic, since both are defined as political positions inconsistent with self-hatred or fear. However, once differences between the members embracing such group identifications are taken into account—differences of class, race, ethnicity, religion, etc.—it becomes more difficult to accept this argument without question. For example, what is one to call avowed feminists, or gay activists, or theorists who are also racist when one discusses their relations with people of color within the group with which all are identified? Is it "just" racism or a race-specific misogyny or homophobia, when what such an individual fears or hates is specific to a gender or sexual identity that is always already racial, too (the black lesbian, for example, is not black and lesbian in some additive or compartmentalized fashion)? Can one simply term the Frantz Fanon of *Black Skin, White Masks* a homophobe, when his fear and revulsion is explicitly directed at white gays and lesbians? Yet *what else* can one call him, given that he "accepts" black gays and lesbians only because he assumes they are acting on economic motives rather than "genuine" sexual desires, which seems to mean they are not "really" homosexual at all? See *Black Skin, White Masks*, trans. Charles Lam Markmann (New York: Grove Press, 1967), 141–209. For a fuller discussion of

Fanon's homophobia, see Fuss; on the debates between the transgender and lesbian communities about how to identify and account for the life and death of the person born Teena Brandon, see Judith Halberstam and Jacob Hale, "Butch/FTM Border Wars: A Note on Collaboration." *GLQ* 4:2 (1998), 283–85, and "Consuming the Living, Dis(re)membering the Dead in the Butch/FTM Borderlands," *GLQ* 4:2 (1998), 311–19.

53. Joseph Boone, "Of Me(n) in Feminism: Who(se) Is the Sex that Writes?" in Boone and Cadden, eds., *Engendering Men*, 23. This essay first appeared in Kauffman, ed., *Gender and Theory, 158–80*, and is reprinted again in Porter, ed., *Between Men and Feminism*, 13–34; an exemplary status.

54. Boone, "Of Men in Feminism," 23.

55. Ibid., 19.

56. Ibid., 17. It is not clear how this might exonerate straight male feminists of color, the other group of "different" men Boone has implied are not recognized by feminists, since Boone does not discuss them.

57. Ibid., 24.

58. Ibid., 22–25.

59. Ibid., 22.

60. Moi, "Men Against Patriarchy," 188.

61. Ibid.

62. Rosi Braidotti, "Envy: Or, with Your Brains and My Looks," in Jardine and Smith, eds., *Men in Feminism*, 238.

63. Jardine and Smith, "A Conversation," 260.

64. Silverman, *Male Subjectivity at the Margins*, 299–338.

65. See Modleski, *Feminism without Women*; Rosi Braidotti, *Patterns of Dissonance: A Study of Women in Contemorary Philosophy*, trans. Elizabeth Guild (New York: Routledge, 1991), especially 98–108; Nancy Miller, "Changing the Subject: Authorship, Writing, and the Reader," in *Feminist Studies, Critical Studies*, ed. Teresa de Lauretis (Bloomington: Indiana University Press, 1986), 102–20; Teresa de Lauretis, *Technologies of Gender: Essays on Theory, Film, and Fiction* (Bloomington: Indiana University Press, 1987), 23–25; Margaret Whitford, *Luce Irigaray: Philosophy in the Feminine* (London: Routledge, 1991).

66. Whitford, *Luce Irigaray*, 137.

67. See Derrida's interview with James Creech, Peggy Kamuf, and Janet Todd, "Deconstruction in America," *Critical Exchange* 17 (1985), 30.

68. On the "deathly patronymic" versus the "living feminine," see Derrida, *The Ear of the Other*, 15-22.

69. See Robert Scholes, "Interpretation: The Question of Protocols," in *The Protocols of Reading* (New Haven: Yale University Press, 1989), and Paul Smith, *Discerning the Subject*, 41-55. Derrida discusses the "steps" of deconstruction himself in *Positions*, trans. Alan Bass (Chicago: University of Chicago Press, 1981), 41–43.

70. Derrida, "Women in the Beehive," 196.

71. Spivak, "Feminism and Deconstruction," 132.

72. Jacques Derrida, "Différance," in *Speech and Phenomena*, trans. Alan Bass (Chicago: University of Chicago Press, 1982), 1–27.

73. See, for example, Laura Mulvey, "Afterthoughts on 'Visual Pleasure and Narrative Cinema' inspired by *Duel in the Sun*," in *Feminism and Film Theory*, ed. Constance Penley (New York: Routledge, 1988), especially 70–71 and 78–79. See also Sarah

Kofman, *The Enigma of Woman: Woman in Freud's Writings*, trans. Catherine Porter (Ithaca: Cornell University Press, 1985), 126–27.

74. Sigmund Freud, "Femininity" (1933), in *New Introductory Lectures on Psychoanalysis*, trans. James Strachey (New York: W. W. Norton, 1965), 116.

75. Ibid.

76. Jacques Lacan, "God and the *Jouissance* of The Woman. A Love Letter," in *Feminine Sexuality: Jacques Lacan and the école freudienne*, ed. Juliet Mitchell and Jacqueline Rose, trans. Jacqueline Rose (New York: W. W. Norton and Co., 1982), 137-161.

77. Derrida, "Choreographies," 68.

78. Luce Irigaray, *This Sex Which Is Not One*, trans. Catherine Porter (Ithaca: Cornell University Press, 1985), 76–77, 133–34; Mary Ann Doane, "Film and the Masquerade —Theorizing the Female Spectator," *Screen* 23:3–4 (1982), 74–88; Mary Russo, "Female Grotesques: Carnival and Theory," in de Lauretis, ed., *Feminist Studies/ Critical Studies*, 213–29; Judith Butler, *Gender Trouble: Feminism and the Subversion of Identity* (New York: Routledge, 1990), especially 142–49, and *Bodies that Matter: On the Discursive Limits of Sex* (New York: Routledge, 1993), especially 223–42.

79. Susan Brownmiller, *Femininity* (New York: Fawcett-Columbine, 1985).

80. Jacques Derrida, *Spurs: Nietzsche's Styles*, trans. Barbara Harlow (Chicago: University of Chicago Press, 1979), 49. This translation is not always satisfactory; I have modified it where it seemed necessary to do so.

81. Otto Fenichel, "The Psychology of Transvestism" (1930), reprt. in *Psychoanalysis and Male Sexuality*, ed. Hendrik M. Ruitenbeek (New Haven: College and University Press, 1966), 204.

82. Derrida, *Spurs*, 49.

83. Anne McClintock, "The Return of Female Fetishism and the Fiction of the Phallus," *New Formations* 19 (1993), 1–21; Lorrain Gamman and Merja Makinen, *Female Fetishism* (New York: New York University Press, 1994). As I note later, however, Derrida does offer certain fetish examples that become metaphors and fantasmatic part objects for the abstraction of the invaginating phallus of sexual différance.

84. Ibid., 59.

85. Ibid.

86. Ibid., 61.

87. Ibid., 53.

88. Octave Mannoni, "Je sais bien, mais quand même," in *Clefs pour l'imaginaire ou l'autre scène* (Paris: Editions du Seuil, 1969), 9–33.

89. Christian Metz, *The Imaginary Signifier: Psychoanalysis and the Cinema*, trans. Celia Britton et al (Bloomington: Indiana University Press, 1982).

90. For a discussion of allegorical figures of truth see Marina Warner, "*Nuda Veritas*," in *Monuments and Maidens: The Allegory of the Female Form* (New York: Atheneum, 1985), 294–328.

91. Jacques Derrida and Verena Andermatt Conley, "Voice II," *Boundary 2*, 12:2 (1984), 85.

92. Gayatri Chakravorty Spivak, "Love Me, Love My Ombre, elle," *Diacritics* 14:4 (1984), 22.

93. Judith Butler elaborates Derridean citation into a Foucauldian theory of gender performativity in both *Gender Trouble* and *Bodies That Matter.*

94. Jacques Derrida, *Given Time: I. Counterfeit Money*, trans. Peggy Kamuf (Chicago: University of Chicago Press, 1992), 7.

95. Derrida, *Spurs*, 137.

96. Derrida, *The Ear of the Other*, 51-52.

97. This is evident throughout most of his writings on woman and the feminine. In *Spurs*, for example, he recommends it for a critique of Heidegger's reading of Nietzsche (83).

98. Jacques Derrida, "Le Facteur de la Vérité," in *The Post Card: From Socrates to Freud and Beyond*, trans. Alan Bass (Chicago: University of Chicago Press, 1987), 441. The title translates as the postman/purveyor/factor of truth.

99. Jacques Derrida, *Positions*, trans. Alan Bass (Chicago: University of Chicago Press, 1981), 86.

100. Barbara Johnson, "The Frame of Reference: Poe, Lacan, Derrida," in *The Purloined Poe: Lacan, Derrida, and Psychoanalytic Reading*, ed. John P. Muller and William J. Richardson (Baltimore: The Johns Hopkins University Press, 1988), 248.

101. Ibid., 219.

102. Ibid.

103. Ibid., 218. Bass translates this slightly differently in *Le Facteur de la Vérité*, 420.

104. Ibid., 249.

105. Spivak, "Responsibility," 25; see also 32.

106. Spivak, "Feminism and Deconstruction," 136.

107. Johnson, The Frame of Reference," 219. The Derridean footnote on Lacan is in *Positions*, 107, note 44. Derrida critiques Lacan again more recently in strikingly similar terms in "For the Love of Lacan," in *Resistances: Of Psychoanalysis*, trans. Peggy Kamuf et al (Stanford: Stanford University Press, 1998), 39–69.

108. Luce Irigaray, *Sexes and Genealogies*, trans. Gillian C. Gill (New York: Columbia University Press, 1993), 42.

109. Johnson, "The Frame of Reference," 248. Bass translates this slightly differently in *Le Facteur de la Vérité*, 441.

110. Ibid., 248.

111. Slavoj, Žižek *The Sublime Object of Ideology* (London: Verso, 1989), 155.

112. Derrida, *Spurs*, 97.

113. See "fetish" in the *Oxford English Dictionary* and *The American Heritage Dictionary of the English Language*. See also William Pietz, "The Problem of the Fetish," *Res 9* (1985), 5–17.

114. Sigmund Freud, "Fetishism" (1927), trans., Joan Riviere in *Sexuality and the Psychology of Love*, ed. Philip Rieff (New York: Collier, 1963), 214.

115. Sigmund Freud, "The 'Uncanny'" (1919), in *On Creativity and the Unconscious: Papers on the Psychology of Art, Literature, Love, Religion*, ed. Benjamin Nelson, trans. Alix Strachey (New York: Harper Torchbooks, 1958), 122–61.

116. For a discussion of woman's penis envy as a masculinist construction, see Luce Irigaray, *Speculum*; and Sarah Kofman, *The Enigma of Woman*. Kofman shares many of Irigaray's conclusions, although she faults the latter for projecting on to Freud, just as Freud projects on to woman, by misquoting what is already a problematic French translation of the German.

117. Jonathan Culler, *On Deconstruction*, 175.

118. Jacques Derrida, *Of Grammatology*, trans. Gayatri Chakravorty Spivak (Baltimore: Johns Hopkins University Press, 1974). Jonathan Culler refers to an "archi-woman" in *On Deconstruction*, 171.

119. Derrida, "Choreographies," 55.

120. Derrida, *Positions*, 41.

121. Ibid.

122. Ibid., 43.

123. Derrida, "Women in the Beehive," 195.

124. Derrida, "Choreographies," 76.

125. Teresa de Lauretis, *Technologies of Gender: Essays on Theory, Film, and Fiction* (Bloomington: Indiana University Press, 1987), 10. Her critique of Derrida is 23–24.

126. Diane Elam discusses a few in a critique of the appeal to "women's experience," *Feminism and Deconstruction: Ms. en Abyme* (London: Routledge, 1994), 61–66.

127. Braidotti, *Patterns of Dissonance*, 106.

128. Gayatri Spivak, "Displacement and the Discourse of Women," in *Displacement: Derrida and After*, ed. Mark Krupnick (Bloomington: Indiana University Press, 1983), 190.

129. Derrida, "Deconstruction in America," 32.

130. Spivak, "Love Me, Love My Ombre, Elle," 24.

131. Derrida argues for the discursive production of bodies in "Choreographies," 70. He makes a similar argument in "Voice II," where he suggests that the colors of voice, like the colors of rhetoric, multiply sexualities, bodies, and meanings (83–85). This argument is not unlike that of Luce Irigaray in "Flesh Colors," in *Sexes and Genealogies*, 151–65. Derrida's may be a deconstructive reconstruction of the feminine like Irigaray's. Of course, for some time transsexual Renée Richards' sex changed with the words of the laws in effect in the countries to which she travelled, and for Lacan too the father's word—"no"—creates the sexes.

132. Jacques Derrida, "Restitutions of the Truth in Pointing *[pointure]*," in *The Truth in Painting*, trans. Geoff Bennington and Ian McLeod (Chicago: University of Chicago Press, 1987), 255–382. This essay and the fetish example is discussed by Gregory Ulmer in *Applied Grammatology: Post(e)-Pedagogy from Jacques Derrida to Joseph Beuys* (Baltimore: The Johns Hopkins University Press, 1985), 11–17.

133. Derrida, *Spurs*, 97.

134. Derrida, "Restitutions of the Truth in Pointing *[pointure]*," 267.

135. On Irigaray and Cixous as essentialist, see Toril Moi, *Sexual/Textual Politics: Feminist Literary Theory* (New York: Methuen, 1985), 102–49.

136. Sarah Kofman, "Ça Cloche," in *Les Fins de l'homme: à partir du travail de Jacques Derrida* (Paris: Editions Gallilée, 1981), 104–5.

137. See Mary Ann Doane, "The Voice in the Cinema: The Articulation of Body and Space," in *Narrative, Apparatus, Ideology*, ed. Philip Rosen (New York: Columbia University Press, 1986), 335–48.

138. For a different and less optimistic interpretation of this, see Robert Stam's discussion of some of the strategies deployed by newscasts to ensure their "truth value" despite the fact that the "enunciator" is not hidden; Stam, "Television News and Its Spectator," in *Regarding Television: Critical Approaches—An Anthology* (Frederick, MD: University of America Publications/American Film Institute, 1983), 23–43. The current trend toward reporters and anchors who are not white, Anglo, and male can support the "mainstream pluralism" characteristic of media news, since they do not disagree with one another or offer alternative perspectives on the stories they report. As long as the reporters' "differences" are at the level of appearance, rather than point of view, they seem to guarantee that the "mainstream" is indeed the center and reasonable mean between the kinds of "extremes" which make the news because they are

seen as extreme. Even their visible differences are minimized by their shared fashion sensibility—still relatively conservative suits—and their unaccented standard English.

139. Jane Gallop, *The Daughter's Seduction: Feminism and Psychoanalysis* (Ithaca: Cornell University Press, 1982), 121.

140. See Marie Delcourt, *Hermaphrodite: Myths and Rites of the Bisexual Figure in Classical Antiquity*, trans. Jennifer Nicholson (London: Studio Books, 1961).

141. Alice Jardine, *Gynesis: Configurations of Modernity* (Ithaca: Cornell University Press, 1985), 191. Both homosexuality and circumcision—and Jewish identity as nonidentity, like woman's—are at stake in Derrida's *Glas*, trans. John P. Leavey Jr. and Richard Rand (Lincoln: University of Nebraska Press, 1986): see also his "Circumfession," in Jacques Derrida and Geoffrey Bennington, *Jacques Derrida*, trans. Geoffrey Bennington (Chicago: University of Chicago Press, 1993).

142. Derrida, *Spurs*, 65.

143. Catherine Millot, *Horsexe: Essay on Transsexuality*, trans. Kenneth Hylton (New York: Autonomedia, Inc., 1990), 65 and 135. See also Charles Shepherdson, who discusses Millot at length in "The *Role* of Gender and the *Imperative* of Sex," *Supposing the Subject*, ed. Joan Copjec (London: Verso, 1994), 158–184.

144. Millot, *Horsexe*, especially 95–100, 122–26, and 135–43.

145. Bernice Haussman, *Changing Sex: Transsexualism, Technology, and the Idea of Gender* (Durham: Duke UP, 1995), 197. The book she critiques is Kate Bornstein, *On Men, Women, and the Rest of Us* (New York: Routledge, 1994).

146. Pat Califia, *SexChanges: The Politics of Transgenderism* (San Franciso: Cleis Press, 1997), 257.

147. Ibid., 273

148. Lee Edelman, "Queer Theory: Unstating Desire," *GLQ* 2:4 (1995), 340; Biddy Martin, *Femininity Played Straight: The Significance of Being Lesbian* (New York: Routledge, 1996), 69.

149. Silverman, *Male Subjectivity at the Margins*, 4.

150. Ibid., 6.

151. Jacques Lacan, *The Seminar of Jacques Lacan: Book 1, Freud's Papers on Technique*, 1953 –1954, ed. Jacques Alain Miller, trans. John Forrester (New York: W. W. Norton, 1988), 126.

152. Ibid., 175.

153. Derrida, "There Is No *One* Narcissism," 199.

154. Stuart Hall, "Cultural Identity and Diaspora," in *Identity: Community, Culture, Difference*, ed. Jonathan Rutherford (London: Lawrence & Wishart, 1990), 230.

155. Derrida, "Women in the Beehive," 198.

156. Frances Bartkowski, "Feminism and Deconstruction: 'A Union Forever Deferred,'" *Enclitic* 4 (1980), 70.

157. As quoted above, Spivak writes that Derrida's good will "cannot turn him quite free of the massive enclosure of the male appropriation of woman's voice," "Displacement and the Discourse of women," 190.

158. Miller, "Changing the Subject"; see also Nancy Miller, "Arachnologies: The Woman, The Text, and the Critic," in *The Poetics of Gender*, ed. Nancy Miller (New York: Columbia University Press, 1986), 270–95, and her debate with Peggy Kamuf on the question of the signature in *Diacritics* 12:2 (1982).

159. Modleski, *Feminism without Women*, 22.

160. Elam, *Feminism and Deconstruction*, 42–66. She briefly compares Derrida's and Irigaray's revisions of the feminine 61–63, and considers Butler on "sex" and transsexuals, intersexuals, and gender blending 49–52 and 56–57.

161. Ibid., 64. Elam's critique of Lacan underlines this. She objects to Lacan's use of Bernini's statue of St. Thereas as his "central example of feminine sexuality" (53), drawing a distinction between "marble slabs" and "the woman herself" (54) that does away with representation and its construction and mediation of woman's relation to her "self," body, and experience, though just a few pages later she insists on it in when she takes certain feminists to task for naïve appeals to "women's experience," as well as when she discusses Paul de Man on autobiography. Most of the book is very critical of any notion of access to an unmediated real.

162. Spivak, "Feminism and Deconstruction," 128–29; my italics. The 1983 essay is "Displacement and the Discourse of Women." See also, "Love Me, Love My Ombre, Elle."

163. For critiques of the familial paradigm, see Hazel Carby, "White Woman Listen! Black Feminism and the Boundaries of Sisterhood," in *The Empire Strikes Back: Race and Racism in 70s Britain* (London: Hutchinson/Centre for Contemporary Cultural Studies, University of Birmingham, 1982), 212–35, and Helena Michie, "Not One of the Family: The Repression of the Other Woman in Feminist Theory," in *Discontented Discourses: Feminism, Textual Intervention, Psychoanalysis*, ed. Marleen S. Barr and Richard Feldstein (Urbana: University of Illinois Press), 15–28.

164. Gayatri Chakravorty Spivak, "French Feminism in an International Frame," *Yale French Studies* 62 (1981), 179.

165. Modleski, *Feminism without Women*, 21.

166. Ibid.

167. Hortense Spillers, "Mama's Baby, Papa's Maybe: An American Grammar Book," *Diacritics* 17:2 (1987), 65–81.

168. Sander L. Gilman, *Difference and Pathology: Stereotypes of Sexuality, Race, and Madness* (Ithaca: Cornell University Press, 1985), 76–108. Gilman notes that working class white women's genitals were also seen as quite different from those of the white middle class woman and aligned them with women who were not white as a "lower form of humanity."

169. Deborah McDowell, "Transferences: Black Feminist Thinking: The 'Practice' of 'Theory'," "*The Changing Same*": Black Women's Literature, Criticism, and Theory* (Bloomington: Indiana University Press, 1995), 162–163.

170. Jacob Hale's "Suggested Rules for Non-Transsexuals Writing about Transsexuals, Transsexuality, Transsexualism, or Trans___" is a web link from Sandy Stone's site at http://www.actlab.utexas.edu/~sandy/hale.rules.html and was live in August 2000.

171. Renata Salecl, *The Spoils of Freedom: Psychoanalysis and Feminism after the Fall of Socialism* (London: Routledge, 1994) 119; 120

172. Spivak, "Feminism and Deconstruction," 133.

173. Ibid., 135; Salecl, *The Spoils of Freedom*, 132.

174. Ibid., 126.

175. Žižek, *The Sublime Object of Ideology*, 87–129.

176. Rey Chow, "Ethics after Idealism," *diacritics* 23:1 (1993), 13–15.

177. Ibid., 19–20

178. Ibid., 20.

179. Derrida and Irigaray both have written about touch or the "aptic." See Jacques

Derrida, "Le Toucher, Touch To-Touch Him," *Paragraph* 16:2 (1993), 122–57, and Luce Irigaray, "This Sex which Is Not One" and "When Our Lips Speak Together," in *This Sex which Is Not One*, trans. Catherine Porter (Ithaca: Cornell University Press, 1985), 23–33 and 205–18; see also her "The Fecundity of the Caress: A Reading of Levinas, *Totality and Infinity*, 'Phenomenology to Eros,'" in *An Ethics of Sexual Difference*, trans. Carolyn Burke and Gillian C. Gill (Ithaca: Cornell University Press, 1993), 185–217. Derrida specifically compares the optic and the aptic 126.

180. Derrida, "There Is No *One* Narcissism," 190.
181. Derrida, "Le Toucher, Touch To-Touch Him," 139

PASSING

O urs is the era of the passing of "passing" as a politically viable response to oppression. It seems fitting that it is a verb with no noun-subject form, since it is an activity whose agent is obscured, immersed in the mainstream, rather than swimming against the tide, invisible to the predatory eye in search of its mark. Passing has become the sign of the victim, the practice of one already complicit with the order of things, prey to its oppressive hierarchies—if it can be seen at all; for the mark of passing successfully is the lack of a mark of passing, of a signifier of some difference from what one seems to be. In fact, passing can only name the very failure of passing, an indication of a certain impossibility at its heart, of the contradictions which constitute it: life/death, being/nonbeing, visibility/invisibility, speech/silence, difference/sameness, knowledge/ignorance, coming out/mimicry. Passing is the effect of a certain affect, an uncanny feeling of uncertainty about a difference that is not quite visible, not quite known, not quite there.

Passing is commonly supposed to result from "closetedness," which Eve Kosofsky Sedgwick describes as "a performance initiated as such by the speech act of a silence—not a particular silence, but a silence that accrues particularity by fits and starts, in relation to the discourse that surrounds and differentially constitutes it."[1] Passing suggests a secret behind a closed door, which it opens as a space of difference in the heart of the same, disrupting identity. Something we cannot quite make out begins to take on shape and color, growing visible in our midst, passing through us, unsettling us, troubling the homogeneity of our group and our identifications with one another, which as Sigmund Freud and others have noted, are the support of group identity.[2] Sometimes that something is one's self, as the focus of an almost nameless anxiety narrows to one's own image, in what Sedgwick calls "circuits of intimate denegation," and one finds oneself—and not the other—in the closet. But to find oneself there is already to come out, to name one's doubts and fears and repudiate them together with the old identity as a mask that deceived no one. Passing is always *passing* through, from one identity to another, uncertainty resolved.

Coming out and mimicry are the critical practices of current interest. They are at the center of arguments about identity politics and postmodernism, essentialism and antiessentialist social constructionism, which structure the discussion of resistance in the wake of passing in many fields today. Participants in these debates voice the desire to be the subjects rather than objects of difference, to speak, write, and desire differently, without reproducing dominant cultures' fetishistic ambivalence about difference, even to be essentially different from the hegemonic subject. They would *fix* resistance (in both senses of the word) by fixing difference—which in the end, can only fetishize it as a play of masking and unmasking. The difference from—but also within—coming out and mimicry, passing passes between and through them like the ghost of a phenomenon, the specter of identities past—and future. As the uncanny experience of the *lack* of an identity, (one is not what one seems, but who notices?) passing is not quite (not) resistance as the act of an agent with a name and an identity. Coming out and mimicry would unmask the face of resistance disguised by passing. They insist on the other's right to be other—to be seen, heard, known, and named as different—affirming that difference, the one directly, the other indirectly, through irony and negation of the same. Each is the other's limit, but a limit passed by passing, which splits and doubles them, as the effect of a symbolic lack which haunts them: the *passing* of the castration complex, not quite not there, the skeleton of the phallus in the closet, not fixed, neutered, or neutralized.

COMING OUT

Coming out, one accepts an identity, declaring and displaying it as a positive difference from a norm that has also served as the measure of superiority. One names oneself, refusing one's assigned or hegemonic name in what Kimberly Bentson describes as a simultaneous unnaming, "affirming at once autonomy and identification in the relation to the past."[3] Of this topos in African-American culture, he writes, "Social and economic freedom [of the former slave]—a truly new self—was incomplete if not authenticated by self-designation. The *unnaming* of the immediate past ('Hatcher's John,' etc.) was reinforced by the insertion of a mysterious initial, a symbol of the unacknowledged, nascent selfhood that had survived and transcended slavery. On the other hand, the association with tropes of American heroism ('Lincoln,' 'Sherman,' etc.) was also an act of *naming*, a staging of self in relation to a specific context of revolutionary affirmation. . . . "[4] After transsexual surgery, Richard Raskind is reborn as Renée Richards; after the Stonewall Riots, the homosexual is gay. Sometimes such renaming involves reclaiming the old name and inflecting it differently, as happened with *queer*, as Judith Butler notes.[5] The hierarchies may even be inverted and the devalorized, revalorized: black is beautiful; women on top. Asserting the right to name oneself this way is asserting the right to be oneself, which is why the fundamental realization of "coming out" is in the use of the phrase itself, as Sedgwick recognizes. According to her, the text on a T-shirt from ACT UP New York, "I am out, therefore I am," functions performatively, rather than constatively; it is in effect a continuing renewal of being through the repetition of the gesture that explicitly affirms one identity and implicitly repudiates another.[6]

In a performance piece that seems to work in a similar way, Adrian Piper has passed out "calling cards" to those who "pass over her racial difference." The cards read:

> Dear Friend:
>   I am black.
>   I am sure that you did not realize this when you made/laughed at/ agreed with that racist remark. In the past I have attempted to alert white people to my racial identity in advance. Unfortunately, this invariably causes them to react to me as pushy, manipulative, or socially inappropriate. Therefore, my policy is to assume that white people do not make these remarks, even when they believe there are no black people present, and to distribute this card when they do.
>   I regret any discomfort my presence is causing you, just as I am sure

you regret the discomfort your racism is causing me.
   Sincerely Yours,
   Adrian Margaret Smith Piper

"Piper's text resists the disappearance of her difference by those who would pass her without her consent," Peggy Phelan explains.[7] Piper's difference goes unremarked because she is camouflaged—but by the others around her, against her will, "disappeared" into the presumptive universal, the unmarked "same." The desire for the whiteness of blackness this passing represents has been described by Frantz Fanon and Homi Bhabha as "mimicry."[8] However, Piper is the object, and not the subject, of such a desire for mimicry, since she has not consented to practice it. She seems to be the victim of a crime, the theft of her identity, in which her desire or will is deeply invested. We have an inalienable right to our desire and identity, according to Sedgwick, who writes, "To alienate conclusively, *definitionally*, from anyone on any theoretical ground the authority to describe and name their own sexual desire is a terribly consequential seizure. In this century, in which sexuality has been made expressive of the essence of both identity and knowledge, it may represent the most intimate violence possible."[9] Unfortunately, our narcissistic investment in our identities and fantasies binds us deeply to others, who have the power to alienate us from ourselves by calling into question the character(s) we are in the fantasies which structure our reality. As a staging of desire, fantasy cannot do without performers and spectators, as well as props. Piper's cards, the ACT UP T-shirt, and other assertions of a "proper" name suggest that it is never enough to name oneself by oneself in a private fantasy. Identity is always dependent upon the other of whom a demand for recognition is made—paradoxically, in terms one calls one's own. As a relation to others, fantasy is necessary public, and the public, therefore, has a fantasmatic dimension.

"NATURAL" SIGNS

The wish for one's own terms, and one's proper identity, the most deeply private property of all, as Sedgwick suggests, can never be satisfied, since both are held in common with others in the community—an effect of the symbolic. We can never be sure what is "coming out" of us for the other—or *from* the other; nevertheless, there persists a paradoxical desire to be self-present through others, to come out to ourselves through the other's recognition of our proper name and image. As signifiers of ourselves, with which we are deeply identified, we wish our name and image to transparently reflect our being, to be naturally bound to it. Such signs are "motivated," rather than "arbitrary" or conventional and artificial. As explained by Ferdinand de Saussure and Charles Sanders Peirce, motivated signs are not supposed to be as susceptible to the disarticulations of signifier and signified, sign and referent, that make communication with arbitrary signs ambiguous. Peirce divides motivated signs into two broad categories: an *iconic* sign is one that resembles its referent, such as a picture, diagram, or onomatopoeia; an *indexical* sign is existentially linked to its referent, with which it is physically contiguous (as when a part substitutes for the whole), or causally connected (as with symptoms, outcomes, or antecedents).[10] Believing that motivated signs are atypical of language, Saussure demonstrates the degree to which they too are arbitrary and conventional, rather than natural.[11] Such a critique calls into question both realism and empiricism, which are based on a faith in the transparency and objectivity of representation. The former fails to register the materiality of the sign that literally substitutes for the real, constituting objects through the codes of our discourses. The latter disregards the materiality of the subject or sign user, whose perception is equally mediated by discursive codes, through which she has been constituted. Each is a cause and effect of the other, since there are no signs except for sign users, who create them by believing that something is meaningful.

In a critique of classic Hollywood cinema, Christian Metz demonstrates that such visual realism is fetishistic. Everything unfolds in the classic realist film so as to promote a disavowal of its fictional status, including that of the masterful "I" with which the spectator identifies, before whose apparently all-seeing eye the action takes place.[12] The spectator in front of the screen experiences a splitting of belief like the fetishist's: "I know very well this is only a fiction, but all the same . . . ," he thinks. The absence of the real in the visual sign is disavowed, just as in fetishism the absence of the maternal phallus—the mother's "difference"—is disavowed, which the subject sees and knows but also fails to acknowledge. There is a splitting of the ego, the system of perception consciousness, as the subject (mis)recognizes what is "right before his eyes," a splitting that characterizes not only cinematic realism but all visual realism or empiricism. The subject is not master of the visual field; something is absent from it—himself as spectator, as Michel Foucault suggests in his analysis of *Las Meninas* in *The Order of Things*. It is this gap that the classical system of representation disguises. According to Foucault, the subject seems to see himself in his substitutes in the Diego Rodriguez de Silva y Velasquez painting, the painter in front of his easel, the visitor on the studio threshold in the background, and the sovereigns in the mirror on the back wall with the artist's finished paintings.[13] Included in the space of the picture, they have necessarily become the spectator's models, since he paints their images on his retina, occupying both the position of the artist who portrayed them on the canvas and the monarchs for whom the spectacle was presented to be re-presented. The representation appears to belong to the spectator as sovereign subject, although they come to him or her from the other (the king and queen, the artist), a phenomenon characteristic of human perception, as Jacques Lacan notes. We cannot see ourselves seeing ourselves. If the subject is in the picture, it is for the other, by whom he is "photographed."[14] The Other is the support of the subject's self-image; in Lacan's phrase "I is another," initially a mirror image with which the infant identifies and then a pronominal shifter or "indicator," as Emile Benveniste terms those elements of speech whose meaning is determined by the discursive context in which they are used.[15] The subject is alienated from a crucial part of himself, the image that represents him and provides him with a self in the first place. He can never reconcile the split between the eye that sees and the eye that is seen; the "I" who speaks (the subject of the enunciation) and the "I" who is spoken (the subject or pronoun of the statement); or the subject of desire and the subject of demand, who must pass through the defiles of the Other's signifiers (desire is what exceeds need in demand, the remaining lack of satisfaction).

In her critique of Metz, Jacqueline Rose emphasizes what he does not: the importance of sexual difference in cinema, whose representations of woman support man's fetishistic belief that castration does not take place for him, although he knows better.[16] When sexual fetishism and realist fetishism are combined, as they are in cinema or empirical studies of sexual difference, sexist representations whose veracity is only an effect of codes pass as the truth of nature. The sexual fetish is indexical rather than iconic: the substitute for the missing phallus is not an ersatz penis but very often the last thing the subject saw before the traumatic vision of the mother's difference, such as underwear or shoes, according to Freud.[17] Cinematic fetishism of women, therefore, condenses the iconic and the indexical in one sign. However, all film and photographic images do, so their "truth" seems to have a double guarantee. Because both are recorded, rather than live, they are marked by what Roland Barthes calls "the photo effect," as John Ellis points out.[18] According to Barthes, the photograph functions as a witness of "what has been," certifying the presence of the past by mortifying the living beings it would immortalize. Its proper tense is the future perfect: this *will have been*. As the agent of that action, the camera-mortician "will have been" in the same space at the same time as what it embalms, preserving the referent's reality through the light rays that have touched the living and the film bodies, creating an existential bond between them. The photograph, Barthes writes, "carries its referent with itself . . . they are glued together, limb by limb, like the condemned man and the corpse."[19] For film critic and theorist

André Bazin, this indexical relation is the basis for a more persuasive argument for cinematic realism than is an appeal to iconicity.[20]

However, indexical signs preserve no more of the real of the referent than iconic signs; they are equally conventional. As Umberto Eco observes, they are based on inferences that come to be socially sanctioned and systematically coded through a discourse, whether of science or "common sense," and it is this cultural coding which transforms them into "semiosic acts."[21] He emphasizes the importance of convention in reading the photograph as "real" by undermining the latter as the natural consequence of "analog" (as opposed to "digital" or purely arbitrary) form: "[A] photograph is perhaps 'motivated' (the traces on the paper are produced by the disposition of the matter in the supposed referent) but it is digitally analyzable, as happens when it is printed through a raster. . . ."[22] Classic Hollywood cinema's realism is no less realistic when a movie is projected from a laser disk rather than film stock, or when an entirely fictional scene manufactured by the computer wizards of special-effects departments is edited together with more conventionally filmed footage. Our inference that the camera was in the space of the mise-en-scène, which therefore "must have been," is simply false in the case of special-effects sequences, and in fact in realist film we are never allowed to see in the diegetic world the camera or anything else that might suggest the staging of the real as a fantasy. The confusion of fact and fiction, sign and referent, is crucial to film's effect of the real, which depends on a fetishistic disavowal of their difference.

Because the signs of recorded visual realism are at once iconic and indexical they seem only to partially substitute for reality, not displacing it completely but simply "supplementing" it, as the fetish does the woman's "lack." The meaning of the real appears almost without mediation in the analog sign, as if the thing were itself through its sign, a little bit of something outside it so transparent it is almost not there. Like the finest veil; it exhibits rather than inhibits the real that is coming out of it by going into it; it does not (sm)other the real in a winding-sheet, as the arbitrary sign does. Such a real sign "demands" no recognition or reading. It is the "natural" language of things by themselves, as themselves, through the supplement. How can a thing be itself through an other? Why does it double itself through an other? As Eco recognizes, the logic of the analog sign as supplement is that of the double, but according to him, doubles do not really exist, and if they did, they would not be signs. "[A]n absolute replica is a rather utopian notion," he writes, "for it is difficult to reconstruct all the properties of a given object right down to its most microscopic characteristics. . . ."[23] Even were that possible a thing cannot be its own sign because the latter is necessarily a supplement, something from "outside," that represents what is absent. Eco clarifies this through a latonic parable, in which the doubles are turned into ghosts of some more real Ideal, of which they are an iconic imitation, lacking some of its properties. "Given a wooden cube of a given size, matter, color, weight, surface structure and so on" he writes, "If I produce another cube possessing all the same properties (that is, if I shape the same continuum according to the same form) I have produced not a sign of the first cube, but simply *another* cube, which may at most represent the first inasmuch as every object may stand for the class of which it is a member, thus being chosen as an example."[24] Doubles are not signs of each other but of an ideal class to which they both belong. By definition, something of the real must be absent in the iconic sign for it to function as a sign at all. The thing that doubles as its own sign splits into an absence and a spectral presence, a ghost of an ideal that re-presents it but misses its vital properties by doing so. The sign, that is, does not represent the real for us; it constitutes it—but as absent, as that which passes through the signifier without a trace except what the codes themselves make perceptible as "the realistic," a mirage to which convention lends reality.

MIRAGES

Lacan describes the iconicity that structures subjectivity and subject-object relations as a matter of "mirages" and doubles. According to him, sometime between the ages of six and eighteen months, the human infant recognizes its image in the mirror and jubilantly identifies with it, receiving from it an impression of itself as having stable boundaries and mastery over itself and its world. The mirror "ideal ego" is "the total form of the body by which the subject anticipates in a mirage the maturation of his power . . . [and] symbolizes the mental permanence of the *I*, at the same time as it prefigures its alienating destination . . . the statue in which man projects himself . . . " through the libido invested in it.[25] This image is at once an iconic and indexical sign: it "resembles" the subject only because it assembles him, fixing him to the gestalt of himself as whole through the libidinal flow that binds him to it as his "self," like Barthes' photograph that mortifes the subject it would immortalize, preserving him in a statue. The mirror other as primordial subject is the foundation for the later identifications with ego-ideals that build up the ego itself. It is an uncertain foundation, however, based on a fundamental misrecognition of identification as identity, confusing spectator and model, the condemned man and his corpse. In fact, it is the mirage that "appropriates" the human being as it attracts the infant libido (what Lacan terms l'hommelette), making it a subject by enclosing it in a fragile shell. Lacan emphasizes this by describing the subject as an effect of impersonation or "mimicry" (his term), which results from and expresses an alienating identification with something outside it, an activity which cannot be reduced to "the supposedly supreme law of adaptation."[26] Sexuality diverges from self-preservation or the pleasure principle, the field of needs, interests, and adaptation to "reality" (the reality principle). There is already something besides self-preservation at work when the subject so radically confounds itself with the other as self-portrait that it *is* the other, or is "itself" only through the other, and attacks "itself" as an other with which it can never be reconciled. The mirror sign imprints itself on the real, constituting the real as a copy or supplement and substitute, like the "absolute replica" Eco thought impossible, which constructs, rather than reconstructs, the properties of what it doubles. The subject is the retroactive cause of what brings it into being, an imitation of a reflection or copy of that for which it "will have been" the original.

The real is therefore the effect of a sign representing another sign. As Eco explains, people mistake for an icon what is a constitutive condition for iconicity, cultural coding itself: "Thus a schematic representation reproduces some of the properties of another schematic representation."[27] There is no Platonic realm of the absent real except through the sign in its difference from itself as another sign that splits and doubles it, leaving a ghostly remainder, which strives to "disalienate" the subject from its alienating ideal ego. The "real" being struggles to shatter the fictional statue it is becoming, the corpse it *will have been.* It can never coincide completely with the ego, nor can the ego be a locus of objective knowledge in the service of "the reality principle," since it is characterized by misrecognition of its self and its objects, a misplaced faith in its own gaze as empiricist. Such misrecognition is constitutive, however. There can be no subject without the narcissistic perception of a similarity where there is difference, nor can there be symbolic communication without the splitting of the real into the similarities and differences of the sign systems that mark out objects for narcissistic subjects. Narcissism must be critiqued and preserved. Lacan finds just such a dialectic in the subject, whose dreams testify to what he describes as "aggressive disintegration in the individual," even as the latter's defenses strive to shore up the fragile ego.[28] Beyond the pleasure principle is the death drive, which must take the self as its object, if the other is to survive—but which must be directed outward, against the other, if the self is to survive, an impasse that Freud articulates clearly in *Civilization and Its Discontents.*[29]

It therefore cannot be surprising that there is a sadomasochistic (aggressive and narcissistic) dimension to the critique of narcissism, which concerns the preservation of self or other, subject or object. Piper's calling cards exemplify this. As Phelan explains, she attacks the narcissism of the white self by calling into question that subject's mastery of the visual field through empiricism.

Piper, Phelan writes, "establishes . . . the failure of racial difference to appear within the narrow range of the visible and registers her refusal to let the visual field *fail* to secure it. The card itself ruptures the given to be seen and exposes the normative force of everyday blindness: if no one looks black, everyone is white."[30] However, Piper repeats what she critiques; she assumes she can see —or hear—who is white, interpellating people as white by giving them her card. She divides the world into black and white, passing over people of color unless they are (black) like her and share her sense of what racism is. Hers is the inverse of white narcissism: if no one looks or acts white, everyone is black. Piper's policy is not so much to assume that white people do not make racist remarks, as her cards claim (otherwise, she would not carry them), but to assume that people of color do not make racist remarks and are all alike in their understanding of racism. She imagines them as her mirror counterparts, what Seyla Benhabib calls the "generalized other," part of a homogeneous collectivity that the expression "people of color" itself creates as the term designating all those who are not white (the "absence" of color, the unmarked universal).[31] Piper abstracts a new universal from concrete differences, "passing" others into whiteness or blackness, whatever they really are, making them into mimic men and women.

NAME-CALLING

The name can no more represent the self's real difference than can the image. Both naming and imaging involve violence, the violence of the "cut" when signs cleave the continuum of the "real" into differences that are culturally significant. Names represent nothing of people's uniqueness; they categorize and therefore reduce specificity, alienating the "real." As Jacques Derrida observes, writing ineluctably effaces the proper name as what is intimately one's own, the index that would point to one person only, bound to him or her in space and time. "The death of absolutely proper naming, recognizing in a language the other as pure other, invoking it as what it is, is the death of the pure idiom reserved for the unique," he writes. "Anterior to the possibility of violence in the current and deriviative sense . . . there is, as the space of its possibility, the violence of the arche-writing, the violence of difference, of classification, and of the system of appellations."[32] Language is public rather than private property, the realm of the iterable rather than the unique. One is white or black, straight or gay, male or female, Dick or Renée, common names for identities held in common, as mutual acts of recognition. There can be no "I" without a "you," and these pronouns gain their meaning from their difference, rather than from any intrinsic link with the subjects whose being they designate, given that anyone can deploy them. The subject is the effect of impersonation, the assumption of an alienating signifier ("I" or "you") and the imitation or repetition of the practices of the apparatus in which it is produced. Nevertheless "I am out, therefore I am" cannot close the gap between performance and utterance, performative and constative, subject and T-shirt, the one who is "outing" and the one who is out, just as Eco's double can only render absent the ideal it represents. "I" will have been out only at the end of the "outing," which is not in its beginning, except retroactively. Being "out" is a Moebius movement of deferral without end and renewal without beginning—the future perfect as past perfected. The subject of the enunciation must pass through the statement in which his "I" is uttered. All subjects therefore are *passing* through the signifers that represent them for an other, to whom a demand for recognition and a question about being is addressed: "(Do you) Hear what I'm saying!? (Do you) See what I am!? What more do you want from me!?"

For whom—and how—is this confidence game staged? Louis Althusser implies that it is "for" the subject, who "*is interpellated as a (free) subject in order that he shall . . . (freely) accept his subjection,* i.e., in order that he shall make the gestures and actions of his subjection 'all by himself.'"[33] However, if we are duped by our act, if we believe our illusions, it is because "the system" requires our subjection so that it may be reproduced. In the final analysis, self-deception is for the Other, the symbolic network, as Slavoj Žižek explains: "[T]hose who should be deceived by the ideological 'illusion' are not primarily concrete individuals but, rather, the big Other."[34] The subject does not have to believe in his act so long as the show goes on—he knows better but some Other does not. This splitting of belief between "I" and "you" (the other) is one form of disavowal, which includes the possible variations on what according to Octave Mannoni is the kernel sentence of the fetishistic fantasy: "I know very well . . . but all the same. . . ."[35] We are in the grip of ideology when we continue to behave in a way consistent with it even if we disavow what we are doing or the beliefs that are supposed to motivate it. We still believe, Metz writes, "but always in the aorist tense . . . the beliefs of 'long ago' irrigate the unbelief of today, but irrigate it by denegation (one could also say *by delegation,* by attributing credulity to . . . former times)."[36] This means that emotions, including belief, can be transferred to others— even to things—"without losing their sincerity," as Žižek observes.[37] The Other can do our believing for us so that our fantasy is not disrupted. But the Other is also ourself, having constituted us through its signifiers; on some Other level, therefore, we still believe—on the level of actions rather than thoughts. No matter how self-consciously we deconstruct identities, no matter how self-reflexively we perform our selves, we are still "doing" them. What's more, we demand that the Other recognize both our identities and our "cynicism" about them—the Other is at once our credulous dupe and the "subject supposed to know" that *we* know better.

This disavowal structures the current version of identity politics. In the postmodern movement, we "know" that coming out is a naively essentialist notion. Since we are always already caught up in a system of conventional differences that preclude the recovery of a "genuine" difference, we can only reverse the discourse that has produced us and embrace the identity we have assumed, as if it represented what we really are. When Jeffrey Weeks opens his book on coming out by describing it as "a historic process, the gradual emergence and articulation of a homosexual identity and public presence," he might well be discussing the discursive production of the homosexual as elaborated by Foucault, rather than any radical reconstruction of gay identity.[38] In Foucauldian terms, coming out is still complicit with the regulation of sexuality even as it functions as a reverse discourse by making demands in the name of the devalued identity constituted by dominant sexual discourses. It involves no real liberation or authentic self-expression but is instead another identity fiction, neither self-generated nor adequate to the diversity and heterogeneity of the interests, desires, and identifications of the subjects who take up its signature. Butler makes this point about the limitations of "queer" as the name in which all the (prospective) members of the gay community would recognize themselves; Lauren Berlant and Elizabeth Freeman express similar reservations about the interpellative power of Queer Nation and the imaginary community it would construct.[39] However, they observe that similar totalizations of identity seem to be a necessary political stratagem in the ongoing war of hegemony and resistance to it. Deploying identity fictions we recognize as such we would practice what Gayatri Chakravorty Spivak has called "strategic essentialism."[40]

As Lacan and Althusser explain, recognition is always misrecognition, the action of the imaginary. Strategic essentialists operate in the realm of choice and conscious knowledge, deliberately differentiating themselves from naive essentialists, who are not supposed to know what they are doing— even when they seem to be doing the very same thing. The naive essentialist is necessarily someone else, even if only a "younger" version of ourselves. Who really is at risk when—"strategically," of course—we take the "risk of essentialism"? What other within the community—or the self—must be excommunicated when we attempt to secure our identity through it? Such stratagems are the province of the ego and inevitably are caught up in aggressive rivalry with the other. R. Radhakrishnan quite rightly worries that when practiced on behalf of ethnic identity, they simply counter one oppression with another: "Doesn't all this sound somehow familiar: the defeat and overthrow of one sovereignty, the emergence and consolidation of an antithetical sovereignty, and the creation of a different, yet the same, repression?."[41] He argues for the critical thematization of the problem of alterity when affirming identity. Such a self-analysis might direct a portion of the death drive against the narcissistic ego. Otherwise, we may be compelled to "act out" over and over again the imaginary struggle between egos, as the death drive is directed against others, given that rivalry can inform morality itself, as Lacan argues in his seminar on the ethics of psychoanalysis. When we do unto others as we would have them do unto us it may be because we love our neighbor as our self, whether or not this is what he wants.[42] There is something beyond the good in the mirror relationship of friendship, something we confront when our friend refuses the good we have wished for him and is not very good to us. He is not my counterpart, after all, if he does not desire my desire. What does he want? What does he want *from me?* What wicked pleasures will he take in me—or from me? I reveal my own evil when I respond to what I fear is his by imposing myself on him, "saving" him from himself by insisting that he enjoy what I do, for his own good—and mine, since I become the instrument of his salvation. As Phillipe Julien explains, "This is a perversion of the love-passion, or, to define it precisely: a pretense to *knowledge (savoir)* about the Other's *jouissance*, which serves to support my devotion to it."[43]

Sedgwick's impulse to privatize desires, identifications, and fantasies is an effort to safeguard them from such an oppressive other, the father who knows best. But as she recognizes in "How to Bring Your Kids Up Gay," they necessarily have a public dimension, especially when they figure in the reverse discourses of countercommunities. "It is worth noting," she writes, "that the gay men [ego psychologist] Richard Friedman admires always have completely discretionary control over everyone else's knowledge of their sexuality; there is no sense that others may have their own intuitions that they are gay . . . no visible participation in gay (physical, cultural, sartorial) semiotics or community. For many contemporary gay people such an existence would be impossible . . . ."[44] Sedgwick articulates a compelling critique of (ego-) psychological therapy undertaken in the name of development and the consolidation of a "core gender identity," which is construed as necessarily heterosexual and masculine for the male child. Yet she implicitly proposes a countertherapeutic mandate when she advocates "supporting gay development" for the "protogay child," envisioning another law of development for another "core gender identity," which is a sexual identity. Would this law be any less repressive, this identity any less "natural" or naturalized, because "perverse"? In his own community, the "other" may be an oppressor, the one whose word is not supposed to be just another law, but a just law: Desire my desire; (be) like me.

SIGNIFYING CLONES

Coming out attempts to *fix* an ideal identity and a community that necessarily recognizes that identity by reflecting it back because everyone shares it. It disavows the split in the self by disavowing the split in discursive address, between self and other, as the other is made the double of the self and her gaze confirms the idealized self-image. When the self and other communicate there is supposed to be no double talk, as Saussure's diagrams of the "speaking circuit" suggest. In them signifiers are always matched with the "proper" signifieds in acts of perfect communication. This is undoubtedly facilitated by the absence in one version of inconvenient human sign producers, who are all too subject to confusion, and their representation in the other as identical talking heads, twins without the desiring bodies that might subject them to Freudian slips of the signifier in their relation to each other.[45] Saussure's ideal speech community is populated by mirror egos, signifying clones. However, as Eco has shown, such doubles signify an ideal they cannot fully embody; they divide each other from their ideal and themselves. The result is the murderous/suicidal rivalry of self and/as other in the imaginary relation, the anxiety of mimicry described by Lacan and Bhabha as each strives to be recognized as the original, the ideal subject who is what he is without the mediation of the Other. It is just this anxiety Barthes articulates in his analysis of the photograph, which "represents that very subtle moment when, to tell the truth, I am neither subject nor object but a subject who feels he is becoming an object: I then experience a micro-version of death . . . I am truly becoming a specter."[46] The subject of the photograph "passes on" because he passes through the object as signifier of some other's desire, whose curious effect is the *passing* of identity itself as it becomes imposture. As Barthes explains it, "In front of the lens, I am at the same time: the one I think I am, the one I want others to think I am, the one the photographer thinks I am, and the one he makes use of to exhibit his art. In other words a strange action: I do not stop imitating myself . . . I invariably suffer from a sensation of inauthenticity, sometimes of imposture . . . "[47] His image, his body is no longer his own; some other is stealing the very stuff of his "self" and using it for his own purposes. What is coming out of Barthes for this other? To what has Barthes consented in posing for him? What right does he have to see Barthes as Barthes cannot see himself, to turn Barthes into a mere facsimile of himself by shooting Barthes with his camera or gaze? Yet how can his mortifying gaze be evaded when it must be solicited so that Barthes can be recognized as himself? There is no "I" without a "you," but no "you" without an eye "through which . . . I am *photo-graphed*," as Lacan says.[48] The Other provides me with the signifiers of my self, which imprint themselves on me (I incorporate them, identify with them), but not without a remainder, the negative that calls into question the ego as positivity, what Lacan calls the stain or *tychic* point on the picture of myself, which is where "you" look at me.[49]

Lacan recounts a parable about himself to illustrate its functioning, a fish story in which the big one does not get away, although it turns out to be only a sardine. As Lacan tells it, when he was in his twenties, and a young, intellectual, he liked to get away and do something that challenged him—and the working classes, against whom he evidently measured himself in the pursuit of their regular occupation. Out on such a fishing expedition one day with a family from Britanny, Lacan was hailed by one of the boat's crew, Petit Jean, who laughed and pointed to something sparkling on the surface of the water: "You see that can? Do you see it? Well, it doesn't see you." As Lacan recognizes with the help of Petit Jean's assertion to the contrary, it did see him and actually gave him the fish-eye, a cold, hard stare that cut him down to size. "It was looking at me at the level of the point of light, the point at which everything that looks at me is situated," he writes, adding, "The point of this little story, as it had occurred to my partner, the fact that he found it so funny and I less so, derives from the fact that, if I am told a story like that one, it is because I, at that moment—as I appeared to those fellows who were earning their livings with great difficulty, in the struggle with what for them was a pitiless nature—looked like nothing on earth. In short, I was rather out of place in the picture."[50] There was something fishy about one of the fishermen in the photo, the *poseur* in the group, whose imposture appeared as such. Thinking to reassure himself with a little game of mimicry, which is linked not only to camouflage but also to travesty and intimidation, as Lacan tells us, he discovered he did not have the biggest one after all. When he pulled in the nets they were empty—not even a sardine in them.[51] In response to the demand for recognition, the other does not always provide a reassuring image of the self as whole, lacking nothing. There is no perfect reciprocity, no purely satisfying sexual or social relation; something is always missing or lacking in one. Beyond the narcissism and paranoia of the imaginary, there is the real, but it cannot be caught in the signifying nets of the symbolic. It remains resistant to meaning, like Eco's absent ideal, driving the subject to new relations with the Other, in which he continues to encounter the trauma Lacan calls *tuché*.[52] The illegible detail or stain on Lacan's picture of himself makes his face a mask and his acts a masquerade that question his very being. It is the mark of his desire for what he does not have and cannot be: no sardines for the would-be analyst, whose desire is for an unsatisfied desire, like that of "the beautiful butcher's wife," the hysteric whose dream of not having the caviar she wanted was analyzed by both Freud and Lacan.[53] As Bhabha argues, drawing on Lacan, mimicry is camouflage, travesty, and intimidation, a (su)stained imitation through which we are hailed into place but also called into question.[54] Beyond our eye is the gaze of the Other, which ensures that the "I" is not secured by vision. I never see what I want or exhibit what is desired in the phallic masquerade, whose effects are ambiguous.

DIFFERENCES

At once worshipped and castrated, the fetish signifies both knowledge and ignorance of difference. The effort to fix identity and community, therefore, must fail, no matter how strict the panoptic (self-)surveillance. Hegemony is always in process, as subcultures engage in a style politics that denaturalizes the apparent universality of the meanings and identities of the dominant culture. Yet subcultures themselves seek to consolidate identity and community through an appeal to counter norms and essences, to motivated rather than purely aribtrary signs, which legitimates and naturalizes certain meanings or "appropriations" of forms and outlaws others as misappropriations or thefts. Kobena Mercer resorts to just such a strategy in his discussion of black hairstyle politics. He seeks to celebrate the diversity of black hairstyles as testimony to "an inventive, improvisational aesthetic" and as resistance to white cultural norms, a resistance that is not grounded in the recovery of a black essence or nature.[55] The Afro or "natural" was no more an iconic or indexical sign of its referent—African ancestry—than was the curly perm, and as he sees it both have been effective weapons in the political struggle over the meaning of blackness through their revalorization of "the ethnic signifier."[56] However, Mercer appeals to the "nature" of black hair when he asserts that only it can be matted into dreadlocks, which is belied by the spread of the style into other racial groups (as happened with corn-rows or braids—and African-American and Caribbean music, as he notes).[57] No hairstyle is a natural or iconic signifier of blackness; the effort to "fix" such signifiers in the nineteenth century was part of a racist science of anthropometry.

Nor is there a style that is indexically bonded to a racial identity, as we might infer from Mercer's discussions of braids. He argues that the Afro was readily depoliticized and incorporated into the mainstream because it—like dread locks—was the product of an "imaginary Africa" and romanticized nature, and as such caught up in a dualistic logic of opposition to European culture.[58] "Neither style had a given reference point in existing African culture," he points out, in which hair is often braided in elaborate styles "reminiscent of the patternings of African textiles and the decorative designs of African ceramics, architecture, and embroidery."[59] Mercer finds a similarity across very different aesthetic realms and ethnic variations within those realms, concluding,

"Underlying these practices is an African approach to the aesthetic."[60] This aesthetic sensibility he discovers functions rather like the expression of a structuralist ur-structure, an "African mind"; it is not the simple empirical fact he presents it as, but the work of his own cultural construction of unity out of diversity. The photos on facing pages elaborating his argument are part of this labor. One details ethnic specificity; it is captioned "Fouta Djallon Peul woman, Guinea." The two on the opposite page perform the African universal; there is only a single caption for both photos, reading, "Contemporary beaded designs, from *African Hairstyles*, Esi Sagay, 1983."[61] The African identity to which the (diasporic) publication title refers is actually the creation of the diaspora, according to Sterling Stuckey, who explains, "Slave ships were the first real incubators of slave unity across the cultural lines, cruelly revealing irreducible links from one ethnic group to the other."[62] Mercer thus participates in the process of opposition and negation he has described, in which "Neo-African" differences from Europe matter more than differences from other Africans. His too is an imaginary Africa and is constructed in relation to European colonial maps of a space whose different peoples were unified under a racial signifier. Mercer knows this, yet disavows it, not only citing Africa as an empirical given but also appealing to historical survivalism, referring to braids as the trace of an indexical relation to that Africa when he writes, "Once the Afro had been ingested, black Americans brought *traditional* braiding and plaiting styles out from under their wraps, introducing novel elements such as beads and feathers into corn-row patterns."[63] If braids in Africa are not all the same, thanks to ethnic differences, braids in America are surely not the same as those in Africa, even without novel elements. Mercer's indexical claim relies on an implicit iconic reduction and is caught up in a counter-hegemonic strategy that cannot be radically outside the logic of hegemony and resistance to it. Braids have a different meaning in Africa than in the diaspora, where they mean "Africa," just as the Afro and dreadlocks do.

Africa is the product of history, and history is the product of historiography, a genre of writing with conventions for creating indexical, cause-effect relations between events it selects and nominates as such. History is therefore a cross-cultural construct—a creole artifact—as Stuart Hall argues: "[C]ultural identity is not a fixed essence at all, lying unchanged outside history and culture. . . . The past continues to speak to us . . . [but] [i]t is always constructed through memory, fantasy, narrative and myth."[64] Forms cannot be permanently normalized, as subculture studies theorist Dick Hebdige has observed.[65] The object of what Eric Lott describes as "love and theft," African-American signifiers are themselves subject to the reappropriation from which Mercer would "save" them.[66] Their resignification is not so much a depoliticization of a style as a different politicization of it, which is not necessarily always conservative. "So who, in this postmodern melee of semiotic appropriation and countercreolization, is imitating whom?" Mercer asks, recognizing the two-way traffic in signs whose inevitable doubleness can secure no identity—or identity politics—on a permanent basis.[67] When there are no traffic cops or natural signs, there can only be reappropriations of contingent signifiers and mimicry of the identities to which they refer as their retroactive origins. The same does not repeat itself without a trace of difference, which unsettles the identity of the subject hailed by a name or an image (mis)recognized as the self.

IDENTITIES

Do meaning and identity take place at all, or are they endlessly deferred, in process? Both Hall and Žižek express reservations about what they describe as the poststructuralist play of the signifier, which they link with Derridean deconstruction. Perhaps recalling Derrida's analysis of writing as violence, Hall emphasizes the metaphorical "cut" or "arrest" of identity and meaning, "the contingent and arbitrary stop—the necessary and temporal 'break' in the infinite semiosis of language."[68] Whereas Hall describes this cut as "strategic," suggesting it might be within our control, Žižek, like Lacan, believes it exceeds our consciousness of it and links it to the law by describing it as symptomatic, neurotic, or perverse. "[T]he fundamental gesture of post-structuralism is to deconstruct every substantial identity . . . ," he writes. "[T]he notion of symptom is the necessary counterpoint to it, the substance of enjoyment, the real kernel around which this signifying interplay is structured."[69] The cut is made by and sutured through the prohibition of the Other, leaving a scar, the mark of symbolic castration. It determines identity as impersonation, the masquerade or display of what one "has" to offer the other, which is a matter of phallic substitutes and fetishes—not what one really wants to give, not what the other really wants to get (there is no sexual relation, as Lacan reiterates). The phallus functions as the occluded signifier of this lack in both the subject and the Other, setting in motion the substitutions and displacements of desire and the identifications with traits that make the subject "lovable" and loving. The effect of symbolic castration is not so much the play of the signifier as the illusion of fixed meaning that stops that play when a signified is attached to a signifier at an anchoring point or *point de caption*. The law would police identities by determining which signs are rightly one's own and which have been stolen, but it is desire and defenses against it that limit semiosis and structure masquerades of having and being that are the substance of our character, our identity—the position we take up in response to the law. Žižek explains the radical contingency of the name through Saul Kripke's notion of "the rigid designator," which ensures identity in difference, beyond all the changes in content or properties time and circumstances make in a person, thing, or action. It is a paradoxical principle of iconicity that ensures the subject always resembles himself, no matter how much the image in the mirror changes. "[T]his guaranteeing the identity of an object in all counterfactual situations—through a change of all its descriptive features—is *the retroactive effect of naming itself*: it is the name itself, the signifier, which supports the identity of the object," Žižek writes.[70] In Lacanian theory, that name is the Name-of-the Father *(nom/non du père)*, which institutes sexual difference and identity as a rigid designation, though with no particular content given in advance, as Lacan suggests in his seminar *Encore* by resorting to logical propositions to define the sexes with respect to the phallic function of castration.[71] Explicating these formulas, Joan Copjec says they preclude the determination of sex by particular attributes: "The principle of sorting is no longer descriptive, i.e., it is not a matter of shared characteristics or a common substance. Whether one falls into the class of males or females depends, rather, on . . . which enunciative position one assumes.[72] Currently *sex* has all but been replaced by *gender* in discussions of sexual difference because *gender* is the word associated with now dominant social constructionist theories. However, Copjec employs the terms that have denoted biological differences once assumed to be beyond empirical givens, rather than constructs, perhaps to underline that sexual difference cannot be changed because it cannot be reduced to changing historical discourses about sex in spite of the fact that the latter is a social construct. This is another way of saying that the phallus is not the penis and no imaginary organ can determine a subject's sexed identity, despite the obstetrician's confident assertions based on just that ("It's a boy!"). Emphasizing this at a different moment in the history of discourses about sex and gender, in *Encore* Lacan prefers a phrasing just the opposite of Copjec's, writing that sex is a matter of "choice," of how one situates or inscribes oneself in a sexed binary.[73] Copjec is concerned sexual difference is now seen as volitional, as if one could decide to do without it or pick something else altogether, a notion conveyed by the title of one of the books by transgender theorist Kate Bornstein, *Gender Outlaw: On Men, Women, and the Rest of Us.* Lacan, on the other hand, wishes to stress taking responsibility for one's desires, which implies liberty despite constraint; Žižek discusses this as the "forced choice of freedom," the paradox of free will even in what seems determined.[74] Sexual identity therefore is a catachresis, not only as a predication without a positive content but also as a freely chosen subjection, like a tragic hero's claiming responsibility for something for which he is not entirely to blame.

In a notorious passage in *Ecrits* Lacan conveys just this mix of free will and social determinism as he describes not just the individual's but our culture's relation to the phallus that structures sexual difference. "It can be said that this signifier is chosen because it is the most tangible element in the real of sexual copulation, and also the most symbolic . . . since it is equivalent . . . to the (logical) copula," Lacan writes. "It might also be said that, by virtue of its turgidity, it is the image of the vital flow as it is transmitted in generation."[75] The godlike creative power of the phallus, which makes human subjects, is here attributed to the penis, at once the element "the most tangible" and the most visible (as "the image of the vital flow") in sexual reproduction, according to Lacan. Through a slip of the signifier, sexual copulation and the logical copula are rendered fungible, so that the penis and phallus become interchangeable. The tangibility of the penis is displaced onto the phallus, and the predication the latter inaugurates—the judgments of existence and the processes of attribution and substitution that constitute language and subjects —is associated with the penis, which is made the progenitor of life itself as its first predicate. By implication, the woman participates in conception only passively, contributing little more than the lifeless matter (the egg) that is animated by "the vital flow" of active sperm, a rather sexist version of reproduction that was lampooned as early as the 1940s by Ruth Herschberger, who narrated a very different, "matriarchal" story, with a large and powerful egg as heroine.[76] As Lacan tells it, the penis-phallus is the proper representative of life and death, and so of desire itself (as eros and the death drive). The real is not entirely absent from such a signifier, which functions as a "fetish," as Lacan himself suggests: "Certainly we should not forget that the organ invested with this signifying function takes on the value of a fetish."[77] If Lacan fetishistically confuses the penis and the phallus—though he once critiqued Ernest Jones for it, as Joël Dor points out—he takes partial responsibility for that desire, not quite openly avowing it as his choice by disguising the agent in the passive syntax of the phrasing ("this signifier is chosen . . ." or in the French, "ce signifiant est choisi").[78] Lacan's "choice" of that fetish is forced; he is constrained to mistake imaginary for symbolic castration because our culture has determined to do so, classifying infants according to the presence or absence of the penis. This reduction of human difference to that anatomical binary is especially evident in medical discourses about intersexuality and to a lesser extent transsexualism. As Suzanne Kessler makes clear in *Lessons from the Intersexed*, "The formulation 'good penis equals male; absence of good penis equals female,' is treated in the literature and by the physicians interviewed as an objective criterion, operative in all cases. There is striking lack of attention to the size and shape requirements of the female genitals other than that the clitoris be not too big . . . and that the vagina be able to receive a penis. . . ."[79] Though today not all MTF (male-to-female) transsexuals are oriented toward surgery, as most once were, it is nevertheless the case that castration, penectomy, and vaginoplasty are still common, an indication that the penis remains for most of us "the absolute insignia of maleness," as Marjorie Garber says, quoting Robert Stoller's recurrent phrase in his influential explanations of transsexualism and transvestism. (Garber shows that the contemporary inability to construct a functioning penis means that FTM transsexuals are not presented with an equivalent surgical choice.)[80] Both sexes confront the fact that the symbolic distinguishes men and women on the basis of the presence and absence of the penis "as a sham referent for the phallus," as Teresa Brennan puts it, a phrase that recalls Lacan's fetishism as she discusses this conflation as one of the "non-contingent" or "transhistorical" parameters for the structure of sexual difference that "set limits on how far the repressed can return . . . ," though they cannot entirely determine psychical reality and the fantasies that express it.[81]

The fetishism of the penis supports the function of the symbolic father as having—at the imaginary level—what the mother lacks and desires. It thus helps catalyze the dissolution of the little boy's fantasy of "being" the mother's phallus, for which "having" the phallus (or, rather, "appearing" to have it, as Lacan emphasizes) ultimately substitutes, enabling the boy to defy the very castration the lacking mother signifies and threatens. As fetish, the penis is a recognition of and a defense against castration, always already caught up in a perverse disvowal of lack and a hysterical parade of virility by which the man stages his claim to having. Lacan almost immediately qualifies his perverse confusion of the penis and phallus by asserting, "All these propositions merely conceal the fact that it can play its role only when veiled . . . ."[82] By reframing his fetishistic claims as symptoms of the fact that the penis is actually not the phallus, he reconstructs the perversion as neurotic, a compromise formation both expressing and defending against desire and the castration anxiety aroused by it. Yet this self-reflexive assertion of neurosis structures his two consecutive paragraphs as an exemplary instance of fetishistic disavowal. Across them, Lacan performs a splitting of the ego: he knows very well the penis is not the phallus and everyone is lacking and desiring, but just the same . . . . Lacan attributes this particular fetishism to both men and women, although fetishism, like all the perversions, is usually said by psychoanalysts to be restricted to men. The typical fetish is that special something in the object, the "shine on the nose" in the case with which Freud opens his essay on the topic, that fascinates the subject. Freud's first and somewhat unusual example does not require that the fetish object make the fetishist's desire her own and therefore most clearly illustrates how the fetish is in the end an "answer of the real," some essentially contingent element of the object, even something projected on to it, that enables the perverse subject to transgress the paternal law and maintain a fantasy that he alone secures the jouissance of the mother, who thus lacks nothing. The fetishist allays his anxiety about his own and the Other's lack with a pretense to knowledge about the Other's desire: the (M)Other enjoys what the father has, the penis as phallus or the "gifts" that serve as its symbol at the anal level. "Where one is caught short, where one cannot, as a result of the lack, give what is to be given, one can always give something else," Lacan explains.[83] If the Father did not have what the mother wanted, how could our symbolic, our identities, have a consistency? What would guarantee sexual difference— or any difference, for the mother might have no desire to turn from her child to someone else for narcissistic satisfaction, prohibiting the child's differentiation?

The anxiety these questions provoke results in the sometimes hysteric disavowal by psychoanalytic theorists of the difference between the phallus and the penis. Like Freud's patient, who "pressed her dress to her body with one hand (as the woman) while trying to tear it off with the other (as the man)," they remind us the penis is not the phallus while insisting that it is especially well suited to play that part.[84] If perversions contain a kernel of neurosis, as Elizabeth Grosz suggests Freud believed by the time he wrote "A Child Is Being Beaten," then hysteric bisexuality could be a symptom of the fetishist's desire as a continuing question about the name of the rigid designator.[85] Am I a boy or a girl? Do I have the means to be the cause of the Other's desire? These questions cannot be separated for the fetishist whose identification with the phallic object can be expressed as transvestism, in which the subject fetishizes himself, as psychoanalyst Otto Fenichel explains.[86] Freud, too, seems to recognize in it a certain indifference to the site of the fetish, as is suggested by his example of the fig leaf, the fetish that covers the genitals of statues of both sexes, and his analysis of the bathing-suit fetish of one of his patients, which he says allowed the patient to disavow the castration of both men and women, presumably because anyone might wear it.[87] Could gender as a phallic masquerade be a form of neurotic transvestism?

Lacan (with Granoff) seems to rule out this possibility in a 1956 essay that predates "The Signification of the Phallus" by just two years, suggesting that there is no neurosis that corresponds to fetishism, let alone one within it, although we might expect a neurotic analogue to it, given that Freud defines neuroses as the negative of perversions.[88] Unlike Lacan, Freud does link fetishism to neurosis: he notes that the fetishist does not simply scotomize the traumatic sight of castration, like a psychotic, but represses it, like a neurotic.[89] He also describes the fetish, like the neurotic symptom, as a compromise formation, contrasting the perversion with psychosis, in which "the true idea which accorded with reality would have been *really* absent."(Ibid.) Curiously, however, what is repressed seems to return in the real for at least some fetishists, albeit in disguised form. There is an element of hallucination in the distinction between women with and without shiny noses, for instance, that we normally associate with psychosis; we might consider whether the same can be said of the difference between a "real" (good enough) penis and a clitoris at stake in intersexual surgeries. The consistency or identity of things has an imaginary as well as symbolic, dimension; indeed, human knowledge itself is paranoid in form, as Lacan reminds us another suggestion that the "normal" shares certain features with psychosis.[90] The generalized fetishism of the penis that is for Lacan at once a cause and effect of symbolic castration and a hysteric parade of virility stabilizes and normalizes the "delusional" misrecognition of the penis structuring patriarchal identities and the perverse and neurotic resistance to them.

Psychosis and the consistency of sexual identity has been the implicit focus of several hours of the *Jerry Springer* talk show, which in one broadcast featured Shawn, a female-to-male transsexual (originally called Tanya) who was not yet taking male hormones and had not made any plans for surgery.[91] "I have always felt like a boy," Shawn asserted at the beginning of the program, a statement typical for transsexuals, who have had to affirm this in order to be eligible for surgery, whether or not it is true. Jerry Springer's response was to declare the statement meaningless, since Shawn was *not* a boy. In an implicit appeal to the rigid designator, Springer explained that whatever he did and felt must be what a man does and feels because he (Springer) *was* a man. As far as he was concerned masculine identity had no essential content—there were no iconic or indexical signs of it—aside from the rigid designator itself; sex was therefore completely arbitrary and absolutely fixed, not amenable to social (and surgical) reconstruction after its initial construction. This sentiment was seconded by a man in the audience who sought to show the absurdity of Shawn's claim by asking, "What if I said I have always felt like a snake?" Yet another man told Shawn he was depriving men of two good women (Shawn appeared on the show with his girlfriend) and alluded to the satisfactions only a real penis could provide. However, Shawn, like Lacan, recognized that "[w]here one is caught short, where one cannot, as a result of the lack, give what is to be given, one can always give something else," and resorted to the now classic line of feminists and sex-therapists, that bigger is not necessarily better.[92] For him, the designator was not so rigid; he simply reappropriated it for his "nub," as he called it. It could substitute for the penis, which also comes up short when measured against the phallus because it is never "good enough."

Obviously, the fetishist believes in *his* particular fetish; what works for one fetishist will not always work for another, as is suggested by the history of the realist fetish—nothing looks more phony to film students today than the classic Hollywood cinema (they believe in the special effects of Industrial Light and Magic instead). Shawn was not going to convert to apostacy the disciples of our patriarchy's rigid designator. As Žižek explains, such conversions are never a matter of rational persuasion in any case, but of transference, which "consists of the illusion that the meaning of a certain element (which was retroactively fixed by the intervention of the master-signifier) was present in it from the very beginning as its immanent essence."[93] Shawn still believes in sexual difference; however, the phallus no longer looks like a "good enough" penis to him, unless it is a penis seen through an anamorphic lens, so that it resembles a "nub." Has what Žižek, echoing Lacan, calls the "rock of castration," upon which psychoanalysis has built its faith, been shifted, perhaps even shattered to bits, by such transgender revisions?[94] Do they render "contingent" what Butler and others have objected to as "transhistorical" in the psychoanalytic theory of sexual defense?[95]

PHALLOCENTRISM IS "NOT-ALL"

Žižek provides several examples of what he calls "not-all," the paradoxically nontotalized totality that an ideological, symbolic discourse is because there is always something that exceeds it, that slips through the signifying net as its intimate "outside," an inconsistency within it that keeps the structure open, in play. That something is the exception that proves the rule: though there is nothing outside the rule and the structure it governs, nevertheless that is "not all" there is. Žižek cites Churchill's famous statement about democracy as one instance of it: "It is true that democracy is the worst of all possible systems; the problem is that no other system would be better!"[96] Can the same be said of phallocentric psychoanalysis? Is phallocentrism all there is to it—or is it "not-all"? Is there something more to psychoanalysis, in excess of the law of castration and the phallic signifier that critics have argued prescribe oppressive gender and sexual norms? Can psychoanalysis account for resistance to those norms and for the production of alternatives to them?

Most feminists who have embraced psychoanalysis have done so because they have valued its theory of resistance despite its phallocentrism, a resistance psychoanalytic theory has located primarily in the unconscious. The unconscious ensures that what Sedgwick worries about in "How to Bring Your Kids Up Gay" can never happen. Though parents may try to raise their kids straight, some always seem to find the other manual in the closet, the one whose title echoes Sedgwick's.[97] The reverse would be equally true—and statistics about the sexual identities of the children of gay and lesbian parents seem to bear this out. As Rose emphasizes, psychoanalysis assumes that demands and the identities in conformity with them are not internalized, "implanted" and "incorporated" (to use Foucault's terms) without a remainder that destabilizes them.[98] For Freud that remainder is the unconscious, which troubles our conscious identity and object relations through the return of what we have repressed (for example, the homosexual object choice he asserts we have all made in our unconscious).[99] Paradoxically, what is excluded or repressed by consciousness is actually included in our speech and acts as the slips of the tongue, parapraxes, mysterious symptoms without organic causes, sudden impulses, and so on that disrupt reason, which the analyst helps the analysand interpret and symbolically integrate.

However, one feminist who has taken issue with the valorization of the unconscious as a force of resistance reminds us that it is the vehicle of normalization as well as resistance, through unconscious attachments to subjection.[100] Developing this argument, Butler notes that psychoanalysis associates the unconscious with what is outside the symbolic; at different points in her work she claims it is linked to the imaginary or to the real. That nonsymbolic status, she asserts, "reifies" the law of castration and sexual difference, rendering it a transhistorical necessity if psychosis is to be avoided, rather than historically contingent and "subject to the discursive rearticulation proper to hegemony," that is, to the labor of production, reproduction, and potential alteration of any element of a social formation from within that social formation's discourses, a process she discusses as "iteration."[101] If the law cannot be changed it will reinscribe as "unintelligible," "abject," and "excluded"—if not psychotic—the resistant identities outside its norms, those of woman, the lesbian, the gay man.[102] The reproduction of normativity and its constitutive outside is an idealist essentialism, Butler argues, "an effort to preclude the possibility of a future for the signifier" through its resignification by those who invest in identity terms but do not reiterate them, instead using them improperly, "calling the aardvark 'Napoleon'"—or a woman a man, and a human a snake, as talk-show host Jerry Springer's audience feared.[103] Normative ideals are not reproduced perfectly because "repetition implies the discontinuity of the material," that is, a space or time of difference in the disciplinary rituals through which the norm is expressed and performatively constituted.[104]

Butler offers as one solution to an essential phallocentrism the resignification of the phallus itself as it fails to be perfectly reproduced. In her discussion of the "lesbian phallus" in *Bodies that Matter*, she disseminates the inseminating, reproductive penis as the phallic guarantor of woman's castration and of heterosexuality. She decenters the organ by deconstructing the hierarchically unified partial drives whose structure Freud outlined as early as 1905 in *Three Essays on the Theory of Sexuality*, recovering the trace of narcissistic investments in other erotogenic zones and enjoyment in aims once primary before they were reorganized as mere forepleasures. The return of the repressed in conversion hysteria (such as Dora's coughing) and other symptomatic and fantasmatic formations, including perversions, in which a sexual function is taken on by body parts other than the genitals (and by nonsexual acts), and as Butler argues, the hypochondriac's narcissistic investment in other body parts detailed in Freud's 1914 essay, "On Narcissism," reveals the fragility of what Freud termed "development" in 1905. "The phallus is then set up as that which confers erotogenicity and signification on these body parts" that function as its substitutes, Butler argues, showing how the phallus serves as an "origin" or prototype that is meant to constrain the metonymic slide between zones (and aims) that structures the rhetoric of the narcissism essay as Freud labors to (re)instate the preeminence of the phallus.[105] That "slide" also informs the "rhetoric" of "sexual development" itself articulated in *Three Essays*, in which the phallus is not just origin but end, since its centrality is destined by maturation. Revealing how plastic and transferable the imaginary power and erotogenicity of the phallus are, Freud undermines his effort to fix and idealize the penis as the phallus by making the former the prototype, both *arche* and *telos*, of the latter's attributes.

Lacan's theory of the phallus is susceptible to the same analysis, Butler asserts. "As an idealization of a body part, the phantasmatic figure of the phallus within Lacan's essay ["The Signification of the Phallus"] undergoes a set of contradictions similar to those which unsettled Freud's analysis of erotogenic body parts," she says.[106] The phallus "is itself instituted through the repudiation of its partial, decentered, and substitutable character," just as it was in Freud.[107] And just as in Freud, it proves to be identical with the penis, though not simply through an imaginary similarity. Rather, theirs is a relation of "determinate negation," since as Butler sees it, in Lacan's major essay on the phallus, "the phallus *must* negate the penis in order to symbolize and signify in its privileged way."[108] Butler concludes that because of this logical (and therefore symbolic) connection, "the phallus requires the penis for its own constitution, the identity of the phallus includes the penis . . . [and] a relation of identity holds between them."[109] Alluding to the feminist critique of the patriarchal symbolic as a masculine imaginary organized around having or being this phallus-penis, Butler suggests that the result of her deconstructive displacement of its transcendental status is "alternative imaginaries," that is, imaginary morphologies and egos (given that the latter are a projection of the former) other than those said to be normative in Western culture.[110] The "lesbian phallus" is one such example, she writes, explaining that it "crosses the orders of *having* and *being* [the phallus]; it both wields the threat of castration (which is in that sense a mode of 'being the phallus,' as women 'are') and suffers from castration anxiety (and so is said 'to have' the phallus, and to fear its loss)" and therefore can "call into question the mutually exclusive trajectories of castration anxiety and penis envy."[111] Butler notes that this also could be true of the phallus of the heterosexual man or woman, deconstructing gender difference.[112] She thus locates the "resistance" of the subject in the "free play" of Lacan's phallic transcendental signifier once it has been separated from the penis and resignified so that the sex/gender structure it seemed to reify is decentered and opened to different sex and gender iterations.

There is only one thing Butler's resignified phallus must not be, and that is the penis-phallus that results from the determinate negation of the penis by the Lacanian phallus. The play of the disseminated phallus is constrained by that one condition, which would suggest, by Butler's reasoning, that it is in a relation of determinate negation to Lacan's determinate negation of the penis, and therefore identical with the latter. Her insistence that there cannot be an absolute break with phallocentrism would seem to confirm this.[113] Butler's ambiguous "denegation" of the penis repeats the disavowal Freud theorizes as characteristic of fetishism, in which castration is at once affirmed and denied. As Freud says in his essay on fetishism, for the fetishist, "the woman still has a penis in spite of all, but this penis is no longer the same as it once was"—it has been negated through castration but also affirmed through the negation of that negation in a process like that in which the Lacanian phallus and the penis are caught up in Butler's critique.[114] The fetish is the penis that is "no longer the same," one that is somewhere else on the woman than on the man because the identity of a "different" corporeal (or fashion) element has been denegated when the fetishist "transferred the importance of the penis to another part of the body," according to Freud, whose description seems to anticipate the reconfiguration of imaginary morphology Butler attributes to the lesbian phallus.[115] The fetish, like Butler's phallus, is also entirely compatible with castration anxiety, as Freud makes clear. "We have come across fetishists who have developed the same fear of castration as nonfetishists," he explains, because disavowal involves "two contrary premises [sic]," and a "splitting of the ego" with regard to reality; for that reason, "fetishism is so often only partially developed."[116] Because the fetishist recognizes reality and does not simply deny it, there may be only a trace of fetishism informing his erotic relations, and the latter may not be as rigidly constrained as they are in clinical cases of the perversion.

Butler's is not the only feminist or queer (re)iteration of fetishism. In 1985 Leo Bersani and Ulysses Dutoit developed a similar "formal model of desire's mobility," which they, like Butler, detached from the penis-phallus.[117] "The crucial point—which makes the fetishistic object different from the phallic symbol—is that the success of the fetish depends on its being seen as authentically different from the missing penis," they assert.[118] Both Parveen Adams and Teresa de Lauretis have drawn on their work to articulate a theory of a lesbian fetishism that would be free from the paternal penis-phallus. In a discussion of lesbian sado-masochism and Della Grace's photo "The Three Graces," Adams argues the dildo disturbs the conventional identification of the penis with the phallus.[119] The dildo, she claims, lacks "the air of masquerading potency that the phallus still attracts to itself"; it "does not cover over castration but reminds us of it."[120] The Della Grace photo instantiates a new, "dildoic" sexuality associated with lesbian sado-masochism. "The women are both phallic and castrated . . . which puts them beyond recognition," Adams says; "the difference in question cannot be the difference of 'having' and 'being.'"[121] Yet Adams's grammar recognizes the women as women despite the claim they are unrecognizable as such. Their ambiguity—and hers—is symptomatic of fetishism as theorized by Freud. They are phallic women, endowed with a denegated penis-phallus somewhere else on their bodies (their bald heads, their piercings and tattoos, as Adams discusses them).

Critiquing Adams, de Lauretis claims that all lesbians, not just lesbian sado-masochists, are fetishists and disavow castration and must be differentiated from men and heterosexual women on the basis of their "freedom from the phallus."[122] Whereas Adams tends to stress the avowal in disavowal, emphasizing the recognition of castration that the dildo, unlike the phallus, affords, de Lauretis privileges the denial in disavowal instead, underscoring the "narcissistically empowered image" of womanhood she believes lesbian fetishism provides.[123] "Failing the mother's narcissistic validation of the daughter's body-image, castration means the lack or loss of the female body; that is to say, the castration complex rewrites in the symbolic a narcissistic wound, a lack of being (Lacan's *manque-à-être*), already established in the imaginary matrix of the body-ego," de Lauretis asserts; "it rewrites it in terms of anatomical ("natural") sexual difference, refiguring as lack of a penis what was first and foremost lack of a lovable body."[124] Through lesbian fetishism—which de Lauretis conflates with "desire" and "love," though she is critical of Paula Bennett for confusing desire and sexual pleasure—the wound is repaired.[125] Lesbian fetishism therefore seems to satisfy desire and restores an imaginary self-perfection; it works like what Lacan calls love, rather than desire, since the latter makes for a lack of satisfaction that disturbs every object relation. While psychoanalysis explains gender as the effect of symbolic castration, de Lauretis locates it in the imaginary or even earlier, which is why she alternates freely between "female" and "feminine," whose different meanings have long been the subject of discussion by feminists, and does not consistently distinguish between "phallus," "paternal phallus," "paternal penis," and "penis" (hence the appeal to "freedom from the phallus" rather than from the paternal penis as the patriarchal solution to the enigma of the mother's desire). The "lovable body" the lesbian lacks is always already female, even if it is not feminine like the mother's. Though the boy's body is not "lovable" in the way the child demands, since he too cannot satisfy the mother's desire, for de Lauretis his insufficiency does not count as castration because he has a penis—despite the fact that it is not the paternal penis (and even the latter requires phallic "supplements" that never fully assuage maternal desire); he too is therefore always already gendered. As in Adams gender is always already recognized before it is performatively (de)constructed. As with Adams too, much of what de Lauretis attributes to lesbian fetishism is characteristic of any fetishism as Freud has described it, particularly those forms which are not severely constraining, in which the fetishism may be so minor as to constitute little more than the material conditions of satisfaction that delimit every object choice and a splitting of the ego more neurotic than perverse.[126]

Each of these feminist and queer (re)iterations of fetishism reproduces the disavowal of castration in Freud and Lacan, for whom the penis and phallus are not entirely distinct, and makes gender at once natural and a social construct. If the resistance to gender norms seems to repeat them, it is a mark of the agency of the letter—and the language community—in the unconscious. When we call an aardvark Napoleon, its identity is both recognized and refused because the phrase suggests that what is actually an aardvark is only being "called" Napoleon. We might conclude that this is just an effect of the limitations of grammar, applying to this example what Butler says about the constraints of grammar in her theorization of the "individual" prior to ideological interpellation.[127] Grammar implies there is always/already an ideological subject who is hailed and thereby constituted as a subject; so too man and woman, having and lacking, seem to be born, rather than made. Yet grammar itself is what testifies to our membership in the community that speaks and is spoken by a given language and shares a world whose meanings and identities that language constitutes. Napoleon is only a madman if no one else believes he is who he says he is, which is the result of what Žižek describes as communal fetishism. "'Being-a-king' is an effect of the network of social relations between a 'king' and his 'subjects'; but—and here is the fetishistic misrecognition—to the participants of this social bond, the relationship appears necessarily in an inverse form," Žižek writes. "They think that they are subjects giving the king royal treatment because the king is already in himself, outside the relationship to his subjects, a king. . . ."[128] The king seems to have a special value outside the social structure which creates it, but his identity is actually the product of his identification with the name by which his subjects hail him. He in turn interpellates them as subjects; mutual recognition—or transference and counter-transference—thus constitutes the reality of king and subjects. That always/already recognition, at once a citation and a performative, (re)produces their shared reality, the "social contract" as the "forced choice of freedom," as Žižek characterizes it, "choosing what is given" in one's history.[129] He explains what little freedom in its ordinary sense this "choice" involves, pointing out that "the subject 'doesn't really do anything,' he only assumes the guilt-responsibility for the given state of things—that is, he accepts it as 'his own work' by a purely formal act. . . ."[130] The psychoanalytic model for this is the tragic heroism of Oedipus, who accepted the blame for the violence resulting from acts for which he was not entirely responsible. Oedipus claimed "his guilt" by acknowledging subjective involvement in the trauma that happened to him when he met up with the desires of others, particularly those of his parents, in a story he thus made his own. We too must come to terms with the desires of our parents as our "cause"—quite literally of our conception—in which fantasies about gender and corporeality (ours and theirs) played a role.

Lacan evokes patriarchal communal fetishism when he tells us that the organ that functions as the phallic signifier of the woman's desire "takes on the value of a fetish." Though the penis is not the phallus, the oedipal structure of the modern Western family invites that misrecognition. Because of the infant's radical prematurity and the origin of the partial drives in the biological needs from which they diverge, the subject's desire is the desire of the mother as the primordial Other. He is determined by and alienated in her signifiers, conforming to her demands in an effort to be what she desires, the imaginary phallic object. The subject only achieves a measure of freedom and subjectivity through the separation from the maternal Other in whom he was alienated, and that is made possible by symbolic castration or lack. Insofar as the mother turns elsewhere for what she wants—in the Western nuclear family, to the father—the child cannot complete her and must recognize his castration, together with the mother's. The Name-of-the-Father (the father's "name" and "no," in the French pun on *nom* and *non*) thus substitutes for the name of the mother's desire as the child identifies with the father, adopting a new relation to the phallus, a relation of (not) having it, rather than (not) being it. With the resolution of the Oedipus and castration complexes, the child is once again alienated, this time in the father's signifying mandate, rather than the mother's, which has been repressed by the paternal identification. However, the subject as split into consciousness and the unconscious has appeared in the difference between maternal and paternal signifiers, as the process of transformation. Lack in the symbolic of an imaginary (proto) signifier, the imaginary phallus, inaugurates the process of substitutive exchanges associated with the symbolic phallus as signifier of the Other's desire, which always remains unsatisfied no matter what is given. The father's penis was identified with the phallus in an ultimately provisional resolution of the enigma of the mother's desire, whose apparent identification with the father's desire seems to account for her separation from the child and serves as an antidote to the anxiety generated by the lack of any answer to the question of desire. The fetish is a momentary arrest of identity and desire, a defense against the lack it screens.

It is its contingency as a phallic signifier that makes the penis a fetish. Something other than the father's desire can signify phallic lack and separate the mother and child; Bruce Fink points out that the castrating phobias Freud finds in Little Hans and other patients serve that function.[131] Something other than the father's penis can serve as the signifier of the mother's desire, the phallus that would satisfy it and fill her lack. Lacan alludes to such phallic supplements and substitutes in 1964 when he discusses gift-giving: "where one cannot, as a result of the lack, give what is to be given, one can always give something else."[132] However, he anticipates them as early as the 1958 essay on the signification of the phallus when he draws attention to the phallic masks and acting that propel the sexual relation into comedic theater, emphasizing "the intervention of an 'appearing' which gets substituted for the 'having,' so as to protect it [the phallus] on one side and mask its lack on the other. . . ."[133] By 1974, in *Encore*, he suggests that the phallus itself is "mere contingency," an analytic construct.[134] Perhaps with that in mind, Žižek declares the phallus a fetish. "Insofar as a fetish is an element that fills in the lack of (the maternal) phallus, the most concise definition of the phallic signifier is that it is a *fetish of itself*: phallus qua 'signifier of castration' as it were gives body to *its own lack*," he writes.[135] The phallus, like the penis, is a disavowal of the lack of the phallus; it is a defense against itself as what cannot be integrated into the symbolic through a signifier and does not have an imaginary gestalt. According to Žižek, then, the phallus always already was the resignification for which Butler calls and that Bersani and Dutoit, Adams, and de Lauretis practice. "The 'identity' of the phallus resides in its own displacement," Žižek says in a discussion of Butler's critique of Lacan.[136] He also affirms as "the fundamental feature" of symbolic castration what he notes Butler "formulate[s] as a *reproach* to Lacan," that the symbolic phallus is "already the loss it fears" because "the fear of possible castration is already castration itself"—just as the fetish is, for Freud, compatible with castration anxiety.[137]

There can be no separation from the phallus as what Žižek terms the "phallus of castration" or separation itself; separation and lack is the kernel of the "real" we cannot avoid as the desire that separates us from the mother and the maternal phallus in which we were alienated.[138] However, the "phallus of co-ordination" that "repeats the operation of imaginary identification with an idealized organ" (whether the penis or the ego itself) can be analyzed in order to effect a separation from it as the master signifier in which one is alienated, such as the Name-of-the-Father, the paternal phallus.[139] Several Lacanian theorists suggest that separation is at work today in the reconfiguration of the modern West's patriarchal nuclear family, as cynicism about the Other and traditional roles and identities reigns supreme. Culture itself performs the work of the analyst, separating the subject from the masks in which desire was alienated. The subject as such a "purified" desire is the subject of the drive, purged not only of its imaginary demands for love but even of its desire as that which must remain unsatisfied in the relation to the other in order to sustain itself as desire. The drive always achieves its aim of jouissance, whatever form it assumes to do so, from dream wish, to perversion, to hysteric conversion symptom. For Žižek, the drive is ultimately Thanatos, a liberation from erotic ties that bind, which the death drive aggressively dissolves. When Thanatos is realized, the libido captivated by the image we love as ourselves is released into entropic decay and the inhuman chemistry that ultimately drives desire. "Do I have to give up me to be loved by you?" asks Kruger's photomontage *Heart (Do I have to give up me to be loved by you?)* (1988). The question appears in white type over an extreme color close up of blood-red tissue that resembles a medical textbook illustration. This image might signify the less than human meat to which the "I" has been reduced by the other, the "you," as the latter makes use of the "I" for his own jouissance. However, it also might represent the very essence of the self behind all the masks the "I" assumes, beyond the narcissism in desire that has attached it to the human form it receives from the other, the lovable self in which love alienates it. That essence would be the horrifying part of the self that enjoys even the pain, loss, and trauma love can inflict, the substance of the pure death drive. Inhuman, it has no face. The face of desire is ultimately nothing but a death mask, obscuring the reality of drives the symbolic cannot name and fully integrate. "*Desire itself is a defense against desire,*" Žižek declares; "the desire structured through fantasy is a defense against . . . this 'pure,' transphantasmatic desire (i.e., the 'death drive' in its pure form)."[140]

The subject, driven toward disintegration and unification, separating and joining, is this split and "impure" desire expressed and disguised by the phallic masquerade. Both Renata Salecl and Paul Verhaeghe argue that the contemporary vogue for piercing and tattooing are subcultural efforts to stabilize identities when the patriarchal symbolic no longer provides identificatory models that might serve as answers to the question of the Other's desire, "What does she want from me?"[141] Through such practices, the postmodern subject separated by radical doubt from one community marks her participation in another whose beliefs she shares, submitting her drives to a law that constitutes desire. "Jouissance is possible only when the boundaries have been put into place to create a limit," Verhaeghe notes, as libido is bound to representations.[142] If psychoanalysis as an ethics of the drive emphasizes separation from every identity as an alienating mask, psychoanalysis as an ethics of desire recognizes that separation is "not all." Even the death drive separates from itself as the life drive, which according to Jean Laplanche was Freud's real discovery in the years leading up to the writing of *Beyond the Pleasure Principle*.[143] Yet Eros becomes a kind of death-in-life when the subject entombs itself in a phallic carapace as a defense against desire, trying to satisfy the Other completely. Analysis separates the subject from that mask and turns it into masquerade, a mere pretense at satisfaction. "The human subject, the subject of the desire that is the essence of man . . . knows how to play with the mask . . .," Lacan says.[144] Masquerade suggests the subject is not the object she seems to be for the Other but different. It implies the Other too is other, not identical with the desire the masquerade pretends to satisfy. Sustaining desire as unsatisfied desire masquerade figures difference—both the subject's and the Other's. Lacan's discussion of the well-known dream of Choang-tsu, the popularizer of philosophical Taoism, seems to speak to this responsibility to difference as a dialectic of imaginary captivation and symbolic separation, the possibility of resemblance, coherence, and an existential link to a world of others, but a world that changes. In the dream, has Choang-tsu netted the butterfly or has it flown off with him? According to Lacan, as long as Choang-tsu can reflect on whether he is a man dreaming he is a butterfly or a butterfly dreaming he is a man, he is not mad.[145] Caught between coming out and mimicry, affirmation and negation of a phallic mask in which he is alienated, Choang-tsu is neither the one nor the other. He knows he is only *passing* through the signifier, on his way to something else that remains an open possibility.

NOTES

1. Eve Kosofsky Sedgewick, *Epistemology of the Closet* (Berkeley: University of California Press, 1990), 3.
2. Sigmund Freud, "Identification," in *Group Psychology and the Analysis of the Ego, 1921*, ed. and trans. James Strachey. (New York: W. W. Norton, 1959). Freud explains the mechanisms of group dynamics he believes to be correctly described, but not accounted for, in the work of his predecessors, primarily Le Bon's *The Crowd: A Study*

of the Popular Mind and McDougall's *The Group Mind* (which he discusses in earlier chapters).

3. Kimberly Benston, "I am what I am: the topos of (un)naming in Afro-American literatur," in *Black Literature and Literary Theory*, ed. Henry Louis gates, Jr. (New York and London: Methuen, 1984), 153

4. Ibid.

5. Judith Butler, *Bodies That Matter: On the Discursive Limits of "Sex,"* (New York: Routledge, 1993), 223.

6. Sedgwick, *Epistemology of the Closet*, 4.

7. Adam Piper, cited in Peggy Phelan, *Unmarked: The Politics of Performance* (London: Routledge, 1993), 97–98; Phelen, 98.

8. See Frantz Fanon, *Black Skin, White Masks*, trans. Charles Lam Markmann (New York: Grove Press, 1967), and Homi Bhabha, "Of Mimicry and Man: The Ambivalence of Colonial Discourse," *The Location of Culture* (London: Routledge, 1994), 85–92.

9. Sedgwick, *Epistemology of the Closet*, 26.

10. See the essays in Charles Sanders Peirce, *The Essential Writings*, ed. E. C. Moore, (New York: Harper and Row, 1972).

11. Ferdinand de Saussure, *Course in General Linguistics*, ed. Charles Bally and Albert Sechehaye with Albert Riedlinger, 1915, trans. Wade Baskin. (1959; reprt. New York: MacGraw-Hill, 1966), 69–70, 131–34; hereafter cited parenthetically as *Course*.

12. Christian Metz, *The Imaginary Signifier: Psychoanalysis and the Cinema*, trans. Celia Britton, Annwyl Williams, Ben Brewster, and Alfred Guzzetti (Bloomington: Indiana University Press, 1982), 69–78.

13. Michel Foucault, *The Order of Things: An Archaeology of the Human Sciences* (1966); trans. (New York: Vintage, 1973), 15.

14. Jacques Lacan, *The Four Fundamental Concepts of Psycho-Analysis* (1973); trans. Alan Sheridan (New York: W. W. Norton, 1978), 106.

15. Jacques Lacan, *Ecrits: A Selection* (1966); trans. Alan Sheridan (New York: W. W. Norton, 1977), 23; Emile Benveniste, *Problems in General Linguistics* (1966); trans. Mary Elizabeth Meek (Coral Gables, FL: University of Miami Press, 1971), 217–20.

16. Jacqueline Rose, *Sexuality in the Field of Vision* (London: Verso, 1986), 217–18.

17. Sigmund Freud, "Fetishism" (1927); trans. Joan Riviere in *Sexuality and the Psychology of Love*, ed. Philip Rieff (New York: Collier, 1963), 217.

18. John Ellis, *Visible Fictions: Cinema, Television, Video*, rev. ed. (London: Routledge, 1992), 58. Barthes himself makes a distinction between the phenomenology of photography and of cinema, which combines the actor's "this has been" with the role's, and denies the pose (and the confusion of life and death) through animation; see *Camera Lucida: Reflections on Photography*, trans. Richard Howard (New York: Hill and Wang, 1981), 78–79. However, he does say, "I can never see or see again in a film certain actors whom I know to be dead without a kind of melancholy; the melancholy of Photography itself (I experience this same emotion listening to the recorded voices of dead singers)" (79).

19. Roland Barthes, *Camera Lucida*, 5–6; 13–14; 85–88.

20. André Bazin, *What Is Cinema?* (1960); ed. and trans. Hugh Gray (Berkeley and Los Angeles: University of California Press, 1967), 9–16.

21. Umberto Eco, *A Theory of Semiotics* (Bloomington: Indiana University Press, 1979), 17.

22. Ibid., 190.
23. Ibid., 180.
24. Ibid.
25. Lacan, *Ecrits*, 2.
26. Ibid., 23; 3. Lacan discusses the "hommelette" (a pun on "little man" and "omelette" as a formless mass) in *The Four Fundamental Concepts of Psycho-Analyis*, 197.
27. Eco, *A Theory of Semiotics*, 213; 208.
28. Lacan, *Ecrits*, 4.
29. Sigmund Freud, *Civilization and Its Discontents* (1930); ed. and trans. James Strachey (New York: W. W. Norton, 1961).
30. Phelan, *Unmarked*, 98. On the visual technologies of race, see Robyn Wiegman, *American Anatomies: Theorizing Race and Gender* (Durham: Duke University Press, 1995), 21–78.
31. Seyla Benhabib, "The Generalized and the Concrete Other: The Kohlberg-Gilligan Controversy and Feminist Theory," in *Feminism as Critique*, ed. Seyla Benhabib and Drucilla Cornell (Minneapolis: University of Minnesota Press, 1987), 77–95.
32. Jacques Derrida, *Of Grammatology* (1967); trans. Gayatri Chakravorty Spivak (Baltimore: Johns Hopkins University Press, 1976), 110.
33. Louis Althusser, *Lenin and Philosophy and Other Essays*, trans. Ben Brewster (New York: Monthly Review Press, 1971), 182; emphasis in the original.
34. Slavoj Žižek, *The Sublime Object of Ideology* (New York: Verso, 1989), 198.
35. See Octave Mannow, *Clefs pour l'imaginaire ou l'autre scène* (Paris: Editions du Seuil, 1969), 9–56.
36. Metz, *The Imaginary Signifier*, 73.
37. Žižek, *The Sublime Object of Ideology*, 34.
38. Jeffrey Weeks, *Coming Out: Homosexual Politics in Britain, from the Nineteenth Century to the Present* (London: Quartet, 1977), i. Foucault discusses the production of sexual identities in *The History of Sexuality: An Introduction*, vol. 1 of *The History of Sexuality*, trans. Robert Hurley (New York: Random House, 1978).
39. Butler, *Bodies that Matter*, 227–30; Lauren Berlant and Elizabeth Freeman, "Queer Nationality," in *Fear of a Queer Planet: Queer Politics and Social Theory*, ed. Michael Warner (Minneapolis: University of Minnesota Press, 1993), 197, 220–25.
40. Gayatri Chakravorty Spivak, "Criticism, Feminism, and the Institution," interview with Elizabeth Grosz in *The Post-Colonial Critic: Interviews, Strategies, Dialogues* (New York: Routledge, 1990), 11. Spivak is more critical of "strategic essentialism" in a later interview; see "In a Word," interview with Ellen Rooney, *Outside in the Teaching Machine* (New York: Routledge, 1993) 13–16.
41. R. Radhakrishnan, "Ethnic Identity and Poststructuralist Differance," *Cultural Critique* 6 (1987), 208.
42. Jacques Lacan, *The Seminar of Jacques Lacan*, Book VII, *The Ethics of Psychoanalysis, 1959–1960*, ed. Jacques-Alain Miller (1986); trans. Dennis Porter (New York: W. W. Norton, 1992), 179–204.
43. Phillipe Julien, *Jacques Lacan's Return to Freud: The Real, The Symbolic, The Imaginary*, trans. Devra Beck Simiu (New York: New York University Press, 1994), 86–87.
44. Eve Kosofsky Sedgwick, "How to Bring Your Kids Up Gay," in Warner, ed., *Fear of a Queer Planet: Queer Politics and Social Theory*, p. 80, n. 5.
45. Saussure, *Course in General Linguistics*, 12; 11.
46. Barthes, *Camera Lucida*, 14.

47. Ibid., 13.

48. Lacan, *The Four Fundamental Concepts of Psycho-Analysis*, 106.

49. Ibid., 74; 77.

50. Ibid., 96; Petit-Jean is quoted 95.

51. Ibid., 98. Of course, in one sense Lacan's net has not come up empty because it is filled with lack. Lacan here repeats the encounter with lack and insufficiency many years later in order to master it. He rewrites the episode so as to make it count differently, to profit from speculating on it, integrating it into the symbolic as an instance of the lack central to the theory of which he is the master.

52. Ibid., 53.

53. Sigmund Freud, *The Interpretation of Dreams*, trans. James Strachey (New York: Avon, 1965), 180–84; Lacan, *Ecrits*, 256–64.

54. In "Of Mimicry and Man," Bhabha describes mimicry as "the sign of a double articulation; a complex strategy of reform, regulation, and discipline, which 'appropriates' the Other as it visualizes power. Mimicry is also the sign of the inappropriate, however, a difference or recalcitrance which coheres the dominant strategic function of colonial power, intensifies surveillance, and poses an immanent threat to both 'normalized' knowledges and disciplinary powers," 86. He opens the essay with a quote from Lacan about mimicry.

55. Kobena Mercer, "Black Hair, Style Politics," in *Welcome to the Jungle: New Positions in Black Cultural Studies* (New York: Routledge, 1994), 128.

56. Ibid., 104.

57. Ibid., 108. After stating that categorically—"Black people's is the only type of hair that can be knotted into such characteristic configurations"—Mercer qualifies it in the next sentence by describing the style as "*not readily available* to white people because their hair does not '*naturally*' grow into such organic-looking shapes and strands" (my emphases). Here, nature is in quotes to remind us of one of Mercer's themes, that it is a cultural construction and one term in a Western binary opposition. The cultural work that goes into hairstyles, as well as the nature/culture opposition, are recalled in the phrase "not readily available. "

58. Ibid., 108–10. For Mercer, this might explain the reappropriation of dread locks by other subcultures, although if it is an iconic sign of blackness, the style should not be subject to such theft.

59. Ibid., 111.

60. Ibid.

61. Ibid., 112–13.

62. Sterling Stuckey, *Slave Culture* (Oxford: Oxford University Press, 1987), 1.

63. Mercer, "Black Hair, Style Politics," 123, my emphasis.

64. Stuart Hall, "Cultural Identity and Diaspora," in *Identity: Community, Culture, Difference*, ed. Jonathan Rutherford (London: Lawrence and Wishart, 1990), 226.

65. Dick Hebidge, *Subculture: The Meaning of Style* (London: Methuen, 1979), 16.

66. Eric Lott, "Love and Theft: The Racial Unconscious of Blackface Minstrelsy." *Representations* 39 (1992): 23–50.

67. Mercer, "Black Hair/Style Politics," 125. For a discussion of just how complex creolization is in the global context of the multidirectional "flow" of people, finance capital, ideas, and mass media images and sounds, see Arjun Appadurai, "Disjuncture and Difference in the Global Cultural Economy," *Modernity at Large: Cultural Dimensions of Globalization* (Minneapolis: University of Minnesota Press, 1996), 27–47.

68. Hall, "Cultural Identity and Diaspora," 230.

69. Žižek, *The Sublime Object of Ideology*, 72.

70. Ibid, 94–95. Rey Chow discusses Žižek's theory as anti-essentialist essentialism in "Ethics after Idealism," *diacritics*, 23:1 (1993), 14. Spivak, on the other hand, maintains that Derrida shows us how the subject is always centered, rather than decentered and undecidable. See, for example, her *The Post-Colonial Critic*, 146, where she asserts, "He is not decentering the subject. . . . There is no way that a subject can be anything but centered. . . ."

71. Jacques Lacan, "God and the Jouissance of The Woman. A Love Letter," *Feminine Sexuality: Jacques Lacan and the école freudienne*, ed. Juliet Mitchell and Jacqueline Rose, trans. Jacqueline Rose (New York: W. W. Norton & Company, 1982), 149–61.

72. Joan Copjec, *Read My Desire: Lacan Against the Historicists* (Cambridge, MA: Massachusetts Institute of Technology Press, 1994), 215.

73. See Lacan, "God and the Jouissance of The Woman," 143; 147; and 150–51.

74. Žižek, *The Sublime Object of Ideology*, 165.

75. Lacan, *Ecrits*, 287.

76. Ruth Herschberger, *Adam's Rib* (New York: Pellegrini and Cudahy, 1948), 75–84.

77. Ibid., 290.

78. Joël Dor, *The Clinical Lacan (The Lacanian Clinical Field)*, ed. Judith Feher Gurewich with Susan Fairfield (Northdale, NH: Jason Aronson, Inc. 1997), 85; Lacan, *Ecrits*, 287; Lacan, *Ecrits II* (Paris: Editions du Seine, 1971), 111.

79. Suzanne Kessler, *Lessons from the Intersexed* (New Brunswick: Rutgers University Press, 1998), 26–27.

80. Marjorie Garber, *Vested Interests: Cross Dressing and Cultural Anxiety* (New York: Routledge, 1992), 94–98.

81. Teresa Brennan, "An Impasse in Psychoanalysis and Feminism," in *A Reader in Feminist Knowledge*, ed. Sneja Gunew (London: Routledge, 1991), 127; ibid.

82. Lacan, *Ecrits*, 288.

83. Lacan, *The Four Fundamental Concepts of Psycho-Analysis*, 104.

84. Sigmund Freud, "Hysterical Phantasies and Their Relation to Bisexuality" (1908), trans. Douglas Bryan in *Dora: An Analysis of a Case of Hysteria*, ed. Philip Rieff (New York: Collier, 1963), 151. For one such hysterical denial, see Richard Boothby, *Death and Desire: Psychoanalytic Theory in Lacan's Return to Freud* (New York: Routledge, 1991). Boothby asserts that what is at stake is a symbolic function, like a differential feature in linguistics, but then argues that the penis is particularly "well-suited" for the job because "even in the male alone . . . [it] embodies a principle of difference in its alternance of flaccidness and erection" and *"aside from the mother's breasts* . . . is the only bodily appendage unsupported by bone and the only appendage incapable of voluntary movement" (153; emphasis added). Because he never explains this "aside," we are left to draw our own conclusions about why breasts cannot function as the "rigid designator" in our culture.

85. Elizabeth Grosz, "Lesbian Fetishism?" in *differences* 3:5 (1991), 53, n. 3.

86. Otto Fenichel, "The Psychology of Transvestism" (1930); reprt. in *Psychoanalysis and Male Sexuality*, ed. Henrik M. Ruitenbeek (New Haven: College and University Press, 1966), 203–20.

87. Freud, "Fetishism," 218–19.

88. See Jacques Lacan and Wladimir Granoff, "Fetishism: The Symbolic, the Imaginary and the Real," in *Perversions: Psychodynamics and Therapy*, ed. Sandor Lorand (New

York: Gramercy, 1956), 265; Sigmund Freud, *Three Essays on the Theory of Sexuality* (1905), ed. and trans. James Strachey (New York: Basic Books, 1965), 31.

89. Freud, "Fetishism," 215–16.

90. Lacan, *Ecrits*, 17,

91. *Jerry Springer*, Metromedia; KCAL broadcast September 13, 1994.

92. Lacan, *The Four Fundamental Concepts of Psycho-Analysis*, 104.

93. Žižek, *The Sublime Object of Ideology*, 102.

94. Ibid., 50.

95. Butler, *Bodies that Matter*, 187–222; see also Judith Butler, *The Psychic Life of Power: Theories in Subjection* (Stanford: Stanford University Press, 1997), especially 83–105.

96. Slavoj Žižek, *Looking Awry: An Introduction to Jacques Lacan through Popular Culture* (Cambridge, MA: MIT Press, 1991), 28.

97. This does not rule out the necessity to oppose gene "therapy" or other treatments which have as their explicit goal the elimination of gender or sexual "dysfunction"— or at the very least to generate public debate about the ethical implications of such "medicine." Currently, scientists are are far more confident there are biological causes of certain kinds of intersexuality than of homosexuality; intersexuals therefore seem a more likely early target of normalizing interventions. Are we prepared to say that every embryo allowed to mature should be clearly sexed and capable of reproduction? What about embryos diagnosed with nonsexual illnesses or conditions that are not curable that we believe to affect adversely the quality of life of the children with them? New diagnostic and therapeutic technologies raise crucial questions about how psychical and physical health will be determined and ensured.

98. Rose, *Sexuality*, 89.

99. Freud, *Three Essays on the Theory of Sexuality*, 11, 1915 note.

100. Butler, *The Psychic Life of Power*, 87.

101. Butler, *Bodies that Matter*, 195.

102. Butler, *The Psychic Life of Power*, 23.

103. Butler, *Bodies that Matter*, 219; 218; see also 230 on the name "queer. "

104. Butler, *The Psychic Life of Power*, 127.

105. Butler, *Bodies that Matter*, 61.

106. Ibid., 73.

107. Ibid., 84.

108. Ibid.

109. Ibid.

110. Ibid., 64; 91.

111. Ibid., 64; 64–65.

112. Ibid., 85.

113. Ibid., 87; see also Butler, *The Subject of Power*, 104.

114. Freud, "Fetishism," 216.

115. Sigmund Freud, "Splitting of the Ego in the Defensive Process," 1938, trans. James Strachey, in *Sexuality and the Psychology of Love*, ed. Philip Rieff (New York: Collier, 1963), 222.

116. Sigmund Freud, *An Outline of Psycho-Analysis*, 1940, ed. and trans. James Strachey (New York: W. W. Norton & Company, 1949), 60.

117. Leo Bersani and Ulysses Dutoit, *The Forms of Violence: Narrative in Assyrian Art and Modern Culture* (New York: Schocken Books, 1985), 72.

118. Ibid., 68.

119. Parveen Adams, *The Emptiness of the Image: Psychoanalysis and Sexual Differences* (New York: Routledge, 1995), 129.
120. Ibid., 135; 137.
121. Ibid., 139.
122. Teresa de Lauretis, *The Practice of Love: Lesbian Sexuality and Perverse Desire* (Bloomington: Indiana University Press, 1994), 225.
123. Ibid., 209.
124. Ibid., 242.
125. Ibid., 233.
126. Adams, *The Emptiness of the Image*, 43; de Lauretis, *The Practice of Love*, 225, footnote 10.
127. Butler, *The Psychic Life of Power*, 111–12 and 117.
128. Žižek, *The Sublime Object of Ideology*, 25.
129. Ibid., 220.
130. Ibid., 218.
131. Bruce Fink, *The Lacanian Subject: Between Language and Jouissance* (Princeton: Princeton University Press, 1995), 56.
132. Lacan, *The Four Fundamental Concepts of Psycho-Analysis*, 104.
133. Lacan, *Ecrits*, 289.
134. Jacques Lacan, *The Seminar of Jacques Lacan*, Book XX: *Encore, 1972–1973: On Feminine Sexuality, The Limits of Love and Knowledge*, ed. Jacques-Alain Miller, trans. Bruce Fink (New York: W. W. Norton & Company, 1998), 94.
135. Slavoj Žižek, *Tarrying with the Negative: Kant, Hegel, and the Critique of Ideology* (Durham: Duke University Press, 1993), 161.
136. Slavoj Žižek, *The Metastases of Enjoyment: Six Essays on Woman and Causality* (London: Verso, 1994), 202.
137. Ibid., 203.
138. Ibid., 202.
139. Ibid.
140. Žižek, *The Sublime Object of Ideology*, 118.
141. Renata Salecl, *(Per)Versions of Love and Hate* (London: Verso, 1998), 150–51 and 159–60; Paul Verhaeghe, *Love in a Time of Loneliness*, trans. Plym Peters and Tony Langham (New York: Other Press, Llc., 1999), 117–19, 182–85. Salecl argues that the contemporary subject plays with imaginary simulacra instead of identifying with symbolic authorities but resorts to cuts in the body (and tattoos) to irreversibly mark the body with a signifier of prohibition as a protest against the idea that identities are changeable. Verhaeghe suggests that the subject engages in a search for a new Other in whom to believe, and that peer groups can be the source of new symbolic norms. These norms control jouissance and the drives, which may also be managed at a more primordial level through rhythm (especially drum beats), piercing, and tattoos.
142. Verhaeghe, *Love in a Time of Loneliness*, 177.
143. Jean Laplanche, *New Foundations for Pyschoanalysis*, trans. David Macey (Oxford: Basil Blackwell, 1989), 146.
144. Lacan, *The Four Fundamental Concepts of Pyschoanalysis*, 107.
145. Ibid., 76.

INDEX